Walking with Purpose

Enabling women to know Christ through Scripture

Dear Friend,

Welcome to *Discovering Our Dignity*, a Bible study highlighting women of the Bible! How I wish I could be going through these lessons with you, hearing your unique insights. I know I'd learn so much from you and your experiences. I'd also be thrilled to watch God meet you right where you are and take you to where He wants you to be. If you come with an open heart, He promises to do a transforming work within you. It will be worth every minute spent studying His Word!

It's amazing to me that no matter how many years ago the women of the Bible walked the earth, they are still able to connect with us and transmit important life lessons. There's something incredibly powerful when we open ourselves up to learning from the women who have gone before us.

We all want to be women of dignity and purpose. No one sets out to be insecure, aimless, or insignificant. But we live in a culture that places value on many things that are out of our control. Beauty, money, fame, and power are celebrated, yet each one of them can be elusive. Could it be that we're looking for significance and worth in the wrong places? During this study, we'll explore what God has to say about where our dignity should come from. In the words of Saint Catherine of Siena, "If we are who we should be . . . we will set the world ablaze!" Let's take some time to hear from the One who created us. He'll point us to the pursuits that will help us experience lives of lasting satisfaction. Are you ready? Let's Discover Our Dignity!

I am blessed to be on the journey with you.

Lisa Brenninkmeyer
Founder, Walking with Purpose

Discovering Our Dignity

www.walkingwithpurpose.com

Authored by Lisa Brenninkmeyer
Cover and page design by True Cotton
Production management by Christine Welsko

IMPRIMATUR   + William E. Lori, S.T.D., Archbishop of Baltimore

ISBN: 978-1-943173-04-4

Discovering Our Dignity

TABLE OF CONTENTS

INTRODUCTION

Welcome to Walking with Purpose...3

The Structure of *Discovering Our Dignity* 3

Study Guide Format and Reference Materials 4

Walking with Purpose™ Courses 5

Walking with Purpose™ Mission Statement..7

About the Author 7

LESSONS

Lesson 1: Connect Coffee Talk: Dignity Through Purpose.. 11

Lesson 2: Eve.. 15

Lesson 3: Sarah 31

Lesson 4: Rebekah 49

Lesson 5: Connect Coffee Talk: Leah and Rachel – Dignity Without Comparison 67

Lesson 6: Leah and Rachel 71

Lesson 7: Rahab 87

Lesson 8: Deborah 103

Lesson 9: Ruth 119

Lesson 10: Connect Coffee Talk: Abigail – Going It Alone... 137

Lesson 11: Abigail 141

Lesson 12: Bathsheba 159

Lesson 13: Tamar... 179

Lesson 14: Connect Coffee Talk: Esther – This Is Your Moment............................... 197

Lesson 15: Esther.. 201

Lesson 16: Mary, the Blessed Mother 219

Lesson 17: The Poor Widow... 239

Lesson 18: Connect Coffee Talk: Martha – Does What I Do Matter? 253

Lesson 19: Martha of Bethany 257

Lesson 20: Mary of Bethany 275

Lesson 21: Mary, the New Eve 297

Lesson 22: Connect Coffee Talk: Mary – Untying the Knot.. 317

APPENDICES

Appendix 1: Saint Thérèse of Lisieux 323

Appendix 2: Scripture Memory 325

Appendix 3: How to Do a Verse Study 333

Appendix 4: Who I Am in Christ 337

Appendix 5: Conversion of Heart 341

ANSWER KEY 345

PRAYER PAGES 381

Welcome to Walking with Purpose

You have many choices when it comes to how you spend your time—thank you for choosing Walking with Purpose. Studying God's Word with an open and receptive heart will bring spiritual growth and enrichment to all aspects of your life, making every moment that you've invested well worth it.

Each one of us comes to this material from our own unique vantage point. You are welcome as you are. No previous experience is necessary. Some of you will find that the questions in this study cause you to think about concepts that are new to you. Others might find much is a review. God meets each one of us where we are, and He is always faithful, taking us to a deeper, better place spiritually, regardless of where we begin.

The Structure of *Discovering Our Dignity*

Discovering Our Dignity is a twenty-two-session course that integrates Scripture with the teachings of the Roman Catholic Church to point us to principles that help us manage life's pace and pressure while living with calm and steadiness.

Discovering Our Dignity is designed for both personal study and interactive group discussion.

If you are going through *Discovering Our Dignity* with a small group in your parish, most weeks will be spent in the group discussing one of the lessons from the *Discovering Our Dignity Study Guide*. Once a month you'll gather for a Connect Coffee, which consists of social time, a DVD presentation of one of the related course talks, and small group discussion of selected questions that relate to the talk.

If you're going through this study either on your own or in a small group, you are welcome to order the DVDs, but you might find it simpler to watch the talks online. The URL for each talk is listed on the Connect Coffee Talk outline within the study guide.

Study Guide Format and Reference Materials

The *Discovering Our Dignity Study Guide* is divided into three sections:

The first section comprises twenty-two lessons. Most lessons are divided into five "days" to help you form a habit of reading and reflecting on God's Word regularly. If you are a woman who has only bits and pieces of time throughout your day to accomplish tasks, you will find this breakdown of the lessons especially helpful. Each day focuses on Scripture readings and related teaching passages, and ends with a Quiet Your Heart reflection. In addition, Day Five includes a lesson conclusion; a resolution section, in which you set a goal for yourself based on a theme of the lesson; and short clips from the *Catechism of the Catholic Church*, which are referenced throughout the lesson to complement the Scripture study. Each lesson ends with a relevant verse study. Instructions for how to do a verse study can be found in Appendix 3.

For the Connect Coffee Talks in the series, accompanying outlines are offered as guides for taking notes. Included are questions to help direct your group's discussion following the talks, as well as URLs for those who would like to view the talks online.

The second section, the appendices, contains supplemental materials referred to during the study, including an article about Saint Thérèse of Lisieux, the patron saint of Walking with Purpose (Appendix 1). Appendix 2, "Scripture Memory," gives instructions on how to memorize Scripture. Two memory verses have been chosen for *Discovering Our Dignity*, and we encourage you to memorize them as you move through the course. Illustrations of the two verses can be found at the back of the study guide, and color versions and phone lock screens can be downloaded from our website.

The third section contains the answer key. You will benefit so much more from the course study if you work through the questions on your own, searching your heart, as this is your very personal journey of faith. The answer key is meant to enhance small group discussion, and provide personal guidance or insight when needed.

At the end of the book are pages on which to write weekly prayer intentions.

The Bible

The recommended Bible translations for use in Walking with Purpose™ studies are: The New American Bible, which is the translation used in the United States for the readings at Mass; The Revised Standard Version, Catholic Edition; and The Jerusalem Bible.

Walking with Purpose™ Courses

Living in the Father's Love, a six-lesson course, is a brief but powerful study meant to revive and refresh us as we discover just how much God loves us! In this study, we learn how the Gospels are deeply relevant to our relationships, both with God and with those we love. A set of DVDs, which includes the opening and closing talks for the study, accompanies this short course. *Living in the Father's Love* is perfect for the season of Advent or Lent, as a summer study, or as an introduction to the twenty-two-session Walking with Purpose™ courses.

Beholding His Glory, a nine-lesson course, shows us how all Scripture points us to our Redeemer, Jesus Christ. As we look at Old Testament people and events, we'll encounter problems that only Christ will solve, needs that only He will satisfy, and promises that only He can deliver. We'll learn to recognize and appreciate God's plan for our own lives, His awe-inspiring majesty, and His desire for personal intimacy with each one of us. A series of three DVDs, which includes supplemental talks for selected lessons in the study guide, accompanies the course. This is the first part of a two-part series and is ideally followed by part two, *Beholding Your King*.

Beholding Your King, a nine-lesson course, picks up where *Beholding His Glory* ends. The story of salvation history is continued as we look at King David, select Psalms, the temple, and many Old Testament prophets and they ways in which they all point to the coming King of Kings, Jesus Christ. A series of three DVDs, which includes supplemental talks for selected lessons in the study guide, accompanies the course.

Opening Your Heart, a twenty-two-lesson introductory course, is designed for women who are brand-new to Walking with Purpose as well as those experienced in Bible study. This course enables all women to take a deep dive into the fundamental questions of our Catholic faith and our relationship with Jesus Christ. Some of the questions that will be explored include: Who is Jesus Christ? Who is the Holy Spirit? How and why should I pray? How can I read the Bible in a meaningful way?" A series of six DVDs, which includes supplemental talks focused on setting priorities and living purposefully, accompanies the course.

Keeping in Balance, a twenty-two-lesson course, takes us on a journey through Scripture as we discover the relevance of Old and New Testament wisdom for daily challenges. This study explores biblical ways that we can manage life's pace and pressure while living with calm and steadiness. A lifestyle of health and holiness awaits. A series of six DVDs, which includes supplemental talks for selected lessons in the study guide, accompanies the course.

Touching the Divine, a twenty-two-lesson course, focuses on the qualities of Jesus revealed through the Gospel of John. This study draws us into a deeper relationship with Jesus as we reflect on His personality. Knowing Christ more intimately will increase our love for Him. John referred to himself as "the disciple whom Jesus loved." As we study, John will teach us how much Jesus loves us, and how His love is the true satisfaction of our souls. A series of six DVDs, which includes supplemental talks for selected lessons in the study guide, accompanies the course.

Discovering Our Dignity, a twenty-two-lesson course, gives us modern-day advice from women of the Bible. Through their stories, recorded in Scripture, they reach out to touch our lives in a tender, honest, and loving way—woman-to-woman. A series of six DVDs, which includes supplemental talks for selected lessons in the study guide, accompanies the course.

Walking with Purpose™ Mission Statement

Walking with Purpose aims to bring women to a deeper personal relationship with Jesus Christ by offering personal studies and small group discussions that link our everyday challenges and struggles with the solutions given to us through the teachings of Christ and the Roman Catholic Church.

About the Author

Lisa Brenninkmeyer, raised as an evangelical Protestant, entered the Catholic Church in 1991. She has led Bible studies in Europe, Mexico, and the United States, and has written curricula for women and children. She founded Walking with Purpose in 2008 out of a desire to see women come to know Christ personally. Her speaking and writing are inspired by a desire to see women transformed as they realize how much God loves them. She holds a BA in psychology from St. Olaf College. She lives with her husband, Leo, and their seven children in St. Augustine, Florida.

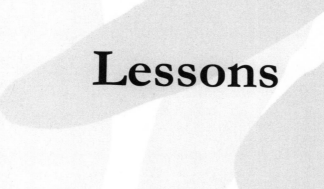

Lessons

Lesson 1: Connect Coffee Talk
DIGNITY THROUGH PURPOSE

Accompanying DVD can be viewed at:
www.walkingwithpurpose.com/courses/videos
Select: *Discovering Our Dignity* – Talk 01 – Dignity Through Purpose

Philippians 1:21: "To live is _____ and to die is _____."

1. The Best GPS

2 Timothy 3:16–17: "All Scripture is _____ and is useful for teaching, for reproof, for correction, for training in righteousness; so that the man [and woman] of God may be adequate, _____ for every _____ _____."

Romans 15:4: "For everything that was written in the past was written to _____ us, so that through endurance and the _____ of the Scriptures we might have _____."

One of the core principles taught by this GPS (the Bible) is:

2. God Has a Calling and a Purpose for Each of Us

A. Our core calling

It is _____ each one of us, but it's not _____ us. It's about _____.

Our CORE CALLING is to be in a relationship with _____.

B. Our feminine calling

    1. To help

       Ezer kenegdo means "a helper who is _____ in _____ and _____ to him."

    2. To nurture

    3. To influence

       Psalm 121:1

C. Our personal calling

3. According to the Catherine of Siena Institute, a spiritual gift is a God-given ability to perform supernatural ministry for Jesus Christ.

Where do spiritual gifts come from?

Why are we given spiritual gifts?

1 Peter 4:10

How can I find out what my gift is?

a. _____

b. _____

Who has spiritual gifts?

1 Corinthians 12:7

Questions for Discussion

1. What kind of a legacy do you want to leave behind at the end of your life? How do you want to be remembered?

2. The three contributions that women make to society based on the way that God has designed us are: helping, nurturing, and influencing. In which of these areas would you most like to grow as you live out your purpose as a woman?

3. Do you think you are carrying burdens that God has not asked you to carry? Could it be that you are trying to carry a burden alone that God has sent help for you to carry?

Lesson 2

EVE

Introduction

I couldn't sleep the other night. Thoughts were rolling around and around in my head. Unfinished to-do lists screamed at me. Concerns about my children and worries that I was falling short in my role as a mother weighed heavily on my heart. Relationships that needed tending, household chores that needed attention, and work deadlines all reminded me that I needed to be *more*. The words "Not good enough . . . not good enough . . . you've wasted time . . . your life is a mess . . . she's so much better than you" whispered in my head. Shame gnawed at my soul.

My first instinct was to get up and start working on my list. True, it was two thirty a.m., but all I could think of was how much I could get done before my household woke up. But I knew my movement as I got out of bed would wake my husband, Leo, and he'd think I was out of my mind. Seeing no good solution to my stress just made me want to give up.

Is there a better way to cope? I believe there is. When I can't sleep at night, or when my stomach is upset during the day because of worries or concerns I am struggling with, God offers me refuge, a place to hide. I get tempted to hide behind my performance (getting up in the middle of the night to work), or under my covers (just giving up), but He calls me out and invites me to hide *in Him*. When faced with the many ways that I fall short, I can choose to rely on myself or to rely on Him.

Eve was faced with the same choice. Her circumstances were different from mine, but she still faced the choice of where to go with her feelings of shame and inadequacy. I don't want to emulate her, but I can definitely learn from her.

As we study Eve's life and choices, let's remember that the book of Genesis was written to reveal spiritual truths to us. It teaches about the mysteries of God's nature, where we come from, the sacredness of marriage, and many other truths. The intention of the author was not to teach science. We are to read Genesis (and all of

Scripture) with open hearts that ask, "God, what do you want me to learn from these passages?"

It is critical that we treat Adam and Eve as people who actually lived. According to the *Catechism of the Catholic Church* 390, "The account of the fall in Genesis 3 uses figurative language, but affirms a primeval event, a deed that took place *at the beginning of the history of man.* Revelation gives us the certainty of faith that the whole of human history is marked by the original fault freely committed by our first parents."[1] This means that the fall was a historical event that took place at the beginning of human history. This event was written about in a language that the people of that time could understand.

It's my prayer that as we study Eve's story, we will not only understand it, but we will grow in wisdom as we apply the truths we learn. May these truths penetrate deeply into our souls, quieting our questions, doubts, worries, and inadequacies that seek to rob us of the peace and dignity that Christ offers to each of us.

Day One
DIGNITY

Read Genesis 1 and 2.

1. In what way was the creation of man different from the creation of animals? See Genesis 1:27.

2. What does it mean to be created in God's own image and likeness? See CCC 225 and CCC 343.

---

[1] *Catechism of the Catholic Church,* revised in accordance with the official Latin text promulgated by Pope John Paul II, 2nd ed. (Vatican City: Libreria Editrice Vaticana, 1997).

3. We can choose to base our dignity on who God says we are or on what the world says has value. What are some of the things our culture says give us dignity?

4. How is the woman described in Genesis 2:18? What is your personal reaction to this description?

5. How does CCC 1605 describe a woman's relationship to a man?

Understanding the meaning of the word *helper* in the original Hebrew sheds important light on this subject. The Hebrew word for helper is *ezer kenegdo*, which means "a helper who is equal in power and ability to him." This term is used twenty-one times in the Old Testament, and only once does it refer to women. It is used seventeen times to refer to God Himself.[2] That's eye-opening, isn't it?

Quiet your heart and enjoy His presence. . . . His love for you is unconditional.

Eve was created as a person with dignity, and so is every woman who has been created since. Yet so many of us, if we were honest, would admit to being plagued at times by feelings of worthlessness. We try to grow in dignity through our accomplishments, our possessions, and our reputations. But none of these things can be counted on; all can be taken away in an instant. When Jesus walked on earth, He offered us a different example to follow. Instead of allowing His sense of worth and dignity to be dictated by what people thought of Him, He kept His focus on what His heavenly Father thought. 1 Peter 2:4 describes Jesus as "rejected by human beings but chosen and precious in the sight of God." Jesus laid down His life for mankind, and what He received in return was rejection. Yet He didn't let that determine His value. He knew He was chosen and precious in the sight of God. Do you know that that is how your heavenly Father sees you? You are chosen and precious in God's eyes. Take a few moments to meditate on this fact. Let Jesus whisper to your heart, "It was not you who chose me, but I who chose you" (John 15:16).

---

2 Examples of this can be found in Psalm 10:14, 30:10, 54:4, 70:5, and 121:2.

Day Two
TEMPTATION

Read Genesis 3:1–6.

1. According to 2 Corinthians 11:3, how did the serpent (Satan) deceive Eve? Do you see ways he employs the same tactic with women today?

Satan began the temptation with a question: "Did God really tell you . . . ?" He whispers questions to us, too. They might seem harmless. What is the danger in playing around with a question in our minds? That depends on the question. One of his favorites is "What if . . . ?" "What if you had married someone else?" "What if you had more money?" "What if God hadn't allowed that loss?" Would life be better? The question plants a seed of doubt in our minds regarding God's goodness. Underlying the subtler question is the real one: "Is God holding out on you? Does He *really* want what's best for you?"

2. Compare Eve's words in Genesis 3:3 with God's words in Genesis 2:16–17. What is the difference between the two? Why is this significant?

3. According to Genesis 3:6, what drove Eve's decision to eat the forbidden fruit?

4. Satan was subtle. Instead of inviting Eve to rebel against God, he asked questions, planted seeds of doubt, and mixed truth with lies. He caught her off guard. He does the same today. He knows better than to tempt God's daughters to curse God and rebel outright. Most of us would recognize such a direct attack and run

the other way. He knows that it's so much more effective if he can plant seeds of doubt and expose us to half-truths. What are some of the doubts that he whispers into the ears of God's precious daughters today?

The enemy of our soul wants us to doubt God's unconditional love for us. He wants us to doubt our dignity based on who we are in Christ. He wants us to doubt that sin has consequences. He wants us to doubt that God will forgive anything if we ask with a contrite heart. He wants us to doubt that inner beauty matters more than physical beauty. He wants us to doubt that *God is enough*, that *He is all we need*.

When we are faced with temptation, we can learn from Eve's mistakes. Each mistake led her further down the path into sin. No doubt Eve struggled with her conscience over the choice before her. The right thing to do would have been to flee, not stay and try to fight the temptation.

Eve's mistakes:

1. **She conversed with temptation.** Remember, Eve had perfect communion with God. If she had kept her eyes on Him and all He'd given her, she would have avoided the conversation with the serpent, which is what led her down the wrong path.

2. **She was careless with God's Word.** Her words, "You must not touch it," were her addition—not God's words.

3. **She looked at the temptation.** Once she started dwelling on the forbidden fruit, her eyes came off of God and His goodness. This weakened her resolve to obey.

4. **She allowed her desires to drive her decision making.** She saw that the tree was good, pleasing to the eye, and desirable. Her desires—rather than God's commands—became her focus.

Quiet your heart and enjoy His presence. . . . He longs to shower you with love.

Take a few moments to ask God to reveal to you an area in your life where you are experiencing temptation. Prayerfully go through Eve's four mistakes, and ask the Holy Spirit to prick your conscience, alerting you to any areas in which you are following her pattern. Remember, "He that is in you is greater than he that is in the world" (1 John 4:4). Although the temptation may seem overpowering, the Holy Spirit who dwells within you is stronger than whoever or whatever is tempting you. But you need to ask for His help. He is waiting to strengthen you from within.

Day Three
CONTENTMENT

Read Genesis 2:16–17 and 3:1–6.

1. Describe God's actions toward Adam and Eve in Genesis 2:16–17.

2. Satan managed to get Eve to shift her focus. Describe how her attention shifted.

3. Use a dictionary and write out the definitions of *discontentment* and *contentment*.

Discontentment:

Contentment:

Satan's message to Eve was, "Are you longing for something more? More knowledge? More wisdom? Then you should be able to have it! Why should you have to experience unfulfilled longings? Take matters into your own hands!" His message is the same to us today. He convinces us that we shouldn't have unfulfilled longings. And our world chimes in, suggesting all sorts of remedies. Do you want something you can't afford? Put it on a credit card. Are you longing for affirmation and attention? Dress seductively to get it. Are you discontent in your marriage? Satisfy your emotional needs with another man.

It's important to note that the longing itself is not sinful. In fact, God put this longing into our hearts to draw us to Him.[3] But we get into trouble when we insist on fulfilling that longing with things of earth, and when we're willing to do whatever it takes to fulfill it, regardless of right or wrong.

4. A. What did Satan promise Eve would receive if she ate the fruit?

   B. What had God already taught Eve according to Genesis 2:16–17?

   C. How had God already made Eve, according to Genesis 1:26?

Do you see what Satan did? He tempted Eve to sin in order to gain something that she *already had*. She was already made in God's image. God had already graciously and lovingly provided this for her. Yet Satan managed to get Eve to take her eyes off the freedom she had and focus instead on the one thing she couldn't have. When her focus shifted, she forgot who she was. She was God's beloved child, made in His image. Oh, the power of deception. She was deceived into believing that sinning against God would give her greater dignity, wisdom, and strength.

Before we are too hard on her, can we see times in our own lives when this has happened? How often do we forget that we are beloved daughters of God, and instead seek to earn dignity in ways other than resting in His grace and mercy? Sometimes we follow Eve's example and do this through poor choices (think of the times a girl will give her body sexually in hopes that she'll be unconditionally loved in return), and sometimes we do this by trying to earn the favor of God through our good deeds. We forget that nothing we can do or give can make God love us more. He already is crazy about us. He already has given us dignity.

We get into trouble when we take our eyes off of what we already have and focus on things we lack. The best antidote to this tendency is gratitude. It sounds simplistic,

---

[3] "You have made us for yourself, oh Lord, and our hearts are restless until they rest in you." Aurelius Augustinus, *The Confessions of St Augustine* (Cambridge: Harvard University Press, 2006).

but the truth is that a heart full of gratitude leaves less room for doubt, discontentment, and unhappiness.

Quiet your heart and enjoy His presence. . . . Bask in His smile as He delights in you.

Dear Lord,

Help me to remember that the only place all my longings and desires will be fulfilled is in heaven, when they've been purified by Your love. Help my unfulfilled desires to draw me toward a longing for heaven with You. Thank You for meeting the deepest longing of my heart.

I know I don't have to wait until heaven to experience something of Your presence and Your filling of my empty places. Help me to cultivate a heart of gratitude. There is much for which I am thankful. These are some of the blessings I acknowledge as coming from Your generous hands. . . .

Day Four
HIDING

Read Genesis 3:7–11.

1. How did Adam and Eve respond when they realized that God was walking in the garden?

2. In Genesis 3:10, why did Adam say he hid? Why was he experiencing that particular emotion?

3. In what ways do we hide from God and others today?

Often it is guilt that causes us to hide. *Guilt* is the act or state of having done a wrong or committed an offense.[4] When faced with our guilt, we have two choices. We can confess it and accept the consequences, or we can hide and try to sweep it all under the carpet. The first option leads to healing. The second can lead us to shame. Shame is defined as "a painful emotion caused by a strong sense of guilt, embarrassment, unworthiness, or disgrace."[5] Guilt can develop into shame, and shame seeps into and erodes our dignity and self-worth.

Shame can develop from guilt over a specific act, but we can also carry shame when we feel we don't measure up. It isn't always that we can point to a specific thing we've done wrong. We may just have a sense that we are walking under a cloud of discouragement, and we don't like ourselves very much. We are vulnerable to this anytime we base our dignity on the wrong things. It's then that we will be tempted to hide behind masks of performance, fake pleasantries, or tough exteriors that communicate, "I don't care."

Our dignity comes from being created in God's image and being adopted as His precious daughters. Does being His daughter mean we'll be perfect? No. We'll make mistakes. We'll fall short. But when we're aware that we are less than we'd hoped, we have a choice. We can hide behind masks, or we can hide somewhere else.

4. Read the following verses, noting where we can go to hide when we need a refuge from our current circumstances. These verses are taken from the Revised Standard Version of the Bible. Other versions may use different translations of the key word *hide*. If yours doesn't use *hide* or *hidden*, don't worry. Just search for the meaning of the passage.

Psalm 17:8

Psalm 27:5

Psalm 32:7

---

[4] *Webster's New World Dictionary* (New York: Prentice Hall Press, 1986), 622.
[5] Jessica L. Tracy, Richard W. Robins, June Price Tangney, *The Self-Conscious Emotions: Theory and Research* (New York: The Guilford Press, 2007), 202.

Psalm 119:114

Colossians 3:3

Because our lives are hidden in Christ, we no longer have to create our own safe places. Those masks that we think protect us only hold us back from healing and wholeness. We think they are safe, but they always fail us. The only thing we can count on is Christ's unfailing love, which will never wane or end. His love is not dependent on what we do or don't do. He's always there for us, waiting to hide us away in His mercy and grace.

Quiet your heart and enjoy His presence. . . . You are precious in His sight.

Meditate on the lyrics of the song "The Shelter." It can be found on iTunes (from the album Come Weary Saints, *produced by Sovereign Grace Music).*

The Shelter

I have a shelter in the storm when troubles pour upon me.
Though fears are rising like a flood, my soul can rest securely.
Oh Jesus, I will hide in you, my place of peace and solace.
No trial is deeper than your love that comforts all my sorrow.

I have a shelter in the storm when all my sins accuse me.
Though justice charges me with guilt your grace will not refuse me.
Oh Jesus I will hide in you, who bore my condemnation.
I find my refuge in your wounds for there I find salvation.

Oh Jesus you have covered me!

I have a shelter in the storm when constant winds would break me.
For in my weakness I have learned, your strength will not forsake me.
Oh Jesus, I will hide in you—the One who bears my burdens.
With faithful hands that cannot fail, you'll bring me home to heaven.

Oh Jesus, I will hide in you—the One who bears my burdens.
With faithful hands that cannot fail, you bring me home to heaven.

Day Five
THE CONSEQUENCES

Read Genesis 3:11–24.

1. When faced with their guilt before God, how did Adam and Eve respond? What would have been a better response?

2. The judgment given to the serpent included a promise for mankind (Genesis 3:14–15). This passage contains our first glimpse of the Redeemer. Write it below and explain its significance.

3. What was the effect of Eve's fall on womankind? See Genesis 3:16 and CCC 400.

4. What judgment was given to the man in Genesis 3:17–19?

5. How did God respond to Adam and Eve's nakedness? See Genesis 3:21.

If it was necessary that the animal die in order for the skins to clothe Adam and Eve, this would be the first example of a substitute in death. An animal died so that Adam and Eve could be covered. Later, animals would be sacrificed to atone for the

Israelites' sins, and ultimately, Christ died as our substitute so that we could stand before God.

6. What was the final consequence of Adam and Eve's sin? See Genesis 3:23–24 and CCC 400.

7. The legacy that Eve left behind was a fallen nature that we all would inherit. What legacy would you like to leave? What is the most important thing you want to pass on to the next generation?

Our own life and how we live it has consequences. We hand on to the next generation our good and our bad. Never underestimate the strength of a woman and her power to influence. We can see the consequences of Adam and Eve's sin: separation from the Father. But they didn't just lose this intimacy for themselves. Their children and all of mankind would bear the consequences of their disobedience. The same is true for us today. Those who suffer the consequences of our actions are most often those we love.

Quiet your heart and enjoy His presence. . . . He is all you need.

Dear Lord,

I wonder if it seemed like such a tiny thing to Eve. It was just a little deviation from the rules— nothing too major. Yet as is so often the case, the consequences snowballed and she was left with enormous regret. Holy Spirit, help me to look at my own life. Are there areas of my life where I am tempted to blame others for my own choices? Are there choices I am making that are going to reap negative consequences for those whom I love? What am I passing on to the next generation? Is it an example of obedience to You or the consequences of going my own way? What legacy will I leave behind?

Conclusion

"Man, tempted by the devil, let his trust in his Creator die in his heart and, abusing his freedom, disobeyed God's command. This is what man's first sin consisted of. All subsequent sin would be disobedience toward God and lack of trust in his goodness" (CCC 397).

What virtue could have protected Eve from all the trouble she got into? It's the same virtue that can keep us from despair, or from taking matters into our own hands. It's the virtue of trust. Underneath Eve's discontentment and susceptibility to temptation was a lack of trust in God. Did He really want the best for her or was He holding back? Was His way truly the one that would lead to freedom and fulfillment? Was He worthy of trust?

Have you ever been in a situation of real need, only to discover that the friend you thought you could count on was nowhere to be found? While you may have continued with the friendship, no doubt your trust in that person was eroded. We trust those who we know are with us and for us, and who will stay by our side in the hard times.

Trust in Christ is never misplaced. He proved to us that He is in it for the long haul, *for our sake*, when He suffered and hung on the cross. He could have taken the easy way out, but He didn't. He stayed on the cross for you. He stayed for me.

In the times when people might desert us, that is when He is nearest. It's a comfort to know that He hears each spoken need. *He hears each spoken need.* Isn't that a comfort? Every detail of our life matters to Him. He cares. We don't always perceive His work, but He always acts on our behalf.

When life seems too much and disappointments weigh heavily on our hearts, and when the future seems scary, God invites us to trust Him enough to hide in Him. He encourages us to shed the masks that conceal our true selves, crawl into His lap, and let Him shelter us in His love.

Don't make Eve's mistake. Don't forget who you are. You are God's beloved daughter. He gave everything so that you could have that privilege. The intimacy that Eve lost in the garden is available to you. God calls to His tired, weak, and wandering daughters, "Come home and rest in my love! Your strength will return as you rest in me. I call you by name. You are mine. All you long for can be found in me. I am worthy of your trust. Hide yourself in my love."

My Resolution

In what specific way will I apply what I learned in this lesson?

Examples:

1. I will identify an area of my life where I am battling temptation. I will look at Eve's mistakes and see if I am making any of them myself. I will determine to flee—and ask for God's strength to help me do so—rather than dabble with temptation.

2. In order to battle discontentment, I will practice the art of thankfulness by starting a gratitude journal. I will write down ten things each day for which I am grateful.

3. I don't want to be like Eve, blaming someone else for my mistakes and hiding instead of saying, "I'm sorry." I will take a step toward reconciling a relationship in my life by writing a letter or making a phone call to apologize. If the one I'm hiding from is God, I will make it my priority this week to take part in the sacrament of reconciliation. No more hiding.

My Resolution:

Catechism Clips

CCC 225 (The Implications of Faith in One God) It means knowing the unity and true dignity of all men: everyone is made in the image and likeness of God.

CCC 343 Man is the summit of the Creator's work, as the inspired account expresses by clearly distinguishing the creation of man from that of the other creatures.

CCC 390 The account of the fall in *Genesis* 3 uses figurative language but affirms a primeval event, a deed that took place *at the beginning of the history of man*. Revelation gives us the certainty of faith that the whole of human history is marked by the original fault freely committed by our first parents.

CCC 397 Man, tempted by the devil, let his trust in his Creator die in his heart and, abusing his freedom, disobeyed God's command. This is what man's first sin consisted of. All subsequent sin would be disobedience toward God and lack of trust in his goodness.

CCC 400 The harmony in which they had found themselves, thanks to original justice, is now destroyed: the control of the soul's spiritual faculties over the body is shattered; the union of man and woman becomes subject to tensions, their relations henceforth marked by lust and dominion. Harmony with creation is broken: visible creation has become alien and hostile to man. Because of man, creation is now subject "to its bondage to decay." Finally, the consequence explicitly foretold for this disobedience will come true: man will "return to the ground," for out of it he was taken. *Death makes its entrance into human history.*

CCC 1605 Holy Scripture affirms that man and woman were created for one another: "It is not good that the man should be alone." The woman, "flesh of his flesh," his equal, his nearest in all things, is given to him by God as a "helpmate"; she thus represents God from whom comes our help.

Verse Study

See Appendix 3 for instructions on how to complete a verse study.

Genesis 1:27

1. Verse:

2. Paraphrase:

3. Questions:

4. Cross-references:

5. Personal Application:

Lesson 3

SARAH

Introduction

Have you ever wanted something so much you were utterly consumed by it? I remember being so homesick after living out of the country for almost ten years that I would have given anything to move back home. Everywhere I went, things brought me to tears. If I saw a pothole in the road, I cried for American streets. If I saw families celebrating together, I longed for my parents and sister with an intense sadness. When I wasn't allowed to drive alone because of safety issues, I cried because of my lack of freedom. Perhaps what made it all the harder was my unknown future. I didn't know when, if ever, things would change. I was surrounded by many blessings, but I couldn't (or wouldn't) see them because my focus was on what I lacked.

As I write, I am in the midst of morning sickness that seems to never go away. It's not morning sickness; it's all-day sickness, and I long for relief. It would be accurate to say that I am utterly consumed by my nausea. I'm waiting, and I'm not sure when it will get better. I'm trying to remain grateful, but it seems that every other minute I'm distracted by my desire to feel normal again.

Your circumstances are no doubt different, but I think we all can relate to wanting something desperately. Even though much can be out of our control, what we do as we wait is really up to us. We can manipulate to get our way. We can break rules (or bend them) to get what we want. We can make everyone around us miserable because misery loves company. Or we can let our longing and waiting drive us closer to the heart of Christ. It's up to us.

Sarah was a woman who longed for something with every fiber of her being. Her arms were empty, and she wanted nothing more than for them to be filled with a baby. Women who lived during that time felt that if they didn't produce children, they had failed. Nothing was as important to Sarah as having a child. Watching other women enjoying what she lacked was painful. There must have been many times when she felt alone in her struggle. "Why?" she must have asked. "Why am I being denied something that is so freely given to everyone else? Isn't it a good thing for me to want a baby? I'm willing to pour out my life for the sake of another. Shouldn't my good desire result in an answer to my prayer?"

As our story opens, things have just gotten harder, not easier, for Sarah. Instead of her arms being filled, she has been taken away from all she knows, all that is familiar. While seeing sisters and friends enjoying motherhood must be painful, there also have been many times when she has been comforted by them in her sorrow. Having to leave them to follow her husband, Abram, must be wrenching.

As we read about Sarah, we might find ourselves asking why. "Why didn't God just give her what her heart desired? Why did she have to experience this unfulfilled longing? Why did she have to wait?" If we're honest, we often want to ask God these same questions about our own situations.

Perhaps the following words from Pope Benedict XVI can shed some light on why we suffer:

> Today, what people have in view is eliminating suffering from the world. For the individual, that means avoiding pain and suffering in whatever way. Yet we must also see that it is in this very way that the world becomes very hard and very cold. Pain is part of being human. Anyone who really wanted to get rid of suffering would have to get rid of love before anything else, because there can be no love without suffering, because it always demands an element of self-sacrifice, because, given temperamental differences and the drama of situations, it will always bring with it renunciation and pain.
>
> When we know that the way of love—this exodus, this going out of oneself—is the true way by which man becomes human, then we also understand that suffering is the process through which we mature. Anyone who has inwardly accepted suffering becomes more mature and more understanding of others, becomes more human. Anyone who has consistently avoided suffering does not understand other people; he becomes hard and selfish.
>
> Love itself is a passion, something we endure. In love I experience first a happiness, a general feeling of happiness. Yet, on the other hand, I am taken out of my comfortable tranquility and have to let myself be reshaped. If we say that suffering is the inner side of love, we then also understand why it is so important to learn how to suffer—and why, conversely, the avoidance of suffering renders someone unfit to cope with life. He would be left with an existential emptiness, which could then only be combined with bitterness, with

rejection, and no longer with any inner acceptance or progress toward maturity.[6]

We long to be mature, faith-filled women. Let's see what we can learn from Sarah's life, and then we will find ways to apply these important principles to our own lives.

Day One
THE LEAVING

Read Genesis 12.

1. What do we discover about Sarai from the following verses?

   Genesis 11:27–29

   Genesis 11:30

   Genesis 12:11, 14

   Genesis 20:12

2. What are some of the things that Sarai gave up when she followed Abram to Canaan? Remember that God spoke directly to Abram, not to Sarai. What might her reaction have been to Abram's announcement that they would be relocating?

---

[6] Benedict XVI, *God and the World* (San Francisco: Ignatius Press, 2002), 322.

3. What was the promise that compelled Abram to obey God? See Genesis 12:2–3. Can you find a connection between Genesis 12:3 and Genesis 3:15?

4. Sarai had given up a lot for this promise. When the good-byes had been said and many miles had been traveled, just when she might have thought the worst was over, famine hit. Abram rerouted them to Egypt, but their problems had just begun.

    A. What was Abram worried would happen?

    B. What was his solution?

    C. Whom was he most concerned about? How might this have made Sarai feel?

5. Have you ever been in a situation in which someone who should have protected you left you in a vulnerable position? How did you respond?

Sarai was taken into Pharaoh's palace, and Abram benefited from her ascent in position. He received flocks, herds, slaves, donkeys, and camels. But God wasn't pleased. He rescued Sarai, even if Abram had dropped the ball. *When* God did this is not clear. What is meant by Pharaoh's words, "I took her for my wife"? We don't know, but we can be sure that this experience had an impact on Abram and Sarai's relationship. God responded by striking Pharaoh and his household with plagues. In a nutshell, Pharaoh's response to Abram was, "Why didn't you just tell me the truth?" The pagan ruler was inflamed by Abram's lack of integrity. May this serve as a warning to us: We are to display character even when it involves risk. That's what it means to be a follower of Christ.

Quiet your heart and enjoy His presence. . . . You are precious in His sight.

What might Abram have done differently? Before we judge him too harshly, let's recognize our own tendency to lie when we feel threatened. No matter how hopeless our situation may seem, God can be trusted to see us through. If doing the right thing means that we are put in a position of greater risk, then it's a perfect time to call on God's promises to provide for us! We may not see a solution, but God, who knows all things, can always provide a way out. "No temptation has overtaken you that is not common to man. God is faithful, and he will not let you be tempted beyond your strength, but with the temptation will also provide the way of escape, that you may be able to endure it" (1 Corinthians 10:13). We have a choice. We can look at God through our difficulties, and the difficulties will make obedience seem impossible. Or we can look at our difficulties through God, knowing that He provides the strength and wisdom we need when we are at the end of our own resources. Put God between you and your difficulty. It'll create a space that helps you realize His perspective on your problems. Wait and see how He displays His power in your life! Take some time to look at your difficulties and temptations in light of God's power to deliver you. Ask Him for the rescue that you need. Affirm your trust in His faithfulness and love. "He who promised is faithful" (Hebrews 10:23).

Day Two
THE WAIT

Read Genesis 15:1–6 and 16:1–6.

1. A. What was the problem stated in Genesis 15:1–2?

    B. What did God promise in Genesis 15:4–5?

2. What was Sarai's solution to the problem? See Genesis 16:1–3.

The plan was for the baby to be born and for Sarai and Abram to adopt the baby as their own. Although this would be the *last* solution a modern-day woman would suggest ("Hey honey, why don't you go sleep with a younger woman?"), this was an accepted practice at that time. According to the *New International Commentary*, "an old Assyrian marriage contract" gave the following instructions: "If within two years she has not procured offspring for him, only she may buy a maid-servant and even later on, after she procures somehow an infant for him, she may sell her wherever she pleases."[7] Since Hagar was her slave, she was Sarai's property. As a result, Hagar's child would belong to Sarai.

3. How had Abram and Sarai most likely ended up with Hagar in the first place? See Genesis 12:16.

4. Do you see any similarities between what Abram did in Egypt and what Sarai did in Genesis 16?

5. What were some of the consequences that occurred when Sarai took matters into her own hands?

The consequence of Sarai's decision to take matters into her own hands would be felt throughout the generations. Ishmael, the son of Abram and Hagar, would later be the father of several prominent Arab tribes, and an ancestor of Muhammad. The relationship between Isaac's and Ishmael's descendants continues to be tense to this day.

Our instinct as women is to help. God created us this way (Genesis 2:18). But there's a fine line between helping and manipulating. Sarai took matters into her own hands

---

[7] Victor P. Hamilton, *The Book of Genesis: Chapters 1–17* (Grand Rapids, MI: William B. Erdman, 1990), 444.

and manipulated the situation. Her motives may have been good, but her methods were not.

6. Have you ever experienced the consequences of running ahead of God and taking matters into your own hands? Share your experience.

Waiting is hard, especially when we feel as if there's nothing we can do to help the situation. We can choose to wait passively or actively for God. Actively waiting means that we pray and exercise the muscle of faith by focusing on God's promises and learning more about His character, which will help us remember how reliable and powerful He is. Remember, "not one word has failed of all His good promises" (1 Kings 8:56).

Quiet your heart and enjoy His presence. . . . Bask in His smile as He delights in you.

If you are waiting for something, here are some promises from Scripture that you can hold on to during this time.

"They who wait for the Lord shall renew their strength, they shall mount up with wings like eagles, they shall run and not be weary, they shall walk and not faint" (Isaiah 40:31).

"Cast all your anxieties on Him, for He cares about you" (1 Peter 5:7).

"I waited patiently for the Lord; He inclined to me and heard my cry. He drew me up from the desolate pit, out of the miry bog, and set my feet upon a rock, making my steps secure. He put a new song in my mouth, a song of praise to our God. Many will see and fear, and put their trust in the Lord. Blessed is the man who makes the Lord his trust" (Psalm 40:1–4a).

"Trust in the Lord with all your heart, and do not rely on your own insight. In all your ways acknowledge Him, and He will make straight your paths" (Proverbs 3:5–6).

Take some time to cast your anxieties on God. If you are finding it hard to wait, share that with Him. He desires honesty and intimacy in His relationship with you. Ask Him to grow your trust and faith, because "without faith, it is impossible to please God" (Hebrews 11:6).

Day Three
THE GOD WHO SEES

Read Genesis 16:7–16.

1. Describe Hagar's circumstances and the emotions she might have been experiencing.

2. Do you think Hagar had much of a choice when it came to Sarai's plan for a child?

3. A. In Genesis 16:1–6, how do Abram and Sarai refer to Hagar?

   B. By contrast, how does God refer to us? See Isaiah 43:1.

It's far easier to mistreat someone when you look at him or her as a part of a group ("Oh, her? She's one of the slaves.") instead of as an individual, made in God's image, with dignity.

4. Do you think Hagar expected to encounter God when she fled to the wilderness? After her treatment by Abram and Sarai, do you think she expected to warrant the attention of their God? It doesn't appear that Hagar fled in pursuit of God, but God was in search of her. She was far from being insignificant to Him; He cared about her plight. God revealed Himself to Hagar in a personal, significant way. She responded by giving Him a name. What was it?

These phrases, "a God of seeing" and "the God of Vision," are translated *El Roi* in Hebrew. This name for God reveals His character as the God who sees. This revelation was life-altering for Hagar. Suddenly she knew that she was not alone. Someone could see her and her difficult circumstances. Someone was watching out for her. And that someone cared about Hagar's present and future.

What difference does El Roi make in our lives today? This name of God reminds us that He is not asleep on the job. When trials and distress enter our lives, He *sees*. Some of us have experienced circumstances that make us wonder if God has forgotten us, if He's gotten busy watching over His other children and missed the tragedy that visited our door. If these thoughts have played in your mind, remember, God's character does not change. God is the same yesterday, today, and forever. The same God who saw Hagar sees you. He sees the hurt that you are experiencing. One day, justice will be served. He promises this in 2 Thessalonians 1:5–10. It is not for us to judge. That is His job. But rest assured, He sees it all.

It's also a comfort to know God as El Roi if you have a loved one who is far from you. It's difficult not knowing what is going on in his or her life, but rest in the knowledge and truth that El Roi is watching over your loved one. He sees.

Quiet your heart and enjoy His presence. . . . His love for you is unconditional.

Dear God, El Roi, the God who sees,

Help me to know You better. Help me grasp this important aspect of Your character. I have hurts that make my heart cry out for justice. Sometimes I long even for revenge. I recognize how this eats me up inside, and I don't want to be this way. Help me to hand over my past to You. Help me to release my anger and hurt to You. You saw it all, and You promise to hold every person accountable for his or her actions. Help me to stop being the judge. Flood my heart with healing. Help me to forgive. Help me to trust. I claim Your promise made in Romans 8:28: "All things work for good for those who love God, who are called according to his purpose." Even in this, as I release my anger, please bring the goodness of healing and freedom into my heart.

Day Four
THE COVENANT

Do you think Sarai wanted to hit a "do over" button in her life? Things hadn't turned out as she had planned. Luckily for her and for us, God keeps His promises, in spite of the ways we mess things up.

Read Genesis 17:1–23 and 18:1–15.

1. A. God had already established a covenant with Abram in Genesis 15:18 ("To your descendants I give this land"). Abram now had a descendant, Ishmael. In the next covenant God made with Abram, what was His promise? See Genesis 17:4.

    B. What promise did God reiterate in Genesis 17:16?

    C. How did Abram immediately respond?

No wonder it was hard to imagine God working in this way through Sarai. Genesis 18:11 tells us that her body was no longer capable of childbearing. Perhaps that's why God changed both Abram's and Sarai's names to Abraham and Sarah. Maybe they both needed to look at one another through fresh eyes. Maybe they needed a reminder that God can do anything, even when hope is gone. God said again, "Your wife Sarah is to bear you a son, and you shall call him Isaac. I will maintain my covenant with him as an everlasting pact, to be his God and the God of his descendants after him."

2. A. What was Abraham's part of the covenant? See Genesis 17:9–10.

    B. How did Abraham respond? See Genesis 17:23.

Circumcision marked Abraham and his descendants as God's people. It was an outward sign of the covenant. It is no coincidence that within a year of Abraham's obedience, he was celebrating the birth of Isaac.

    C. According to Deuteronomy 30:6, what kind of circumcision did God ultimately want for His people?

    D. Can you see ways in which we might settle for an "outward sign" instead of experiencing circumcision of the heart?

3. Who came to visit Abraham and Sarah in Genesis 18:1–15?

4. When Sarah laughed at the thought of having a child in her old age, what was the Lord's response? See Genesis 18:14.

5. Do you believe in miracles? Why or why not?

Quiet your heart and enjoy His presence. . . . He is all you need.

God did the impossible for Sarah. Isaac's birth is recorded in Genesis 21. It wasn't according to Sarah's timetable, and it wasn't in the way that she expected. But He came through for her. Scripture is full of promises for you and for me. How He'll choose to fulfill them in our lives is unlikely to be the way we would predict. "For my thoughts are not your thoughts, nor are your ways my ways, says the Lord. As high as the heavens are above the earth, so high are my ways above your ways and my thoughts above your thoughts" (Isaiah 55:8–9). We may not understand His methods or timing, but we can be assured that His way is always best.

Is there something in your life that seems impossible? Talk to God about it. Ask Him to purify your heart so that your desires are in keeping with His will.

"For all the promises of God find their Yes in [Christ]" (2 Corinthians 1:20).

Day Five
THE LEGACY

1. How is Sarah remembered, according to Hebrews 11:11?

Clearly, something happened between the time that Sarah laughed at the thought of giving birth to a child (Genesis 18:12) and the actual conception. This verse tells us that she was given the power to conceive because she considered God faithful. The moving of God's hand to bless her was connected to her faith. Scripture doesn't record exactly how that change in Sarah's heart occurred. Perhaps her laughter wasn't rooted in doubt over what *God* was capable of doing but in what God could do through *her*. Sometimes that's what blocks our faith. It isn't that we doubt that God is powerful and able to do miracles. We just don't feel worthy of them, or we think He would never choose to do those things in our lives.

2. What encouragement do the following verses offer us when we doubt that God is willing to intersect our lives with His power?

Lamentations 3:22–23

2 Corinthians 12:9

Ephesians 1:11 (NAB)

Jeremiah 29:11

3. What is the definition of faith? See Hebrews 11:1 and CCC 1813 and 1814.

4. Why should we desire to be women of faith? See Hebrews 11:6, and give an example from your own life of the value of having faith.

5. In what sense is faith a grace? See CCC 153.

Quiet your heart and enjoy His presence. . . . He longs to shower you with love.

Enjoying God's presence, which is one way to describe spending time with Him in prayer, allows us to get to know Him better. Another way to know Him is by reading Scripture, as it reveals His heart and character. Why is it important that we get to know God? According to CCC 158, "It is intrinsic to faith that a believer desires to know better the One in whom he has put his faith and to understand better what He has revealed; a more penetrating knowledge will in turn call forth a greater faith, increasingly set afire by love."

Meditate on the following verses. Talk to God about what these verses reveal about who He is. Allow these truths to sink deep into your heart, strengthening your faith in the One who "will never forsake you or abandon you" (Hebrews 13:5).

"I love you, LORD, my strength, LORD, my rock, my fortress, my deliverer, my God, my rock of refuge, my shield, my saving horn, my stronghold!" (Psalm 18:1–2)

"The Lord is a stronghold for the oppressed, a stronghold in times of trouble" (Psalm 9:9).

"Though the mountains leave their place and the hills be shaken, my love shall never leave you nor my covenant of peace be shaken, says the Lord, who has mercy on you" (Isaiah 54:10).

"May the God of peace himself make you perfectly holy and may you entirely, spirit, soul, and body, be reserved blameless for the coming of our Lord Jesus Christ. The one who calls you is faithful, and he will also accomplish it" (1 Thessalonians 5:23–24).

Conclusion

Sarah made some big mistakes. People were hurt in the process, and the consequences were long term. We can look at Sarah in judgment, or we can look in the mirror to conclude that there's no such thing as a perfect person. But fortunately, there is a perfect God with a perfect plan.

God's perfect plan wasn't thwarted even when Sarah and Abraham made mistakes. His love and faithfulness weren't based on their performance. Yes, consequences of their wrong actions were felt, but God wasn't limited by them.

We can receive both a warning and hope as we reflect on Sarah's life. We aren't the only ones who feel the consequences of our actions. They affect our families, sometimes for generations to come. Our influence can be for good or ill. We can pass a baton of faith, wisdom, and contentment, or we can pass one of judgment, anger, unforgiveness, and a critical spirit. How will we be remembered? What kind of legacy are we passing along?

Any of us who have messed up, who look back on life decisions with regret, can receive hope when observing what God did in spite of Sarah's mistakes. He can do the same with our mixed-up lives. God enters our imperfection, and if we let Him, He takes all the broken pieces and makes them into something beautiful. He has a perfect plan for each of our lives, and if we want to experience it, we need only surrender the reins to Him. When we try to take matters into our own hands, we rarely end up with the happy ending we desire. But if we allow God to order our steps, He promises to guide us to what will bring us the greatest fulfillment and joy.

My Resolution

In what specific way will I apply what I learned in this lesson?

Examples:

1. I will begin each day with a focus on hope by reading the following Bible verses:

   "This is the day the Lord has made, let us rejoice and be glad in it!" (Psalm 118:24)

   "Is anything too marvelous for the Lord to do?" (Genesis 18:14)

2. Instead of rushing into a decision and taking matters into my own hands, I will go to adoration and spend time asking for God's direction and wisdom.

3. I want to know God better so that my faith in Him grows. I'll write one of the Bible verses from Day Five on a card and carry it with me, reminding myself of God's faithfulness.

My Resolution:

Catechism Clips

CCC 153 When St. Peter confessed that Jesus is the Christ, the Son of the living God, Jesus declared to him that this revelation did not come "from flesh and blood," but from "my Father who is in heaven." Faith is a gift of God, a supernatural virtue infused by him. "Before this faith can be exercised, man must have the grace of God to move and assist him; he must have the interior helps of the Holy Spirit, who moves the heart and converts it to God, who opens the eyes of the mind and 'makes it easy for all to accept and believe the truth.'"

CCC 158 "Faith seeks understanding": it is intrinsic to faith that a believer desires to know better the One in whom he has put his faith and to understand better what He has revealed; a more penetrating knowledge will in turn call forth a greater faith, increasingly set afire by love. The grace of faith opens "the eyes of your hearts" to a lively understanding of the contents of Revelation: that is, of the totality of God's plan and the mysteries of faith, of their connection with each other and with Christ, the center of the revealed mystery. "The same Holy Spirit constantly perfects faith by his gifts, so that Revelation may be more and more profoundly understood." In the words of St. Augustine, "I believe, in order to understand; and I understand, the better to believe."

CCC 1813 The theological virtues are the foundation of Christian moral activity; they animate it and give it its special character. They inform and give life to all the moral virtues. They are infused by God into the souls of the faithful to make them capable of acting as his children and of meriting eternal life. They are the pledge of the presence and action of the Holy Spirit in the faculties of the human being. There are three theological virtues: faith, hope, and charity.

CCC 1814 Faith is the theological virtue by which we believe in God and believe all that he has said and revealed to us, and that [the] Holy Church proposes for our belief, because he is truth itself. By faith "man freely commits his entire self to God." For this reason the believer seeks to know and do God's will. "The righteous shall live by faith." Living faith "work[s] through charity."

Verse Study

See Appendix 3 for instructions on how to complete a verse study.

Hebrews 11:11

1. Verse:

2. Paraphrase:

3. Questions:

4. Cross-references:

5. Personal Application:

Lesson 4

REBEKAH

Introduction

It all started out so perfectly: a storybook romance, followed by many children and a home filled with traditions and happy memories. But something happened. There was a mistake . . . a failure . . . a sin. And the glory of their life seemed snuffed out. She wanted someone to pay. She wanted to escape. So she did what she had to. At least that's what she told herself—because to admit failure, to seek and give forgiveness, to face the pain head-on, was too agonizing. And in the end, she lost it all. In grasping for vindication and escaping in the bottle, she lost the family that she so treasured. She was left alone.

So many of our stories start well. But then something eludes us. A desire is denied, or something happens that seems insurmountable. We grasp at what we think we need, what we think will satisfy the ache within us. But when we seek to fill that ache with anything other than God Himself, we end up disappointed.

Rebekah's story had a good beginning, too. Genesis 24 introduces us to a hardworking woman filled with initiative and ready to go the extra mile. She was chosen and delighted in. But like her mother-in-law, Sarah, when she really wanted something, she did whatever it took to get it. Heartache resulted.

Thankfully, the story doesn't end with her shortcomings. Threaded throughout every page we see our sovereign God, always working things out according to His purposes. He isn't limited by Rebekah's failures, and His plan isn't thwarted by ours, either. So, "are we to continue in sin that grace may abound? By no means!" (Romans 6:1–2) But what a blessing it is to know that forgiveness and a fresh start are always available. If we will go to Him with our heartache and unmet desires, He will rewrite our stories. He will take our crooked lines and rather than just drawing something straight, He'll create a masterpiece.

Day One
A WORTHY WOMAN

Read Genesis 24:1–27.

1. When Abraham was in search of a wife for his son Isaac, what were the things that were most important to him?

2. What qualities do you think are most important to look for in a spouse? If you have children, how are you teaching them what qualities they should be looking for?

3. Eliezer was looking for the ideal woman for Isaac. What do we learn from 1 Peter 3:3–4 about what God values in a woman?

4. Eliezer's first response was to ask God for guidance in his search for a bride for Isaac. He had learned a lot about God from Abraham's example. The people in your family and your closest friends observe your relationship with God. What are they learning about God from watching you?

5. What sign did Eliezer ask for from God? See Genesis 24:12–14.

6. What do we learn about Rebekah's character from her response to Eliezer? Bear in mind that a camel can drink up to twenty-five gallons of water.

Quiet your heart and enjoy His presence. . . . You are precious in His sight.

My dear daughter,

You receive so many messages that say your worth and value are determined by your physical beauty and accomplishments. I want to remind you that I look at things differently. "The Lord does not look at the things people look at. People look at the outward appearance, but the Lord looks at the heart" (1 Samuel 16:7). I see the many times you serve and go the extra mile. I delight in your willingness to sacrifice your own needs and desires for the sake of others. When I look at you, I say to myself, "She is beautiful!" Please don't veil your face before me, insisting that when I say, "She is beautiful," I am talking about someone else. I mean you.

~Your adoring Father

Day Two
PREPARING THE BRIDE

Read Genesis 24:28–67.

1. What thoughts might have been running through Rebekah's head as she heard Eliezer describe the reason for his journey and his perspective on their meeting?

2. A. What gifts were given to Rebekah as she prepared to become Isaac's bride? See Genesis 24:53.

B. In 2 Corinthians 11:2, Saint Paul is addressing the Church. How does he describe the relationship between the Church and Christ?

C. According to Revelation 19:6–9, what are we to wear for the wedding day of the Lamb (Jesus)?

D. What are some of the gifts our Bridegroom has given us to help us prepare to meet Him at the wedding feast? See Isaiah 61:10, Galatians 3:27, Ephesians 1:13–14, and Galatians 5:22–23.

To prepare us to meet Him face-to-face, Jesus offers us redemption and forgiveness, "in accord with the riches of his grace that he lavished upon us" (Ephesians 1:7–8). What a beautiful image—God lavishing us with grace. I'm sure that Rebekah loved her gold and silver jewelry and fabulous clothes, but nothing compares to the riches that God pours out on each one of His beloved daughters.

3. After Rebekah was given to Eliezer by Laban and his household, how quickly did Eliezer want to leave? What timetable did Rebekah's family prefer? What was Rebekah's response?

4. Stepping into the unknown and leaving all that Rebekah loved required a leap of faith. Yet, she didn't hesitate. Is there an area of your life where God has asked you to step out in faith? Are you delaying or are you responding with immediate obedience?

Quiet your heart and enjoy His presence. . . . Bask in His smile as He delights in you.

Take a few moments to talk with God about an area of your life where it is difficult for you to obey Him. Faith means that we believe something that we can't see, and it is the virtue we need when we are finding it hard to do things God's way instead of our own. Remember that blessing always follows obedience. Ask God to help you to shift your perspective from the unknown and the things you fear and onto His all-sufficiency and continuous provision of all that you need.

Day Three
UNEXPECTED ANSWERS

Read Genesis 25:19–22.

1. What blessing did Rebekah's family wish for her as she left for her new life with Isaac? See Genesis 24:60.

2. Was that blessing immediately experienced in her new marriage?

3. While she dealt with the heartache of infertility, what are two lessons that Rebekah had to learn about God's plan? See Isaiah 55:8–9 and Ecclesiastes 3:1.

4. A. The heartache of wanting a child when your womb and arms are empty is a raw pain. The ache is often intensified when having children seems to come so easily to many women, often to those who don't want them. Wanting something and having to wait for it is a form of suffering. Is there something for which you long? Is there a prayer in your heart that has yet been unanswered?

B. How do Saint Paul's words in Philippians encourage us to spend our time of waiting?

Philippians 4:6–7

Philippians 4:8

Philippians 4:11–13

5. God answered Isaac's prayer, but that didn't mean that things were easy. Rebekah's pregnancy was uncomfortable and difficult. She made this clear when she said, "If it is thus, why do I live?" (Genesis 25:22, RSV) In other words, "If this miserable state I'm in is the way our prayer was answered, what's the point? I'm still unhappy!" Sometimes the answer to our prayers isn't what we expect.

About seven months ago, I said the following to the Lord: "My heart's desire is to be totally abandoned to your will. I want to be like Saint Thérèse of Lisieux. I want to be able to say (and mean it!), 'If the Lord offered me the choice, I would not choose anything: I want nothing but what He wants. It is what He does that I love.'"[8]

I asked God to work in my life to help me to abandon my will to His. He answered me, but not in the way that I would have planned. He brought a challenging circumstance into my life, one that affected my health, my emotions, my productivity, my pride, and my ability to control my life. At the same time, I was no longer experiencing many of the comforts of His presence. By this I don't mean that He left me, because His Word says that He will *never* leave us or forsake us (Hebrews 13:5), but I didn't feel or sense His presence as I usually did. I related to Rebekah's words. In this place of darkness, stripped of all the things I wanted to offer God (such as my service and beautiful prayers), all I could offer Him was empty hands of surrender. But wasn't that exactly the place I had wanted to go?

---

[8] Father Jean C. J. d'Elbée, *I Believe in Love* (Manchester, NH: Sophia Institute Press, 2001) 87.

The answer to my prayer was His plan, in His timing, in His way . . . but I didn't find it easy.

What about you? Have you ever experienced an answer to a prayer that turned out to be other than what you expected? Share that experience here.

Quiet your heart and enjoy His presence. . . . His love for you is unconditional.

A dear friend of mine is also experiencing an unexpected answer to a heartfelt prayer. Her circumstance is stretching her, and although she recognizes that she is making spiritual progress, it's also hard. She wrote me the following:

God is showing me all kinds of things through this. A friend sent this thought to me and it has been amazing: "Ask the Lord, 'What is it that You want to be to me in this situation that You could not be to me in any other?' and He will show Himself to you in new ways through this."

If you are in a season of waiting, or if you are in the midst of a circumstance that you don't like, ask God the same question. What does He want to be to you in this situation that He could not be in any other? Each season of our lives has opportunities for us to get to know God in a new, personal way. The uniqueness of this particular circumstance has within it a distinctive opportunity to grow in intimacy with Christ. Ask Him for the eyes to see it and the heart to embrace Him within it.

Day Four
INSTANT GRATIFICATION

Read Genesis 25:23–32.

1. What prophecy did God share with Rebekah regarding the babies in her womb? See Genesis 25:23.

2. List all the things you learn about Esau and Jacob from Genesis 25:25–28.

   Esau:

   Jacob:

3. What are some reasons a parent might prefer one child to another? What are some of the things that result from favoritism within a family?

4. We may naturally feel a certain way, but if those feelings are likely to result in strife within our families, then we need to change the way we think in order to change the way we feel. As women, we are easily driven by our feelings and emotions, acting as if we have no choice in the matter. Only by taking the time to dwell on what is true and right are we strengthened to do the God-honoring thing, regardless of what we are feeling in the moment. "Finally brethren, whatever is true, whatever is honorable, whatever is lovely, whatever is gracious, if there is any excellence, if there is anything worthy of praise, think about these things" (Philippians 4:8). Disciplining the mind to dwell on a child's good characteristics helps to control the feelings that could drive a mother's behavior toward favoritism. What further light does CCC 1803 shed on these truths?

5. Describe the events of Genesis 25:29–34 in terms of what Esau valued and devalued. See Hebrews 12:16 for added insight.

Halley's Bible Handbook describes the deal as follows: "Esau's transfer of his birthright for a meal demonstrated that he was 'godless' (Hebrews 12:16), since at the heart of the birthright were the covenant promises that Isaac had inherited from Abraham. The owner of the birthright, generally the firstborn, also received at least a double portion of the father's wealth at the time of the father's death."[9]

6. Esau isn't the only one to struggle with long-term good versus short-term gain. God has given His children "redemption through his blood, the forgiveness of our trespasses, according to the riches of his grace which he lavished upon us" (Ephesians 1:8). He then has placed the Holy Spirit in our hearts as a guarantee that we will receive an eternal inheritance (Ephesians 1:14 and 2 Corinthians 1:22). While we wait for our inheritance, He asks us to "Look carefully then how you walk, not as unwise men but as wise, making the most of the time, because the days are evil. Therefore do not be foolish, but understand what the will of the Lord is" (Ephesians 5:15–17).

But it's so tempting to forget all that and live in a way that makes us happy in the moment! It's truly difficult to delay gratification. What are some of the things that tempt us to settle for instant satisfaction instead of the true blessing of godly living?

---

[9] Henry H. Halley, *Halley's Bible Handbook* (Grand Rapids, MI: Zondervan, 2007), 118.

Quiet your heart and enjoy His presence. . . . He is all you need.

The First Principle and Foundation

The goal of our life is to live with God forever.
God, who loves us, gave us life.
Our own response of love allows God's life
To flow into us without limit.

All the things in this world are gifts of God,
Presented to us so that we can know God more easily
And make a return of love more readily.

As a result, we appreciate and use all these gifts of God
Insofar as they help us develop as loving persons.
But if any of these gifts become the center of our lives,
They displace God
And so hinder our growth toward our goal.

In everyday life, then, we must hold ourselves in balance
before all of these created gifts insofar as we have a choice
and are not bound by some obligation.
We should not fix our desires on health or sickness,
Wealth or poverty, success or failure, a long life or a short one.
For everything has the potential of calling forth in us
A deeper response to our life in God.

Our only desire and our one choice should be this:
I want and I choose what better leads to God's deepening his life in me.[10]

—Saint Ignatius as paraphrased by David L. Fleming, SJ

---

[10] Michael Harter, SJ, *Hearts on Fire: Praying with Jesuits* (St. Louis: Loyola Press, 1993), 9.

Day Five
BLESSING AT ANY COST

Read Genesis 27:1–28:5.

1. God had promised that Jacob would be blessed, but instead of trusting God to work out His purposes with His timing and method, Rebekah took matters into her own hands. In her mind, the end justified the means. God doesn't see things that way. What insights do we gain from the following verses regarding trusting God instead of taking matters into our own hands?

   Psalm 33:9–11

   Proverbs 3:5–6

   Proverbs 14:12

2. Think back to a time when you were tempted to do whatever it took to achieve your desired end. When you gave it your all, what happened?

3. Describe Esau's reaction to the loss of his blessing.

4. We all can imagine Esau's bitter feelings as he realized what had happened. The unfairness of the situation was enough to cause deep resentment. Ultimately, however, resentment and anger do the most harm to the person holding those emotions. They begin to drive a bitter root deep into the heart, which then affects all relationships. What are we to do when we have been wronged? What is the

proper way to handle anger and bitterness? See Ephesians 4:31, Hebrews 12:15, and Proverbs 16:32.

The only way we can live out the truth in those Bible verses is by maintaining a clear picture of all that God has forgiven in us. We need to forgive so that a root of bitterness doesn't grow deep in our hearts. It's more commendable to be a woman who can rule her spirit (her emotions and will) than to be a person who can subdue a city.

5. What did Rebekah give up to arrange for Jacob's blessing by his father?

Does your heart cry out for justice when you read this story? Doesn't it seem wrong that the blessing is passed to Jacob through an act of deception and fraud? While it may seem wrong, it's important to know that God did not bless Rebekah and Jacob's plan. What we see here is simply the fact that God's plans cannot be thwarted by anyone. Remember the prophecy given to Rebekah in Genesis 25:23? God had declared at that time that Jacob would be the stronger and the blessing was to go to him. God had decided that the elder (Esau) was to serve the younger (Jacob). God's plan came to pass, and Jacob received the blessing. But had Rebekah not manipulated the situation and instead trusted God to work, she could have enjoyed seeing His will come to pass without personal heartache. Taking matters into our own hands and manipulating situations isn't worth it. Even when the prize is so desirable, it's always better to trust God and wait.

Quiet your heart and enjoy His presence. . . . He longs to shower you with love.

Having faith means believing with all our hearts that it can be done. Trust is the assurance that it will be done. We have faith in God when we know that He can do all things for our good. And we trust Him when we rest in the assurance that He will do all things for our good. When we say we have great faith in a person's abilities or potential, we mean we have great faith in what he or she can do. But trust is believing that the person will do it. There is a difference.

We do not suffer purely when we are full of anxiety. This is something from which we must be delivered in order to rejoice always. It is trust in God that delivers us from anxiety. Again we see the insufficiency of earth to fulfill the Word of God. We see that only God is sufficient to fulfill His promises. Then we rejoice because we know that He will do so. We do not know how, we do not know when, we do not even know if we will have the sense to see it, but we know that He will. —Mother Mary Francis, PCC[11]

Ask God to help you to trust Him in an area of your life where you are tempted to worry. You may not know how He'll help, you may not know when, but ask Him to grow your belief that He will.

Conclusion

Oh, how I relate to Rebekah. The love a mother has for her child, her desire to protect and provide for that child at any cost, can be all-consuming. It's a good desire, but when we are willing to manipulate to protect and provide, we'll have to deal with some nasty consequences.

I recently shared one of my parenting struggles with a friend. I explained that my husband and I had caught one of our children in a string of lies that added up to months of deception. We had said that simply saying "I'm sorry" wasn't enough. It was necessary, we felt, for that child to come clean—to talk through the specific ways in which we had been deceived. The response? A door slammed in anger. I wasn't sure when, if ever, the true apology would come. I shared with my friend how frustrating this was to me.

I talked about how through this experience, I had seen how much I had controlled and manipulated my husband during these very same months. He had known our child was up to something, and the lengths I had gone to as I advocated for and defended our child had crossed a line. I had undermined Leo, disrespected him, and battled him at every turn. "I'm so disgusted with myself! I've told him I'm sorry, but I haven't gone into all the details. It would just be too hard to lay it all out!"

My friend started to laugh. "Can't you see? You are expecting behavior from your child that you can't—or won't—even do yourself!" It made me think of Matthew 7:5: "You hypocrite, first take the plank out of your own eye, and then you will see clearly to remove the speck from your brother's eye."

---

[11] Mother Mary Francis, PCC, *Come, Lord Jesus: Meditations on the Art of Waiting* (San Francisco: Ignatius Press, 2010).

Note that Jesus doesn't say we are to do nothing about the speck in our child's eye. But He puts things in the proper order, so that we go to our child in the right spirit—a spirit of humility. This helps us to discipline with love, not harshness, and with humility, not pride.

Dan Allender writes of this in his book *How Children Raise Parents*:

> Without an awareness of our deep impotence, we are full of self-satisfaction and arrogance. But strength that has been tempered by failure will be generous and tender, nourishing and kind. . . .
>
> We must also have the ability to confess to our children that there is real hope for love in brokenness. It's one thing to admit failure. (Some do so with such frequency and pathetic demand, it's almost worse than not admitting failure at all.) But to confess failure, truly, is to hunger for redemption.
>
> And redemption is not merely change, nor is it knowing that one is forgiven. There are some who change only to become proud and demanding of others to do the same. Others know they are forgiven and use that as an excuse to perpetrate the same harm again and again, expecting no personal consequences. True redemption involves being struck dumb by the enormity of our failure and then struck even dumber by the enormity of the heart of God that cancels our debt. Redemption brings a level of gratitude that frees the heart to desire the sweet balm of forgiveness for oneself and others. It frees the heart to extend to others what has been so freely given to us.
>
> Redemption is the soil that enables our children to see our failures and therefore face their own.[12]

This is the lesson we learn from Rebekah. God can make use of everything—even our mistakes—in His salvific plan. We all make poor choices sometimes. How we respond to them makes all the difference. Can we be authentic? Can we admit our failure? By doing so, we can give others hope for love in their brokenness. How grateful we are for the enormous heart of God that cancels our debt and redeems our failures.

---

[12] Dan B. Allender, *How Children Raise Parents* (Colorado Springs: Waterbrook Press, 2003), 104.

My Resolution

In what specific way will I apply what I learned in this lesson?

Examples:

1. Instead of trying to hide my failures, I will seek authenticity in my relationships. Most important, I'll be authentic in my relationship with God, going to reconciliation to confess to Him what I've done or failed to do. I will also be honest with the people in my life, living transparently rather than covering up where I fall short.

2. I will pray an Act of Faith prayer every morning to strengthen my soul so that I can trust God in areas of life that cause me anxiety.

   Act of Faith prayer:

   > O my God, I firmly believe that Thou art one God in three divine Persons, Father, Son, and Holy Spirit; I believe that Thy Divine Son became man, and died for our sins, and that He will come to judge the living and the dead. I believe these and all the truths which the Holy Catholic Church teaches, because Thou hast revealed them, who canst neither deceive nor be deceived. Amen.

3. In order to live out Philippians 4:8, I will begin my day by thanking God for the many blessings in my life.

   "Whatever is true, whatever is honorable, whatever is just, whatever is pure, whatever is lovely, whatever is gracious, if there is any excellence, if there is anything worthy of praise, think about these things" (Philippians 4:8).

My Resolution:

Catechism Clip

CCC 1803 "Whatever is true, whatever is honorable, whatever is just, whatever is pure, whatever is lovely, whatever is gracious, if there is any excellence, if there is anything worthy of praise, think about these things."

A virtue is an habitual and firm disposition to do the good. It allows the person not only to perform good acts, but to give the best of himself. The virtuous person tends toward the good with all his sensory and spiritual powers; he pursues the good and chooses it in concrete actions.

The goal of a virtuous life is to become like God.

Verse Study

See Appendix 3 for instructions on how to complete a verse study.

Philippians 4:8

1. Verse:

2. Paraphrase:

3. Questions:

4. Cross-references:

5. Personal Application:

Lesson 5: Connect Coffee Talk

LEAH AND RACHEL – DIGNITY WITHOUT COMPARISON

Accompanying DVD can be viewed at:
www.walkingwithpurpose.com/courses/videos
Select: *Discovering Our Dignity* – Talk 02 – Leah and Rachel – Dignity Without Comparison

Please read Genesis 29:16–30:2 before watching the video. Lesson 6 will allow you to follow up with a deeper dive into this passage.

At the root of so many of our struggles, we are really searching for _____ and _____.

1. **Comparison**

2. **Insecurity**

The opposite of dignity is _____.

Our insecurity comes from _____.

A fear of failure can lead to _____ behavior.

Seeking security in our reputations causes us to fear _____ and _____.

Sometimes our desire for acceptance is so great that we'll take _____ if we can't get _____.

3. Why God Is the Answer to Our Quest for Dignity

God is the answer to our quest for dignity because He is the only source of true, lasting security.

Romans 12:2

Proverbs 31:25

2 Corinthians 12:9–10

Psalm 8:3–8

Questions for Discussion

1. Comparison and competition robbed Rachel and Leah of what could have been a wonderful relationship between sisters. Have you experienced the same thing, either within your family or among friends? What steps do you think women can take to rid their relationships of comparison and competition?

2. Can you identify any area in your life where an underlying fear is causing you to feel insecure? Fear of failure? Fear of being alone? Fear of not being or having enough? Fear of rejection?

3. God has clothed you with dignity and honor (Psalm 8:3–8). Have you experienced the difference it makes when your mind is renewed by focusing on how God sees you? What can you do differently this week to make sure that you are edifying your soul instead of feeding your insecurities?

Lesson 6

LEAH AND RACHEL

Introduction

As Rebekah reflected on what she was going to be left with when Jacob departed for Haran, she wasn't pleased with her company. Her son Esau had married a Hittite woman who disgusted her. She said that if Jacob did the same, her life wouldn't be worth living. Isaac stepped in and had the following parting words for Jacob:

> "Do not marry a Canaanite woman. Go at once to Paddan Aram, to the house of your mother's father Bethuel. Take a wife for yourself there, from among the daughters of Laban, your mother's brother. May God Almighty bless you and make you fruitful and increase your numbers until you become a community of peoples. May he give you and your descendants the blessing given to Abraham, so that you may take possession of the land where you now live as an alien, the land God gave to Abraham." Then Isaac sent Jacob on his way, and he went to Paddan Aram, to Laban son of Bethuel the Aramean, the brother of Rebekah, who was the mother of Jacob and Esau (Genesis 28:1–5).

Rebekah wanted Jacob to marry someone who was similar to her in heritage. Foreign wives brought with them their own traditions and culture, and the differences caused a rub in family relationships.

Because I was a "foreign wife," I can understand that cultural differences add a certain stress to the melding of two lives in marriage. But even in a marriage in which both husband and wife come from the same background, there are always dissimilarities. So often, opposites attract, and then those very things that initially seemed so fresh later become annoying.

Jacob was soon to find that even though his wives would come from his mother's culture, there would be many bumps along the road. Every marriage experiences this. We can differ in terms of the importance of faith in daily life, the way we want to raise children, the way we resolve conflict, gender roles—even in the way we use toothpaste. God faithfully offers us an opportunity to turn these frustrations into good. In fact, our closest relationships have the most potential for teaching and changing us for the good. As we bump up against one another and find that the fit isn't perfect, God can use that "rubbing" to polish us so that we "shine as lights in the world" (Philippians 2:15). It can be easier to take the bitter with the sweet when we see the good produced in us as our character is softened and molded through adversity.

Day One
LOVE AT FIRST SIGHT

Read Genesis 29:1–20.

1. Why didn't the shepherds immediately get down to the business of watering their sheep?

2. What was the first thing Jacob did when he set eyes on Rachel? What was the second thing he did?

Nothing brings out the strength of a man like trying to impress a lady. I can remember my first-grade Halloween party at school. One of my classmates, Albert, had come dressed as Superman. He flexed and showed all the girls his muscles, and we oohed and aahed appropriately. But that wasn't enough. He needed to show us just how strong he was, so first-grader Albert walked over to the large fish tank and lifted it above his head. Unfortunately, the strength it took to get the fish tank up was all the strength he had, and as he tried to hold it there, his muscles wobbled, and the whole thing came crashing down. Fish were flopping all over the room, and suddenly Albert didn't seem quite so amazing to the girls.

Lucky for Jacob, his show of strength resulted in sweeping Rachel off her feet. I love educator Leon Kass' take on the scene:

> Jacob's boldness with the boulder is matched by his boldness with the woman. The flock he waters, but the woman he kisses. To protect Jacob's reputation, commentators have been at pains to insist that this was a genteel kiss, a sign of

respect or familiar affection. And Jacob truly had every reason to be overjoyed to have arrived safely and to have met up with his kin; the tears he weeps could be tears of joyous relief, his lifted voice could be an expression of thanksgiving. Indeed, Jacob could well take this fortuitous meeting—a perfect answer in the perfect place at the perfect moment—as a sign that Rachel is his destiny. But his kiss is bold in any case, and, considered as a sequel to his superhuman heroics with the stone, it looks to be love-inspired. He kisses Rachel even before speaking to her. In fact, this is the only instance in biblical narrative in which a man kisses a woman who is neither his wife nor his mother. Jacob acts on strong and immediate passion, and Rachel allows it. Only after the kiss and the weeping does Jacob speak, identifying himself as her father's kin and as Rebekah's son. Rachel, who has apparently remained speechless, runs home to tell her father.[13]

3. List what you learn about Leah and Rachel from Genesis 29:16–17.

4. What might it have been like for Leah to grow up with a sister like Rachel?

5. Living in the shadow of another woman's beauty or ability can be a hard cross to bear. Have you ever had a relationship in which this was your experience? Or do you relate more to Rachel? Have you been the woman casting the shadow?

---

[13] Leon R. Kass, *The Beginning of Wisdom: Reading Genesis* (New York: Free Press, 2003), 313.

6. How are the seven years served by Jacob for Rachel's hand in marriage described?

Quiet your heart and enjoy His presence. . . . You are precious in His eyes.

If you have been living in another woman's shadow, you may think that you have no choice in the matter. We can imagine that Leah felt her "second best" position was inescapable. Rachel was the apple of Jacob's eye. Leah might have been older, and it may have been expected that she would marry first, but where was the man who considered her the special one? He was nowhere to be found. Where do we go when we don't feel special? What can console us when it seems that we're always passed by? We can call out to the lover of our soul, "Keep me as the apple of your eye. Hide me in the shadow of your wings" (Psalm 17:8). Take a few moments to meditate on the fact that you are the apple of the eye of the Creator of the universe. He invites you to spend some time in the shadow of His wings, a place where your innermost being is treasured and loved.

Day Two
THE DECEIVER IS DECEIVED

Read Genesis 29:21–35.

1. A. Based on what you learned in Lesson 4 on Rebekah, what irony do you see in Laban's deception of Jacob?

   B. When have you recognized your own sin by seeing a magnified version of it in another person? Maybe you saw it in your child or a close friend. How did that make you feel?

2. You may wonder how it's possible that Jacob didn't figure out that his bride was actually Leah until the next morning. It was likely due to the fact that a bride was veiled when she was brought to her bridegroom. Needless to say, Jacob felt cheated. How do you think Leah felt when she saw his reaction to her unveiled face?

Regardless of whether Leah had been a willing accomplice or had been forced by her father to marry Jacob, she had just given her virginity to him, in hopes that she'd receive protection and love in return. Instead, she was rejected, undesired, unsought. And within a week, she was displaced as Jacob was allowed also to marry Rachel.

3. "Jacob then consummated his marriage with Rachel also, and he loved her more than Leah" (Genesis 29:30). What a mess. What a recipe for heartache! Names carried great significance in Old Testament times. Record the names Leah chose for her sons and their meanings.

   Son's name: **Name's meaning:**

4. What do these names and meanings reveal about the progression of Leah's expectations, her relationship with God, and her perspective on her situation?

5. Leah hoped for love in a loveless marriage. How does a woman today stay faithful to her marriage vows when she doesn't feel loved by her husband?

It's essential to fill the love tank with unconditional love from God. Every woman is chosen and loved by God. If we base our self-worth on what any person thinks of us, we'll spend our lives riding a roller coaster of emotions. But if we start every day drinking deeply of God's love, we'll be able to stay steady even when other people don't love us as they should.

Quiet your heart and enjoy His presence. . . . Bask in His smile as He delights in you.

We all struggle with relationships that are less than perfect. Can you think of one in your life that you wish was better? Have you asked God to intervene, but the situation has remained the same? In the words of Alice Mathews, author of A Woman God Can Use, *"God often works in our lives, not by giving us a perfect situation, but by showing His power and love in our very imperfect situations."[14] Ask God to give you insight into His purposes in this struggle. Ask for eyes to see His power and love being displayed in the midst of your difficulties.*

Day Three
DESPERATE MEASURES

Read Genesis 30:1–24.

1. Which emotions did Rachel display because of her barrenness?

2. Where did Jacob encourage Rachel to look for the source of fertility?

---

[14] Alice Mathews, *A Woman God Can Use* (Nashville, TN: Thomas Nelson, 1990), 23.

3. What insights can we gain from CCC 2374, 2378, and 2379, which reveal the teachings of the Catholic Church regarding fertility?

"Sorrow, suffering, is but a kiss of Jesus—a sign that you have come so close to Jesus that He can kiss you. . . . So let us be happy when Jesus stoops down to kiss us. I hope we are close enough that He can do it." —Blessed Teresa of Calcutta

If you are suffering the cross of infertility, perhaps this resource will be helpful:

Hannah's Tears Ministry: Catholic Infertility Support
hannahstearsinfertilitysupport.blogspot.com/

4. Do you think it's easy or difficult to trust God with your fertility? Why?

5. It was culturally acceptable for Rachel to give her maid, Bilhah, and for Leah to give her maid, Zilpah, to Jacob to produce children on their behalf. But that doesn't mean that God approved or that it was good for the family. In time, God's people came to understand that marriage is a lifelong, exclusive commitment between one man and one woman. Still, our modern culture downplays the devastating effects of infidelity and adultery in marriage. At the end of CCC 2380, adultery is said to be an image of another sin. What is it?

6. "Then God remembered Rachel; he heard her prayer and made her fruitful. She conceived and bore a son" (Genesis 30:22–23). What change took place in Rachel between Genesis 30:1 and Genesis 30:22?

Quiet your heart and enjoy His presence. . . . His love for you is unconditional.

As you reflect on the cross that you are carrying, meditate on the following verses. Discuss them with the Lord. Ask Him to fill your heart with peace as you trust in His goodness and His plan for your life.

"With full voice I cry to the Lord; with full voice I beseech the Lord. Before God I pour out my complaint, lay bare my distress. My spirit is faint within me, but you know my path" (Psalm 142:2–3).

"In his mind a man plans his course, but the Lord directs his steps" (Proverbs 16:9).

"In the same way, the Spirit too comes to the aid of our weakness; for we do not know how to pray as we ought, but the Spirit itself intercedes with inexpressible groanings. And the one who searches hearts knows what is the intention of the Spirit, because it intercedes for the holy ones according to God's will" (Romans 8:26–27).

Day Four
FLEEING IN SECRET

In Genesis 30:25–43, Jacob asked Laban to send him back to his homeland, Canaan, with his wives and children. Laban acknowledged that he had grown prosperous because of Jacob's labors, and he asked Jacob what he could give him in return. Jacob asked for all of the speckled, spotted goats and black lambs from the flock. Jacob knew these animals were rare, but he didn't think he was asking for too much. Laban agreed, but that very day, he removed all the goats that were speckled or spotted, as well as every black lamb, and he put them in the care of his sons. Jacob continued to care for Laban's flocks even though he had been cheated out of these wages. God blessed him, and the offspring of the animals in his care were born speckled, spotted, and dark. Jacob then separated his animals from Laban's, and in time he grew rich.

Read Genesis 31:1–24.

1. What was prompting Jacob to leave Laban and return home to Canaan?

2. It seems that jealousy was a trait that ran in the family. Rachel, Leah, and their brothers all struggled with it. How does Romans 12:15 recommend that we deal with the emotion of jealousy? Do you find this difficult? Why or why not?

It's hard to rejoice with those who rejoice when God has given the other person exactly what we are longing for. Is it even possible? God would not have commanded it if it weren't. To understand how to adjust our mind-set so that we can keep jealousy at bay and instead be happy for others' successes, we can look at Romans 11:33–36: "O the depth of the riches and wisdom and knowledge of God! How unsearchable are his judgments and how inscrutable his ways! 'For who has been his counselor?' 'Or who has given a gift to him that he might be repaid?' For from him and to him are all things. To him be glory forever. Amen."

Verses like this remind us that we need to look at life through the wide lens of God's mercy. He doesn't owe us anything, yet He has blessed us with so much. We haven't gotten what we deserve. Instead of the punishment we should receive for our poor choices, we receive mercy and grace. When discontentment and jealousy spring up in our hearts, it's time to reflect on all that God has given us and what a privilege it is to be His beloved daughter. What is our reference point? Is it what we wish we had, or what we've already been given by God?

3. Where did Jacob believe his blessings came from? Reflecting on his history, in what way is this evidence of spiritual growth in his life?

4. Rachel and Leah finally agreed on something! How did they respond to Jacob's words in Genesis 31:5–13?

5. Jacob, Rachel, and Leah all came to a point of trusting God to lead them after it became clear that they had no other choice. God's plan was better than anything they could come up with! Have you ever experienced coming to the end of your resources, and only then being able to take the leap of faith required to trust in God's plan? Share your story.

6. When Jacob and his wives left, no one said good-bye. Had God commanded that Jacob leave in secret?

Quiet your heart and enjoy His presence. . . . He is all you need.

God's power was not limited by Laban's deceitful ways. We can take comfort in this fact when we are mistreated. God is a just judge, and He is able to meet our needs and help us to thrive even in the midst of unfair treatment. Is there an area of your life in which you feel maltreated? Does it seem that manipulative, deceitful people get ahead in life, and honesty doesn't yield the same results? Take some time to talk to God about your situation. Be reminded of His ability to overcome any obstacle. Remember that His power and plan is never thwarted by man's sin and deceit.

Day Five
A COVENANT AND A NEW BEGINNING

Read Genesis 31:25–54.

1. Why did Laban decide not to harm Jacob, and instead choose to talk with him to reach a resolution?

2. What did Jacob say would happen to the person found with Laban's household idols?

The household idols (Hebrew *teraphim*) were small figurines. Often, idols like these were used for divination purposes. While Rachel's theft might indicate that she, too, was a worshipper of these foreign gods, more likely she was after items she considered monetarily significant. The Nuzi tablets (Hurrian law from contemporary Mesopotamia) link control of household idols with inheritance rights, supporting the view that Rachel's theft was prompted more by financial motives than by spiritual belief.[15]

3. Why might Laban not have made Rachel stand up when he came to inspect her tent? See Leviticus 15:19–24.

4. What did each party agree to in the covenant between Jacob and Laban? How did they mark the covenant?

---

[15] Dorothy Kelley Patterson and Rhonda Harrington Kelley, *Women's Evangelical Commentary: Old Testament* (Nashville, TN: Holman Reference, 2011), 73.

5. A chapter in Jacob's life ended when he made the covenant with Laban. He would no longer have to deal with Laban's deceit and envy. Jacob had the opportunity to turn over a new leaf in his *own* life, as up to this point, much of what he had done was characterized by deceit. His new beginning is described in Genesis 32:28. Prior to this passage, he wrestled all night with God. Describe what changed for Jacob.

6. Rachel probably thought that she had a fresh start ahead of her, too. As she looked to the future, she must have been excited at the thought of seeing Joseph grow up. Her joy increased with her second pregnancy. But things didn't go as planned. "Rachel began to be in labor and to suffer great distress. When her pangs were most severe, her mid-wife said to her, 'Have no fear! This time, too, you have a son.' With her last breath—for she was at the point of death—she called him Ben-oni" (Genesis 35:16–18). She never had the chance to raise her second son, Benjamin. Her life and death are reminders that the time for a fresh start is now. We often think we have so much time in which to get our hearts right with God, but the truth is, we don't know the future. Is there an area of your life that you know needs changing, but you have put off getting serious about it? What is holding you back from full obedience?

Quiet your heart and enjoy His presence. . . . He longs to shower you with love.

When we are ready to turn away from a sinful pattern and embrace total obedience to God, He promises us a fresh start. That's the beauty of the sacrament of reconciliation. When we confess our sins, they are forgiven. The slate is wiped clean. We're given a new beginning. We experience the greatest fruit in reconciliation when we've taken the time to prepare well. Take some time to examine your conscience, asking the Holy Spirit to reveal to you any area of your life that needs His healing grace.

"Therefore, if anyone is in Christ, he is a new creation. The old has gone, the new has come!" (2 Corinthians 5:17)

"Remember not the events of the past, the things of long ago consider not; See, I am doing something new! Now it springs forth, do you not perceive it? In the desert I make a way, in the wasteland, rivers" (Isaiah 43:18–19).

"I, even I, am he who blots out your transgressions, for my own sake, and remembers your sins no more" (Isaiah 43:25).

Conclusion

If I were to summarize Leah's and Rachel's heartaches, I would say that they both spent a great deal of time longing for something that seemed very far out of reach. They both had good desires. It wasn't as if they were pining for material possessions or power. One wanted the love, or at least the respect, of her husband. The other longed for a child.

When Rachel and Leah were at their lowest point, neither of them could see what God could see. God knew that Rachel wouldn't live past her second child's birth. Each year before Benjamin's birth was a gift. She experienced more time with her beloved Jacob than she would have if she'd gotten pregnant right away. Leah didn't feel honored, but she would be a part of a lineage remembered throughout history. David, Israel's greatest king, would come from her son Judah. And from King David would come the Lion of the Tribe of Judah, Jesus Christ. What greater honor could there be?

When God says "no" or "wait" to our heartfelt requests, we long to see the whys behind His decisions. We might focus on the fact that what we are asking for is a good thing. We might think of His power, and point out that it wouldn't be very hard for Him to say yes to this one request. We can easily let our thoughts dwell entirely on what we don't have, instead of all that we have received already.

I've had many times in prayer when God has said no to my request. During the lowest points of those experiences, I have cried out to Him, "You promised in 1 Corinthians 10:13 that because of your faithfulness, you would never send me more than I can bear! This is it! I'm telling you, this is more than I can bear. I'm going to sink under this pain and disappointment and grief."

God impressed on my heart the following: My suffering was *not* more than I could bear, although it might have been *as much* as I could bear. Most important, I would only be able to walk through this valley if I leaned entirely on Him. And that is when

He showed me His faithfulness. I experienced Him as Emmanuel, God with us. I felt His closeness as He strengthened me and helped me, upholding me with His righteous right hand (Isaiah 41:10).

Romans 8:28 promises us, "We know that in everything God works for good with those that love Him, who are called according to His purpose." It doesn't say that everything that happens to us is good. But it assures us that with time, and with our cooperation, God can bring amazing things out of our most desperate hours.

My Resolution

In what specific way will I apply what I learned in this lesson?

Examples:

1. To remind myself how special I am in God's eyes, I'll read Psalm 139 each morning and meditate on it.

2. In order to receive encouragement from the Lord, I'll write down one of the following verses and carry it with me. I'll read it whenever the cross I bear starts to feel too heavy.

    "With full voice I cry to the Lord; with full voice I beseech the Lord. Before God I pour out my complaint, lay bare my distress. My spirit is faint within me, but you know my path" (Psalm 142:2–4).

    "Fear not, for I have redeemed you; I have summoned you by name; you are mine. When you pass through the waters, I will be with you; and when you pass through the rivers, they will not sweep over you. When you walk through the fire, you will not be burned; the flames will not set you ablaze" (Isaiah 43:1–2).

3. I'll write down the examination of conscience that I did in the *Quiet Your Heart* section of Day Five, and bring it with me to the sacrament of reconciliation.

My Resolution:

Catechism Clips

CCC 2374 Couples who discover that they are sterile suffer greatly. "What will you give me," asks Abraham of God, "for I continue childless?" And Rachel cries to her husband Jacob, "Give me children, or I shall die!"

CCC 2378 A child is not something *owed* to one, but is a *gift*. The "supreme gift of marriage" is a human person. A child may not be considered a piece of property, an idea to which an alleged "right to a child" would lead. In this area, only the child possesses genuine rights: the right "to be the fruit of the specific act of the conjugal love of his parents," and "the right to be respected as a person from the moment of his conception."

CCC 2379 The Gospel shows that physical sterility is not an absolute evil. Spouses who still suffer from infertility after exhausting legitimate medical procedures should unite themselves with the Lord's Cross, the course of all spiritual fecundity. They can give expression to their generosity by adopting abandoned children or performing demanding services for others.

CCC 2380 Adultery refers to marital infidelity. When two partners, of whom at least one is married to another party, have sexual relations—even transient ones—they commit adultery. Christ condemns even adultery of mere desire. The sixth commandment and the New Testament forbid adultery absolutely. The prophets denounce the gravity of adultery; they see it as an image of the sin of idolatry.

Verse Study

See Appendix 3 for instructions on how to complete a verse study.

Genesis 31:42

1. Verse:

2. Paraphrase:

3. Questions:

4. Cross-references:

5. Personal Application:

Lesson 7

RAHAB

Introduction

Much time had passed between the births of Rachel's and Leah's children in Genesis and Rahab's story in the book of Joshua. To set the scene:

Jacob's sons, called the sons of Israel, grew up and experienced famine in their land. Joseph, Rachel's first son, had been so irritating to his brothers that earlier they had sold him into slavery in Egypt. When the brothers needed food because of the famine, their father, Jacob, sent them to Egypt, where food was plentiful. Because Pharaoh favored Joseph, his brothers and their families were given food and allowed to stay in Egypt. As time passed, their numbers multiplied. A new Egyptian leader came into power and Joseph was forgotten. The Israelites fell out of favor and were enslaved by the Egyptians. It took God's miracles and Moses' obedience to free them. God had heard their cries, and promised to bring them home.

The miracles that God performed were astonishing and displayed His limitless power. Yet when the Israelites were faced with the size and strength of the people living in the land that God had promised to them, they were overcome with fear. Spies were sent to scope out the land. They returned, assuring everyone that the land was fruitful and desirable, but they reported that "the people who dwell in the land are strong, and the cities are fortified and very large . . . we are not able to go up against the people; for they are stronger than we" (Numbers 13:28, 31). Only two spies had faith in God's power to bring them victory: Joshua and Caleb. They were overruled.

The Israelites' doubt in God's ability to deliver them to the Promised Land resulted in their wandering for forty years in the desert. The entire generation that had doubted died in the wilderness. Only Moses, Joshua, and Caleb survived.

As faith grew, so did the victories. The Israelites conquered the King of Arad, the King of the Amorites, King Og of Bashen, King Balak of Moab, and the five Kings of Midian. Moses died, and Joshua became the leader. Their time had finally come. Joshua prepared the people to claim the Promised Land. All that stood between them was the Jordan River and the thick walls of the city of Jericho.

Across the Jordan lived the same people who had so terrified the Israelites when they had scouted the land years ago. But things were different now. Behind the tall walls of Jericho, the people had heard the stories of the Israelites' victories. From their vantage point, the residents of Jericho could see the Israelites camped across the Jordan River in Shittim. As they waited to see what the Israelite army would do, they quaked in fear.

Rahab was one of the citizens of Jericho. She, too, had heard the stories of the Israelites and their God. But her reaction differed from that of her countrymen. The stories made her yearn for the Israelite God. While her profession, prostitution, left her stripped of dignity, something in her longed to be swept up and protected by the God who was coming. Would He care about her? Was she disqualified from His love? She was a harlot. She wasn't one of His people. She lived on the wrong side of the river. Yet in spite of everything stacked against her, she hoped.

For those of us who have felt disqualified to be loved by God, for those of us ashamed of our past, for those of us who desperately need a rescue, may Rahab's story remind us that our God looks for a tender heart of faith. There is hope for us all, regardless of where we come from. What matters is where we are headed.

Day One
A SPLIT-SECOND DECISION

Read Joshua 2.

1. Carefully read Joshua 2:2–3. How much time did Rahab have to determine her course of action regarding the Israelite spies?

2. Rahab's split-second decision was shaped by her view of herself, of her world, and of God. What she believed gave her courage. What belief caused Rahab to hide the spies, risking her life by betraying her country?

3. Many times in our lives, we will be faced with choices that require a split-second decision. We won't always have the luxury of consulting a friend or mulling over the pros and cons. What we decide to do will be determined by what we have previously decided we most value in ourselves, what we believe about our world, and what we believe about God.

    For example, when a woman gets to her car, she realizes she was given too much change at the grocery store. What does she choose to do? Think about how her values and beliefs might shape her decision.

    If she values her honesty and integrity more than anything, she'll probably return the money to the store, even if it means she'll be inconvenienced or late to her next appointment. But if she finds it more important to always be on time, she might justify pocketing the money, figuring that it wasn't her fault she was given too much.

    She might think about how unfair the world often is, remembering the time she had bought milk at the store and found that it had already turned sour in spite of being before the sell-by date. She might tell herself that keeping the money is simply making things fair—a reimbursement of sorts.

    She might wonder if God is really interested in the details of her life. If so, then would He really care if she kept the money?

    What is the character quality that you most esteem? Can you think of a time in your life when your belief in the importance of that character quality and your beliefs about God shaped a quick decision?

4. We are highly unlikely to make the right decisions when risk is involved, unless we agree with Rahab's words in Joshua 2:11: "The Lord your God is he who is God in heaven above and on earth beneath." Rahab believed that God was the One in charge both in heaven and on earth. Do we believe this? Do we believe that He is the One who can be counted on? Do we believe that His is the only approval we should seek?

The following are some questions we can ask ourselves when faced with a decision. Look up the corresponding Scriptures for added insight and record your thoughts below.

A. What does God think about my decision?

Philippians 4:6–7

James 1:5

B. What character issues are at stake?

James 3:13–18

C. Which decision is a better one if I look at it from an eternal perspective?

John 6:27, CCC 679

Quiet your heart and enjoy His presence. . . . You are precious in His sight.

"But the eyes of the Lord are on those who fear Him, on those whose hope is in His unfailing love" (Psalm 33:18).

"For the eyes of the Lord run to and fro throughout the whole earth to show Himself strong on behalf of those whose heart is loyal to Him" (2 Chronicles 16:9).

Was it a mere coincidence that the two Israelite spies were drawn to the house of Rahab? No. God had seen past the walls of Jericho, through the ungodly culture surrounding her, beyond her bad choices, and into her heart. When He looked at her heart, He saw what pleased Him most: faith.

Rahab's faith moved God's heart and hand, and she was promised rescue. But remember, her faith led to action. "Faith is a step, not just a statement."[16] True faith is reflected in our decisions.

Are you facing a choice right now? Take time to discuss it with the Lord, and ask yourself the questions listed in number 4:

What does God think about my decision?
What character issues are at stake?
Which decision is a better one if I look at it from an eternal perspective?

Day Two
PREPARING TO CROSS

Read Joshua 3.

The Ark of the Covenant is described in detail in Exodus 25:10–22. God commanded Moses to have the Israelites build the Ark of the Covenant out of acacia wood overlaid with gold. Rings of gold held wooden poles also covered with gold. This was topped with a mercy seat of pure gold, on top of which were two golden cherubim. The cherubim had wings spread out, overshadowing the mercy seat. God told the Israelites to keep three things in the Ark of the Covenant: the tablets with the Ten Commandments, a jar of manna, and Aaron's staff, which had budded.

1. What was the significance of the Ark of the Covenant? See Exodus 25:21–22, Leviticus 16:1–3, and Joshua 3:3–4.

2. A. What did Joshua command the Israelites to do before the journey over the Jordan would begin? See Joshua 3:5.

---

[16] Mathews, *A Woman God Can Use*, 42.

B. In what way can we sanctify ourselves before we stand in the presence of God in the Eucharist? Why is this important? How does receiving the Eucharist sanctify us? See CCC 1393, 1394, and 1395.

3. What were some of the reasons God chose to bring the Israelites through the Jordan River in a miraculous way? See Joshua 3:7, 10.

4. What was symbolized by the Ark of the Covenant going into the water before the people crossed?

5. A. What did the priests have to do before the miracle occurred?

B. What might have happened if the priests had been too afraid to step into the flood-level waters? Often, God asks us to step out and trust Him, and to move forward even though we don't see proof that He'll take care of us. What "river" is in front of you? What is holding you back from stepping forward in faith?

Quiet your heart and enjoy His presence. . . . His love for you is unconditional.

Many times God will ask us to wait for His timing. And we are wise to do so. But sometimes, we miss His blessing because we are still waiting, even when He has asked us to move. In order for Abraham to experience the blessings that God had promised, he had to move. He had to take the step of faith and leave his homeland. In order for the Israelites to experience deliverance from the Pharaoh of Egypt, they had to step out into the teeming Red Sea. In order for God to roll back the Jordan, the priests had to step into the floodwaters. In each of these cases, there was a key to unlocking the fulfillment of God's promise. That key was the same one that rescued Rahab: faith. It takes faith to step out into the unknown. But when we take that step, God's power is unleashed on our behalf.

Dear God,

Thank You that "in all these things, we are more than conquerors through him who loved us . . . neither death, nor life, nor angels, nor principalities, nor things present, nor things to come, nor powers, nor height, nor depth, nor anything else in all creation, will be able to separate us from the love of God in Christ Jesus our Lord" (Romans 8:36–37). It's because You love me that I can have faith in whatever You ask me to do. My emotions may be full of fear, but when I meditate on how much You love me, I know You'd never ask me to do anything that wasn't ultimately for my good. Others may fail me. No human love is perfect. But Yours is, and because of that, I trust in You.

Day Three
STONES OF REMEMBRANCE

Read Joshua 4.

1. A. After crossing the Jordan, what did Joshua ask a representative from each of the tribes of Israel to do?

   B. What was the reason for doing this?

C. Where else was a pile of stones placed and by whom?

2. According to Joshua 4:24, why did God part the Red Sea and the Jordan River?

3. We erect monuments (memorial stones) to honor people who have done great things in our world. George Washington is honored with an obelisk in Washington, D.C., towering at a height of 556 feet. Below, I paraphrase a lesson on "Stones of Remembrance," taught by pastor Todd Phillips.

> George Washington's monument was modeled after the Egyptian obelisk, a monolithic pillar capped with a pyramid. Obelisks and pyramids were sacred constructions to the Egyptians. Built by slaves, they were believed to contain sacred powers that would transform the men they honored. Joshua was familiar with the Egyptian obelisks and pyramids. His blood and sweat had gone into the construction of their bricks. He became a great military leader, but he had begun as an Egyptian slave, a common laborer.
>
> After leaving Egypt, the Israelites prepared for battle against the Amalakites. Joshua was chosen to lead the army. He had no military background, but as long as Moses' arms were raised in prayer, Joshua was strong and courageous.
>
> At the end of the battle, Moses raised a memorial stone—not for Joshua, but for God. It was an altar, a sacrificial monument, to honor God, Jehovah Nissi (meaning "the Lord is my banner"). This monument was to remind the people of the real victor of the battle: the one true God.
>
> Joshua wasn't given the honor of being remembered; rather, he was given the challenge to remember. Why? Because the people he was leading tended to forget easily. Joshua was the one who would lead the people into the Promised Land. By that point, Moses was gone, and almost all the people of that generation had died. Joshua was to be the spiritual memory for his people.

We, too, are called to be spiritual memories. Saint Paul and Saint Peter refer to the body of Christ as a living sacrifice or living stone. We are to be sacred constructions that honor the Lord. We are to be stones of remembrance— seeking not to be remembered, but to live in such a way that our God is remembered and honored.[17]

What are practical ways that our lives can serve as stones of remembrance?

4. What object could you put in your home as a "memorial stone" to help you to remember God's faithfulness to you?

5. Has anyone ever looked at your life and asked you why you are the way you are? Have they asked for an explanation for what they see in you? If so, what explanation have you given them?

Quiet your heart and enjoy His presence. . . . Bask in His smile as He delights in you.

Memorial stones were erected to give the Israelites an opportunity to share the truth of God's faithfulness with the next generation—their children and grandchildren. We, too, are given the responsibility to pass on the baton of faith to those who follow us. This is the greatest inheritance that we can give. Take some time to reflect on the spiritual inheritance you are leaving behind. Part of this inheritance is your testimony—your story of God's faithfulness in your life. Another aspect of it is the truths that you have learned about God. Talk to God about the ways in which you can pass on your faith to others, especially the children in your life.

---

[17] "Joshua—Stones of Remembrance w Teaching by Todd Phillips—Ministry Videos," GodTube video, 4:18, posted by "bluefishtv," October 1, 2010, http://www.godtube.com/watch/?v=21FEJNNU.

Day Four
STRENGTH IN WEAKNESS

Read Joshua 5.

1. Why did Joshua circumcise the Israelite men? See Joshua 5:4–7.

2. In what sense is the timing of the circumcision interesting?

3. The Israelite men couldn't trust in their own strength as they recovered. Where did they have to place their trust? By contrast, where were the people of Jericho placing their trust? Where did Rahab place hers?

4. God often takes us to a place of weakness in order to show us His strength. Can you share a time when He has done this in your life?

5. A. How did Joshua show respect for the commander of the army of the Lord? What other time was someone commanded to remove his sandals because he was standing on holy ground? See Exodus 3:4–5.

   B. How do we show respect for God in our actions and attitudes?

Quiet your heart and enjoy His presence. . . . He is all you need.

We live in a culture that sees strength as standing up and asserting our rights. God looks at things differently. Isaiah 30:15 says, "In quietness and trust shall be your strength." We can be quiet because we trust that God is on our side and fights our battles. Is there any area of your life where you are desperate to fight? There are times when God asks us to stand up and speak boldly, but not always. It takes great strength to refrain from saying whatever comes to mind. It takes immense strength from God to resist getting in the last word when we have the perfect comeback on the tip of our tongue. Take your battles to the Lord in prayer. Ask Him to show you if He wants you to do something, or if He wants you to rest. Either way, He'll provide the strength you need.

Day Five
THE RESCUE

Read Joshua 6.

1. What might have been going through Rahab's mind as she watched the Israelites march around Jericho for six days with no evidence of any more action?

2. Why do you think God chose this strategy as the means of bringing the Israelites to victory over Jericho?

3. As the Israelites marched, Rahab hung the scarlet cord from her window. What other rescues does the color of the cord bring to mind? See Exodus 12:1–13, Leviticus 4:32–34, Hebrews 9:22, and Ephesians 1:7.

4. Where were Rahab and her family placed after the rescue? Why? Was this a permanent situation?

5. According to Hebrews 11:31 and James 2:25, why was Rahab rescued?

Quiet your heart and enjoy His presence. . . . He longs to shower you with love.

Think of how thrilled Rahab must have been when she was invited to become a part of the Israelite community. It must have been beyond her wildest dreams. During her time of waiting in Jericho, she believed that God was real, but she also knew that she didn't belong to Him. The wait must have enhanced her ultimate joy. Rahab, who had made her living trading her dignity for money, became one of the chosen ones. God wanted her in spite of her past.

And He wants you. Regardless of where you've been, He wants you. Take a moment to meditate on Saint Thérèse of Lisieux's words:

> *May today there be peace within.*
> *May you trust God that you are exactly where you are meant to be.*
> *May you not forget the infinite possibilities that are born of faith.*
> *May you use those gifts that you have received, and pass on the love that has been given to you.*
> *May you be content knowing you are a child of God.*
> *Let this presence settle into your bones, and allow your soul the freedom to sing, dance, praise and love.*
> *It is there for each and every one of us.*

Conclusion

"Rahab and Salmon had a son, Boaz.
Boaz was the father of Obed;
Obed, the father of Jesse;
Jesse, the father of King David.
And from the line of King David of the tribe of Judah
Came the promised Messiah,
Jesus Christ our Savior and Lord."[18]

Who would have thought that Rahab would not only be rescued, but would be given one of the greatest honors possible among the Israelites? For a nation of people focused on genealogy, you would think that God would have chosen more pristine characters to be Christ's ancestors, but God doesn't look at things the way man does.

His choice of Rahab teaches us something very important: When He looks at us, He sees our potential. He knows that within each of us lies a destiny that will bring fulfillment and joy. He also knows that the key to discovering it is found in a relationship with Him. He looks for women hungering for closeness with Him. Our past does not disqualify us from a magnificent future with Him. As Father Jean d'Elbée says in *I Believe in Love*, "He looks much more at what we are than at what we do; and we are, in His eyes, what we sincerely want to be for Him."[19] He sees our hearts.

What do we sincerely want to be for Him? God saw Rahab's heart, and He knew there was nothing she would hold back if she could be rescued by Him. She risked it all. What if she'd been caught hiding the spies? What if someone had noticed her hanging a scarlet cord out her window? She cast all her fears at His feet and hoped.

Where do we place our hope? Are we willing to trust God regardless of what He asks of us? Rahab let go, not just of her old lifestyle but also of the things that gave her security. She practiced abandonment. Our past doesn't disqualify us, but when we cling to anything other than God for security, we miss out on the magnificent rescue that He desires for us.

There's often much that we *can* control. But instead of trying to paint our own destinies, can we offer the paintbrush to God and ask Him to create a masterpiece of the broken bits of our lives and make us whole? The Creator of the universe draws

---

[18] Francine Rivers, *Unashamed* (Wheaton, IL: Tyndale House, 2000), 129.
[19] D'Elbée, *I Believe in Love*, 83.

the most beautiful pictures, and as the author of life, He will write a better story than we ever could.

My Resolution

In what specific way will I apply what I learned in this lesson?

Examples:

1. I will identify an area in my life where God has asked me to step out in obedience. I resolve to obey, and to take that initial step of faith. Each time I am overcome by fear, I'll pray an Act of Faith.

2. I will begin a journal, listing my stones of remembrance—the times God has come through for me and proven His faithfulness.

3. I will write out my testimony—my personal story of God's faithfulness in my life. I'll pray about how I can most effectively share this with the next generation.

My Resolution:

Catechism Clips

CCC 679 Christ is Lord of eternal life. Full right to pass definitive judgment on the works and hearts of men belongs to him as redeemer of the world. He "acquired" this right by his cross. The Father has given "all judgment to the Son." Yet the Son did not come to judge, but to save and to give the life he has in himself. By rejecting grace in this life, one already judges oneself, receives according to one's works, and can even condemn oneself for all eternity by rejecting the Spirit of love.

CCC 1393 Holy Communion separates us from sin. The body of Christ we receive in Holy Communion is "given up for us," and the blood we drink "shed for the many for the forgiveness of sins." For this reason the Eucharist cannot unite us to Christ without at the same time cleansing us from past sins and preserving us from future sins:

For as often as we eat this bread and drink the cup, we proclaim the death of the Lord. If we proclaim the Lord's death, we proclaim the forgiveness of sins. If, as often as his blood is poured out, it is poured for the forgiveness of sins, I should always receive it, so that it may always forgive my sins. Because I always sin, I should always have a remedy.

CCC 1394 As bodily nourishment restores lost strength, so the Eucharist strengthens our charity, which tends to be weakened in daily life; and this living charity wipes away venial sins. By giving himself to us Christ revives our love and enables us to break our disordered attachments to creatures and root ourselves in him:

Since Christ died for us out of love, when we celebrate the memorial of his death at the moment of sacrifice we ask that love may be granted to us by the coming of the Holy Spirit. We humbly pray that in the strength of this love by which Christ willed to die for us, we, by receiving the gift of the Holy Spirit, may be able to consider the world as crucified for us, and to be ourselves as crucified to the world. . . . Having received the gift of love, let us die to sin and live for God.

CCC 1395 By the same charity that it enkindles in us, the Eucharist preserves us from future mortal sins. The more we share the life of Christ and progress in his friendship, the more difficult it is to break away from him by mortal sin. The Eucharist is not ordered to the forgiveness of mortal sins—that is proper to the sacrament of Reconciliation. The Eucharist is properly the sacrament of those who are in full communion with the Church.

Verse Study

See Appendix 3 for instructions on how to complete a verse study.

Philippians 3:7–8

1. Verse:

2. Paraphrase:

3. Questions:

4. Cross-references:

5. Personal Application:

Lesson 8

DEBORAH

Introduction

While our story of Rahab ended with the Israelites' determination to obey God fully in order to experience all He had promised them, much had changed by the time of Deborah. Deborah lived during the period when Israel was ruled by judges. These were dark days for Israel, and "everyone did as he saw fit" (Judges 17:6). This generation "knew neither the Lord nor what he had done for Israel" (Judges 2:10).

After Jericho fell, God gave the Israelites victory after victory as they claimed the Promised Land. They had one recurring problem: They didn't obey God. God had commanded them to conquer the entire Promised Land and to drive out their enemies. He warned them that failing to do so would result in serious future difficulties. But the Israelites grew tired and complacent (total obedience is such hard work), and settled for "good enough." They got rid of most of their enemies—wasn't that sufficient? It reminds me of a little phrase I've used when training my children in obedience. "How do we obey? Straightaway, *all* the way, and with a happy spirit." The Israelites didn't obey *all* the way, and as a result, they were surrounded by enemies who influenced them with the worship of other gods. This was the Israelites' downfall. As they fell into the pattern of complacency and began to adopt their neighbors' practice of worshipping idols, God allowed painful consequences to teach them how important total obedience is. Time and time again, the Israelites fell into patterns of sin, and God allowed the surrounding nations to conquer and oppress them.

When the Israelites experienced the punishment of the surrounding nations' oppression, they cried out to God for help. In response, He raised up judges to deliver them. These godly men and women were leaders who led their people out of bondage. Deborah was a judge who played a key role in Israel's deliverance from the Canaanites.

May we be inspired by her bravery, wisdom, and strength, and accept the challenge to pursue total obedience to God. Just as the Israelites were tempted to settle for "good enough," we can fall into the trap of mediocrity. God's grace is always available, but if we want to live the abundant life that He promises in John 10:10 ("I have come that they may have life, and have it abundantly"), our total obedience is essential.

Day One
PARTIAL OBEDIENCE

Read Judges 4:1–3 and 5:6–7.

1. Describe the oppression the Israelites were experiencing based on Judges 4:1–3 and 5:6–7.

2. What had God commanded of the Israelites in Numbers 33:52? Based on the information given in the Introduction, why would a loving God command this?

3. According to Judges 1:27–33, did the Israelites obey?

4. The Israelites were now experiencing the consequences of settling for "good enough" instead of pursuing total obedience. Partial obedience is always so tempting. "At least I made an effort. At least I tried," we convince ourselves. But the consequences of this can prove disastrous. Is there an area in your life where God is asking you to obey Him and you are tempted to compromise?

As we journey on the road toward God's will for our lives, we'll be offered many "halfway houses" where we're invited to stop and settle for a while. Sometimes we convince ourselves that to obey halfway means we'll at least receive half the blessings of obedience. But this isn't the case. To receive the blessings of obedience to God we need to obey Him fully. One can assume that once the Israelites experienced the oppression by the Canaanites, they would want to go back and thoroughly drive them out of their land. But it was too late. Obeying straightaway is the only kind of true obedience. Delayed obedience is disobedience. When God asks us to do something, He promises to bless us if we do what He has asked when He asks us. Our part is to obey immediately. He can always be counted on to do His part.

Quiet your heart and enjoy His presence. . . . He longs to shower you with love.

Sometimes God lets us know loud and clear which path of obedience He wants us to take. Sometimes His direction is whispered and only a quieted heart is able to hear it. What is He whispering in your ear today? Are you quiet enough to hear it?

A whisper can hardly be heard, so it must be felt as a faint and steady pressure upon the heart and mind, like the touch of a morning breeze calmly moving across the soul. And when it is heeded, it quietly grows clearer in the inner ear of the heart. God's voice is directed to the ear of love, and true love is intent upon hearing even the faintest whisper. . . .

So when you are about to say something in conversation with others, and you sense a gentle restraint from His quiet whisper, heed the restraint and refrain from speaking. And when you are about to pursue some course of action that seems perfectly clear and right, yet you sense in your spirit another path being suggested with the force of quiet conviction, heed that conviction. Follow the alternate course, even if the change of plans appears to be absolute folly from the perspective of human wisdom. . . .

Therefore if you desire to know God's voice, never consider the final outcome or the possible results. Obey Him even when He asks you to move while you still see only darkness, for He Himself will be a glorious light within you. Then there will quickly spring up within your heart a knowledge of God and a fellowship with Him, which will be overpowering enough in themselves to hold you and Him together, even in the most severe tests and under the strongest pressures of life.[20]

---

[20] L. B. Cowman, *Streams in the Desert* (Grand Rapids, MI: Zondervan, 1997) 373–4.

Day Two
GIFTED TO SERVE

Read Judges 4:4–5.

1. How is Deborah described in Judges 4:4?

Deborah had been given grace by God to act as His prophet. She exercised this gift of prophecy for the good of her people and nation. Prophecy is one of the charisms, or spiritual gifts, mentioned in Scripture. According to Sherry Weddell, author of *The Catholic Spiritual Gifts Inventory*, "The charism of Prophecy empowers a Christian to be a channel of divine truth and wisdom by communicating a word or call of God to individuals or a group through inspired words or actions."[21]

The word *charism* is defined in the glossary of the *Catechism of the Catholic Church* as "a specific gift or grace of the Holy Spirit which directly or indirectly benefits the Church, given in order to help a person live out the Christian life, or to serve the common good in building up the Church."[22]

2. According to CCC 951 and 1 Corinthians 12:7, are all baptized Christians given charisms, or are they given only to special people, like Deborah?

---

[21] Sherry Weddell, *The Catholic Spiritual Gifts Inventory* (Colorado Springs: Siena Institute Press, 1998), 45.
[22] *Catechism of the Catholic Church*, 870.

3. According to CCC 799, what is the purpose of a charism?

4. Many of the charisms are listed in Romans 12:4–8, 1 Corinthians 12:4–11, and Ephesians 4:11–14. Record them in the space below.

5. How is Deborah's spiritual gift of prophecy described in 1 Corinthians 14:3?

Each of us has been created by God for a unique purpose. There is something that God wants each one of us to do to further His kingdom in our generation. We are equipped with spiritual gifts, or charisms, to help us to fulfill that call. Some of us go through life and completely miss out on what we have been created for. It's our responsibility to explore how God has uniquely gifted us, and then seek out what His purpose for us might be. I recommend the resources provided by the Catherine of Siena Institute to help in the discernment process. They can be found at www.siena.org/Called-Gifted/called-a-gifted.

6. When we know how we have been uniquely gifted, we still have to battle complacency. Life gets busy, and it can be hard to take the time to go out into the world and make a difference there. Author Jeanne Hendricks likes to ask herself this question: "Do I grasp the truth that the world 'out there' will eventually be my world 'in here' if nothing is done?"[23] What pressing needs of the times we live in are most apparent to you? If you could help one group of people in the world, who would it be and why?

---

[23] Jeanne Hendricks, *A Mother's Legacy* (Carol Stream, IL: NavPress, 1988), 82.

Quiet your heart and enjoy His presence. . . . He is all you need.

Our unique purpose will be different from Deborah's. It's unlikely that we'll be called on to lead our nation in battle. But wherever God has put us, we'll be best able to meet the needs "out there" if we know that we have been called and equipped by God. We need to continually seek the delicate balance of keeping an eye on the needs of the times while keeping our hearts focused on our relationships with God. It's His presence within us that makes it possible for us to fulfill the calling and purpose that He gives us. When we try to do things in our own strength, we are completely missing the secret of the Christian life. God wants to do the work in and through us. He wants us to continually rely on the power and strength of the Holy Spirit.

My precious daughter,

I know that the challenges and needs you face can be overwhelming. But don't despair! I never ask anything of you without providing exactly what you need in order to obey. I measure each task before you, and then give you the grace you need to fulfill it. You get into trouble when you set out in your own strength without filling up with grace through the sacraments and prayer. I offer grace to you continually, but you need to make the decision to receive it. Never forget my Son's words in John 15:5: "I am the vine, and you are the branches. Whoever remains in me and I in him, will bear much fruit, because without me you can do nothing." That doesn't mean that you'll never accomplish anything by the world's standards. Examples abound of people who do all sorts of wonderful things while completely ignoring me. What it means is that you will do nothing of lasting value—nothing that counts for eternity—unless you do it through continual dependence on me. It's not your strength that I value most; that is simply a gift that I've given you. I'm most delighted by your humble dependence on me. If you can only grab hold of me with one little finger of faith, it is enough to make my power yours. With my power, you'll be able to accomplish the act of service that seems overwhelming when you face it alone.

~Your devoted Father

Day Three
THE BATTLE IS THE LORD'S

Read Judges 4:6–24.

Background information: Deborah judged under a specific palm tree, which was located in the mountain region of Ephraim in the south of Israel. Barak was from the region of Naphtali, located in the north of Israel. The worst of the oppression by the Canaanites took place in the north.

1. Whose commands was Deborah communicating to Barak? Why was this important?

2. Judges 4:15–16 describes Barak's victory. Additional insight is gained from Judges 5:4–5 and 19–22. What did God do in order to give Barak the victory?

3. A. What two facts do we learn about the Kenite Heber from verses 11 and 17?

   B. Based on those facts, why were Jael's actions surprising?

4. From a human perspective, there didn't seem to be any hope of victory for the Israelites. Had Barak given in to fear, dwelled on the what-ifs, and not stepped out in obedience, the Israelites would have remained under the Canaanites' oppression. All involved learned the lesson that when God is on your side, nothing is impossible. Are you facing what appears to be an impossible or hopeless situation? If so, describe it below.

How do the following verses apply to the obstacles and battles we face?

Job 42:2

Jeremiah 32:17

John 14:13

Quiet your heart and enjoy His presence. . . . His love for you is unconditional.

"Lord, there is no one like you to help the powerless against the mighty" (2 Chronicles 14:11).

When facing daunting obstacles, it's wise to check our focus. Are we dwelling on the problems and difficulties, or are we remaining focused on God's power to do anything? A local radio station often says, "Don't tell God how big the mountain is; tell the mountain how big your God is." We can remind God that we are absolutely counting on Him. Remind Him of the truth of His Word in Scripture: "There's no one like you to help!" Perhaps you are in a situation in which your difficulties have risen to an alarming level. Instead of facing these trials alone, put God between you and your difficulty. Then when the obstacles advance, they will only press you closer to your loving Savior's heart.

Day Four
SELF-LEADERSHIP

Read Judges 5:1–15.

1. To whom did Deborah and Barak give credit for the victory? What character trait does this reveal?

Humility is an essential trait in a leader. Deborah exemplified this through her immediate praise of God after the victory. There's another subtle indication of her humility in Judges 5:6, when she referred to their current time as "the days of Shamgar, son of Anath," not "the days of Deborah." Shamgar had been the previous judge.

When we lead, we need to find a way to remain humble, keeping our attention on God while still focusing on ourselves enough to make wise and prudent choices. If you are about to tune out this next section because you don't consider yourself a leader, please reconsider. We all have a sphere of influence, in which people around us are affected by the way we live. If you are a mother, you are a leader. If you live in a neighborhood, there are people around you whom you influence. If you are in any kind of a community, you are surrounded by people who are affected by you, for good or for bad.

One of the hardest aspects of leadership is self-leadership. We can get so busy focusing on those we are leading that we lose sight of the attention we need to pay to ourselves. By this, I don't mean that we need to indulge ourselves, although a balanced woman will take time out for fun and refreshment. I'm referring to something that goes much deeper.

Bill Hybels addresses this in his book *Courageous Leadership*, quoting Daniel Goleman, the author of *Emotional Intelligence*. Goleman researched why some leaders develop to their furthest potential, while others seem to stagnate and not progress. This is what Goleman concluded:

> The difference has to do with (you guessed it) self-leadership. He calls it "emotional self-control." According to Goleman, this form of self-control is exhibited by leaders when they persevere in leadership despite overwhelming opposition or discouragement; when they refuse to give up during times of crisis; when they manage to hold ego at bay; and when they stay focused on their mission rather than being distracted by other people's agendas. Goleman contends that exceptional leaders distinguish themselves because they "know their strengths, their limits, and their weaknesses."[24]

2. What insights do the following verses give in terms of self-leadership?

Mark 1:35

---

[24] Bill Hybels, *Courageous Leadership* (Grand Rapids, MI: Zondervan, 2009), 184.

Acts 20:24

Matthew 25:14–30

1 Peter 5:5

Quiet your heart and enjoy His presence. . . . Bask in His smile as He delights in you.

Deborah had the additional challenge of leading Israel while still being a faithful wife and most likely a mother. The balance couldn't have been easy. Needs surrounded her constantly. We, like Deborah, need to continually check our pace and seek balance. No one can create this balance for us. It is our responsibility to know when to say no and when to withdraw for times of refreshment. When our hearts are passionate about the needs around us, we can foolishly assume that God will always bless our efforts, even when we go at an unhealthy pace. The truth is, God has given us the ability to reason and act with prudence. When we take on too much and start to compromise in other important areas of life, we'll suffer, and so will those closest to us. Take some time in God's presence to check your pace. Is it sustainable? Are you giving your best to those outside your home, while those closest to you are only getting the leftovers? Ask God to give you insight into the things He is calling you to and the things you've committed yourself to doing that aren't His call. Then commit to making the necessary changes to bring balance back to your life.

Day Five
SPIRITUAL MOTHERHOOD

Read Judges 5:6–31.

1. A. How did Deborah describe herself in Judges 5:7?

   B. She faced a spiritual battle in Israel, described in Judges 5:8. What was it?

2. Two mothers, Deborah and the mother of Sisera, are highlighted in this passage (Judges 5:28–30). Contrast the viewpoints of these two women.

While not every woman is a mother in the biological or adoptive sense, all women can experience spiritual motherhood. Author Katrina Zeno describes this in her article "Why Woman":

> The Catholic Church has always encouraged spiritual motherhood, only under a different title—the corporal and spiritual works of mercy. Giving food to the hungry, drink to the thirsty, etc., emphasize caring for a person's tangible needs while counseling the doubtful, instructing the ignorant, comforting the sorrowful, etc., nurture others in less tangible, but still critical ways.

> When looking for the consummate model of femininity and motherhood, Pope John Paul II turns to Mary. Feminine receptivity and relationship find their ultimate expression and fulfillment in her. Mary's *fiat* welcomed the Holy Spirit into the empty space within and conceived a new kind of fruitfulness, a fruitfulness of the Spirit. Her union with God brought the human body of Christ into the world.

> Every woman is called to be overshadowed by the Spirit so as to be abundantly fruitful, to be a Christ-bearer. The transformation of society and culture into a civilization of love and a culture of life begins here: with the empty space within. Whether a woman is 8 or 88, the sacred space within has a purpose—to

be filled with the Spirit (and Eucharistic body) of Christ so she can go forth to nurture the emotional, moral, cultural, and spiritual lives of others. Then all human society will be enriched, and peace will flourish as women reveal the mystery of life—to be in human and divine relationship.[25]

3. A spiritual mother enters the battle between good and evil that rages in our world. She acts as a force for good, using spiritual weapons instead of a tent peg and hammer. How is this battle described in Ephesians 6:12? Have you ever experienced this as you have tried to make a difference in the world? Explain.

4. Describe the spiritual protection and weapons available to us as outlined in Ephesians 6:13–17.

5. We are foolish to engage in this spiritual battle without any weapons. One of our most powerful weapons is prayer. Our hard work and good intentions only go so far. There will always be obstacles and problems in our world that will be bigger than our ability to solve them. When we are worried or overwhelmed by concerns or fears, we are being called to turn to God in prayer. When we pray, the power of God penetrates the lives of our loved ones. He works through our powerlessness.

How do the following verses encourage you in your prayer life?

"Pour out your heart like water in the presence of the Lord; Lift up your hands to him for the lives of your little ones" (Lamentations 2:19).

---

[25] Katrina Zeno, "Why Woman," theologyofthebody.net.

John 15:16: "It was not you who chose me, but I who chose you and appointed you to go and bear fruit that will remain, so that whatever you ask the Father in my name he may give you."

"The fervent prayer of a righteous person is very powerful" (James 5:16).

Quiet your heart and enjoy His presence. . . . You are precious in His sight.

Every detail of our lives—past, present, and future—is important to God. When we turn to Him in prayer, we can present our current concerns, areas from our past that need healing, and future needs. He stands ready to come to our aid, and asks that we trust and not doubt, as it says in James 1:6: "But he should ask in faith, not doubting, for the one who doubts is like a wave of the sea that is driven and tossed about by the wind." When we struggle with doubt, we can pray the words of the desperate father in Mark 9:24: "I do believe, help my unbelief!" Doubt comes from questioning whether God is really all-powerful and all-loving. The more time we spend with God, the more we will grow in trust. Take some time to present your requests to God. What is on your heart today? Pass your burdens over to Him.

Conclusion

There will be times in each of our lives when we'll be called to stand up and lead. Some will be dramatic, some will be quiet, and many will require bravery and strength that we may feel we lack. The following story of Mary Slessor, a missionary in the early 1900s, is inspiring. Mary worked with the Okoyong tribe deep in the rain forest in what is now Nigeria. One evening, she heard drumming as she walked home from the marketplace. Following the sounds, she encountered a horrific sight: masked men tightening the cords that tied a terrified girl, stretched spread-eagle, to stakes in the ground. James Buchan describes the scene in his book *The Expendable Mary Slessor*.

The oil was boiling on a fire nearby and a masked man was ladling some of it into a pot. It was a scene which would have daunted the bravest of people: the ring of seated chiefs, the masked men grotesque in the flicker of the fire and of the torches, the laughing, drunken warriors, the screaming, the drumming, and the sexual excitement and anticipation of the spectators. It is possible that if Mary had known what she was going to find, she would have thought it wiser to stay away. . . . But as she stood inside the circle and the chiefs saw her, it did not occur to Mary to turn back. . . . She walked out and got between the fire and the girl. What a film sequence it would have made. The hush as everyone stared at the small white woman. Then the explosion of chatter as the crowd babbled their amazement. . . . The masked man began to swing the ladle round his head and to caper towards Mary. She stood and stared at him. The ladle whistled nearer and nearer her head. The crowd looked on in silence. The Egbo man dodged from side to side, his eyes staring at her through the holes in the mask. He had the choice of striking her with the ladle or of retreating. Mary stared back at him. He retreated. Mary walked towards him on her way to where Edem [the chief] was sitting, and he almost fell over himself to get out of her way. Such a show of power from a mere woman astounded the crowd. They had never seen anything like it before. . . . The girl's punishment now became a trivial matter compared to this exhibition of the power of the white woman's God. The chiefs allowed Mary to take the girl into her own custody pending further consideration of her case. In a few days, in typical Okoyong fashion, the palaver was forgotten and the girl slipped quietly back to her husband.[26]

What gave Mary the strength and courage to stand between the masked man and the girl? It is the same power that is available to each of us today. When we face challenges and are called to lead, we often feel that we don't have what it takes to do what is needed. It's then that we need to remember the truth contained in Ephesians 1:19–20: God offers "his incomparably great power for us who believe. That power is like the working of his mighty strength, which he exerted in Christ when he raised him from the dead and seated him at his right hand in the heavenly realms." When God calls us to step out of our comfort zones and make a difference for Him in our hurting world, we must resist the temptation to rely on our own strength and abilities, which will be no match for the task. We *must* draw on the strength of the indwelling Holy Spirit. As someone once wisely said, "God doesn't call the equipped; He equips the called." He did it for Mary Slessor. He did it for Deborah. He'll do it for you.

"The one who calls you is faithful, and *he will do it*" (1 Thessalonians 5:24).

---

[26] Mathews, *A Woman God Can Use*, 49–51.

My Resolution

In what specific way will I apply what I learned in this lesson?

Examples:

1. Instead of focusing on my difficulties and obstacles, I will go to adoration and focus on Christ. I'll meditate on the incredible power that His sacrifice on the cross made available to me. Because of all He did for me, I can tap into God's strength and power. I'll put Christ in the midst of my problems.

2. I will take the time to study and discern my charisms/spiritual gifts. I'll bring this to the Lord in prayer daily, asking Him where He wants me to serve Him.

3. Each night before I go to sleep, I'll review my day before the Lord in prayer. I'll ask the Holy Spirit to give me insight into the times that I obeyed fully and immediately, and into areas of my life where I am only partially obeying.

My Resolution:

Catechism Clips

CCC 799 Whether extraordinary or simple and humble, charisms are graces of the Holy Spirit which directly or indirectly benefit the Church, ordered as they are to her building up, to the good of men, and to the needs of the world.

CCC 951 *Communion of charisms.* Within the communion of the Church, the Holy Spirit "distributes special graces among the faithful of every rank" for the building up of the Church. Now, "to each is given the manifestation of the Spirit for the common good."

Verse Study

See Appendix 3 for instructions on how to complete a verse study.

Romans 8:37

1. Verse:

2. Paraphrase:

3. Questions:

4. Cross-references:

5. Personal Application:

Lesson 9

RUTH

Introduction

I don't want to open a can of worms, but have you ever wondered if God is "for" women? Have there been times when you've questioned if He values men more? His apostles were all men. Has this caused you to feel less valuable because you are female?

These questions have been asked by women throughout history. Does God care about women as much as He cares about men? Does He consider a woman's contributions to be as important as a man's? What is a woman's place in God's plan for the world?

The lessons we learn from Ruth increase in significance when we see that she lived in a patriarchal society whose regard for women left much to be desired. In the ancient world, women were second-class citizens, valued for their ability to produce male heirs who would carry on the family name and bring economic stability. A woman's dignity found its source in a man. Not being married and not having children carried an enormous stigma. If we want to grasp the full scope of the lessons contained in Ruth, we must look at her story with an eye toward the culture within which she lived. As we do this, we'll see a radical affirmation of God's love for His daughters and His desire to see them play significant roles in His plan of redemption.

The book of Ruth addresses the following questions:

Can a woman lose her usefulness?
What lessons can we learn from women who struggle with infertility?
Does God care about the details of our lives, or just the big picture?
Does it matter to God how we do things, as long as the end result is what He wants?
What do we do when we feel like so many people are depending on us and the weight of responsibility is overwhelming?

Far from being just a love story in which Ruth is rescued by her Prince Charming, her tale is one of a steadfast, strong woman who makes radical choices that change the world.

Day One
LEANNESS AND LOSS

Note: Ruth lived during the period when Israel was ruled by judges.

Read Ruth 1:1–5.

1. A. What caused Elimelech and his family to leave Bethlehem (which means "house of bread") to live in Moab?

   B. In Deuteronomy 28:22–24, what had God warned would happen to the Israelites if they weren't faithful to Him?

The Israelites had embraced the pagan gods of the surrounding nations and turned their backs on God. This began a recurring cycle throughout the Old Testament: The Israelites would turn away from God, resulting in cursing and punishment. The difficult circumstances would cause the Israelites to cry out to God, and He would rescue them. But it never took long for the cycle to begin again, and the Israelites would turn back to idols.

Nothing is said in the book of Ruth to suggest that Elimelech, Naomi, or their two sons were personally involved in this idolatry. But just as good things, such as rain and sun, fall on the good and bad alike, faithful followers of God experienced the consequences of the nation's descent into idolatry.

2. Circumstances were certainly dire if the country of Moab was appealing to Elimelech and Naomi. Read the following passages for some background about Moab.

Genesis 19:30–38

Deuteronomy 23:3–6

Judges 3:12–14

The people of Israel didn't exactly feel warm and fuzzy toward the Moabites. Not only did they have a history of not getting along with one another (to put it mildly), the Moabites worshipped the god Chemosh. They believed that Chemosh was appeased through child sacrifice, an act that was abhorrent to the Israelites, who valued children and considered them a sign of God's blessing.

3. List the heartaches that Naomi experienced in these five short verses.

It's so easy to read these verses and gloss over the pain they represent. How often have we glibly said, "I'm starving!" with no real idea of what that feels like? If we want to imagine what Naomi went through, we need to picture famine in Africa, and think of what mothers are willing to do in order to feed their emaciated children with bloated bellies.

Because we haven't gotten to really know Naomi, it's easy to read of her widowhood without much emotion. But think about its consequences for her. She lived in a culture that deferred to men. She had no rights. She couldn't own property. She had no voice. Her only hope was that her sons would provide for her. But wait! She had lost them, too. She was without hope and without protection. According to the world around her, her value as a person had diminished because of her losses.

4. Many women today are facing the challenges of life (and parenthood) alone, and we often gloss over their pain as quickly as we read of Naomi's tragedies. What are some of the issues a woman faces when she is alone?

5. What is God's view of a widow? When widowhood or anything else alters a woman's life, does it change how God sees her?

Throughout Scripture, God instructs His people to treat widows with kindness and high regard. But He doesn't see a widow just as a needy woman who should be helped. He sees her potential to contribute to His purposes. In the New Testament, Saint Paul even goes so far as to suggest that a woman will be "happier if she remains as she is" (1 Corinthians 7:40), not because men are unpleasant, but because her singleness gives her more time and focus to spend on God's work. We can continue to live for God's purposes regardless of our station in life.

Quiet your heart and enjoy His presence. . . . He is all you need.

God has a purpose for each one of us, regardless of our circumstances. He desires that we be His hands and feet in whatever position we find ourselves. Take some time to meditate on the unique challenges and opportunities that your status (single, widowed, married, religious) brings you. Ask the Lord to open your eyes to His purposes in your life. God is doing big things in our world, and He is doing many of them through His daughters. Much goes unseen by all but Him, but that doesn't mean it lacks eternal significance. Even if we are bedridden with illness, we can still serve God through the ministry of prayer. Ask Him to open your eyes to the infinite possibilities around you!

Day Two
EMPTY YET LOYAL

Read Ruth 1:4–22.

1. The pain of Ruth's and Orpah's childlessness isn't highlighted in this passage, but we know it was there. Mahlon and Chilion died before leaving either wife a child. Barrenness would have been especially painful for Ruth and Orpah in their ancient culture, which placed the blame at the feet of the women, never the men. Tragically, their society would have labeled them as failures. The ache of infertility is as real today as it was then. Some call infertility the "silent epidemic," because often it's only the couple and their doctor who know. What do you think goes on in the soul of a woman who fails to conceive or to bring a baby to term?

Author Carolyn Custis James can relate to Ruth's and Orpah's pain from her own experience. She writes of lessons learned through her infertility in her book *The Gospel of Ruth*:

> Even when we can pinpoint "something good" that came out of a tragedy, it *never* balances out what we have lost. How could anything compensate Naomi for the loss of her husband and sons? What could possibly make up for Job's losses of his children and his workers? Can any trade-off fill the void in a woman's heart when her longings for a child go unanswered and her husband rejects her and turns to another woman?

> No, the balance sheet *always* comes up short when we try to confine God in some delicate balancing act where the physical blessings we receive match and somehow overcome our losses. We live in the realm of faith, and that means trusting God for who he is and not because things equal out or we have satisfying answers to our questions. Faith may want answers, but somehow it is able to survive without them. That's at least part of the wisdom the barren woman imparts to us.

> We also learn from barren women that God uses suffering to open our eyes to see more of him than we would under rosier conditions. At some point, we grow weary of tears and our thrashings die down. We are quiet—not because

we've gotten answers to our troubling questions, but because we are spent. When we are in pain, we may get the sense that God has vanished from our lives. In truth, the opposite has happened. *God meets us in our pain.*[27]

2. Which of the lessons mentioned in the preceding excerpt are especially helpful to you as you reflect on difficult circumstances in your own life?

3. What reasons did Naomi give to Ruth and Orpah to try to persuade them to go back to their families in Moab?

4. What was the most sensible decision for Ruth and Orpah to make? Why?

5. In Ruth 1:16–17, Ruth's entire center of gravity shifted. What do you think became her source of security and identity?

---

[27] Carolyn Custis James, *The Gospel of Ruth* (Grand Rapids, MI: Zondervan, 2008), 84–5.

Quiet your heart and enjoy His presence. . . . He longs to shower you with love.

"I shall look at the world through tears. Perhaps I shall see things that dry-eyed I could not see."[28] *We decide how we respond to pain, loss, and disappointment. These circumstances offer us many choices. We can choose to lean on the Lord, to grow bitter, to let the heart grow numb, or to be overcome with anger, to name a few. What will be your choice? Can you take a moment and ask God to reveal to you lessons in your hurt that you might miss if you were dry-eyed? Can you ask Him to use every bit of your pain to teach you something you'd otherwise not learn?*

Day Three
PROVIDENCE AND PROVISION

Read Ruth 2.

1. Give an explanation of what it means to "glean" based on Leviticus 23:22.

2. A. In which field did Ruth happen to glean?

   B. What is divine providence? See CCC 321.

   C. When you read that Ruth happened to end up in the field of Boaz, did that strike you as a stroke of luck, or as the divine providence of God? When small miracles happen in your life, are you more apt to credit God or attribute it to chance? What light does Romans 8:28 shed on this issue?

---

[28] Ibid.

It can be difficult to believe in the divine providence of God. We often wonder if He really is in control. We might wonder if He really is directing things with a motivation of love for us. We sometimes question whether His plan is really what's best for us. If we were honest, many of us would admit that we often want more than Jesus' words. We want some proof. We want to see this truth in action with our own eyes. But do we give God the opportunity to show Himself to us in this way? In the words of Saint John of the Cross, "As long as a person who must jump with a parachute does not jump out into the void, he cannot feel that the cords of the parachute will support him, because the parachute has not yet had the chance to open. One must first jump and it is only later that one feels carried. And so it is in the spiritual life: 'God gives in the measure that we expect of him.'"[29] When we insist on controlling everything in our lives, we miss the opportunity to see how faithful and able God is to help us in any situation. Sometimes tragedy and difficulty is the greatest gift, because it forces us to admit that we really aren't in control, and then we are able to see the miracle of God's providence and provision.

3. What did Boaz's question about Ruth in 2:5 reveal about the culture's view of women?

4. Why had Ruth earned Boaz's concern?

What a surprise Naomi received when Ruth arrived with not just enough grain for dinner, but ready-cooked leftovers and extra grain as well! Ruth had gathered an ephah of grain, which was twenty-six quarts, enough to sustain them both for about five days. God had provided more than they could ask for or imagine. He promises the same provision for us in Ephesians 3:20: "Now to him who is able to do immeasurably more than all we ask or imagine, according to his power that is at work within us, to him be glory in the church and in Christ Jesus to all generations, forever and ever!"

---

[29] Father Jacques Philippe, *Searching for and Maintaining Peace* (Staten Island, NY: Fathers and Brothers of the Society of St. Paul, 2002), 28.

5. Not only did God provide more food than Ruth and Naomi had expected, but Ruth had gleaned in the fields of a man who was a near relative of Naomi, one of their redeemers. The Hebrew word for *redeemer, go'el,* is also translated *kinsman redeemer.* A kinsman redeemer was responsible for protecting the interests of his family. He had to be a blood relative, he had to have the financial means to support the widow, and he had to be willing to redeem her. In what ways is Christ our kinsman redeemer?

Quiet your heart and enjoy His presence. . . . His love for you is unconditional.

After honoring Ruth for all she had done for Naomi, Boaz blessed her by saying, "The Lord recompense you for what you have done, and a full reward be given you by the Lord, the God of Israel, under whose wings you have come to take refuge" (Ruth 2:12). Ruth had left behind her father, mother, and homeland, but God would not leave her without protection and care. This reflects a common Old Testament teaching that applies to us today. Psalm 57:1 says, "Be merciful to me, O God, be merciful to me, for in thee my soul takes refuge; in the shadow of thy wings I will take refuge."

My precious one,

My offer of refuge under my wings is always available for you. How I hope that you won't turn me away or substitute some other protection or shelter for the one I long to give you. I offered the same to the people of Jerusalem when I walked the earth. Their resistance to my offer grieved me deeply. I remember saying, "O Jerusalem, Jerusalem, killing the prophets and stoning those who are sent to you! How often would I have gathered your children together as a hen gathers her brood under her wings, and you would not."[30] But to fit under my wings meant bowing down, and they preferred to rely on themselves. Where do you seek shelter if not under my wings? Remember, only I am unchanging. I will never leave you or forsake you. Take refuge with me. It is a place of total safety. Let the mask drop. Leave all attempts at self-sufficiency at the door. Come as you are. My love for you cannot be shaken.

~Jesus

---

[30] Matthew 23:37.

Day Four
TRUSTING YET ACTIVE

Read Ruth 3.

1. Ruth trusted in God's providence, but what steps did she take in Ruth 3 to participate in the working out of her salvation?

Saint Paul applied this principle to all followers of Christ in Philippians 2:12–13: "Therefore, my beloved, as you have always obeyed, so now, not only as in my presence but much more in my absence, work out your own salvation with fear and trembling; for God is at work in you, both to will and to work for his good pleasure." This verse shows how law and grace work together. According to CCC 1949, "Divine help comes to him in Christ through the law that guides him and the grace that sustains him." CCC 1963 says, "According to Christian tradition, the Law is holy, spiritual, and good, yet still imperfect. Like a tutor it shows what must be done, but does not of itself give the strength, the grace of the Spirit, to fulfill it."

2. A. What motivated Ruth to leave her homeland, do the backbreaking work of gleaning, and then take a risk by approaching Boaz and asking for his provision?

   B. As mentioned previously, we are to work out our own salvation. What should be our motivation for the good things we do? Where does that motivation come from? See CCC 1972.

C. According to CCC 1972, by what means do we get the strength of grace to live as we should?

D. Can you share an experience in which you received strength of grace to do what you needed to do through the means of faith and the sacraments?

In Ruth 3:9, Ruth asked Boaz to place the corner of his garment over her. In that cultural setting, when a man did this it signified his readiness to marry the woman he covered. Ruth, instead of seducing Boaz, as some commentators believe Naomi was suggesting, appealed to Boaz's sense of responsibility. She reminded him of a provision in the law described in Deuteronomy 25, which stated that if a man died without a son to inherit his property and carry on the family name, then his brother had a responsibility to marry the widow and father a child with her so that the name of his brother would carry on. Boaz was not Mahlon or Chilion's brother, but he was a relative, and was therefore able to redeem Ruth in this way.

Ruth's response to Naomi's suggestion is a beautiful combination of trust in God's providence and willingness to do her part. She didn't sit at home waiting for God to act. She did what she could. But the way that she did her part was hugely important. It isn't too big a stretch to think that many a woman would have "used what she had" to catch a husband. It happened then, and it happens now. Why? Because so often it works. There they were in the dark. Boaz was merry, as the Bible politely puts it, and Ruth had taken care to smell and look her best. Where does your imagination take you? To put it nicely, there are *a lot* of ways that Ruth could have suggested to Boaz that marrying her was a great idea. But she didn't seduce or manipulate him. The way she asked mattered.

When we know where we want to get to, it's a huge temptation to get there using methods that aren't the best. We live in a culture that often degrades women, and this trains us to seek or regain power by whatever means we can. We hear the message loud and clear that we are only as good as we are sexually desirable. Many women have bought into this false message, and have exploited themselves and given away their mystery for the sake of power, admiration, or what they think is love. We need to wholeheartedly reject this notion and remember that God bases our worth and dignity on our hearts, not on our outward appearance. Our motives and methods matter.

3. How did Boaz respond to Ruth's request?

4. Boaz didn't seem to be fazed by Ruth's foreign background. What might have contributed to his compassion and open-mindedness? See Matthew 1:5.

Quiet your heart and enjoy His presence. . . . You are precious in His sight.

When Ruth reported to Naomi all that had happened, Naomi assured her that Boaz would not let the matter rest until he had figured it out. She knew Boaz to be a man of character, a man of his word. If he said he would do something, he would do it.

Isn't it wonderful that we have a Savior we can count on in the same way? Whatever God promises us, He will do. He is unchanging, and He is completely faithful to His Word.

Meditate on the following promises of God, and thank Him for being true to His Word.

God promises He will give you the strength to do all He asks of you.
"The Lord alone is God; God alone is our defense. He is the God who makes me strong, who makes my pathway safe. He makes me sure-footed as a deer; he keeps me safe on the mountains. He trains me for battle, so that I can use the strongest bow" (Psalm 18:31–34, GNT).

God promises to protect you.
"I look to the mountains; where will my help come from? My help comes from the Lord, who made heaven and earth. He will not let you fall; your protector is always awake. The protector of Israel never dozes or sleeps. The Lord will guard you; he is by your side to protect you. The sun will not hurt you during the day, nor the moon during the night. The Lord will protect you from all danger; he will keep you safe. He will protect you as you come and go now and forever" (Psalm 121).

God promises to forgive you.
"There is no other god like you, O Lord; you forgive the sins of your people who have survived. You do not stay angry forever, but you take pleasure in showing us your constant love" (Micah 7:18).

He promises to love you unconditionally.
"The Lord's unfailing love and mercy still continue,
Fresh as the morning, as sure as the sunrise.
The Lord is all I have, and so in him I put my hope" (Lamentations 3:22–24).

Day Five
BLESSING AND PURPOSE

Read Ruth 4.

1. What caused the next of kin to decline the offer to redeem Elimelech's property?

2. How did God provide for Ruth and fulfill her longings?

3. What long-term blessing came from Ruth and Boaz's marriage? See Ruth 4:17–22 and Matthew 1:1–16.

4. Naomi became Obed's nurse. She passed on her faith to him and trained him, and he in turn passed on the faith to his son, Jesse. Jesse had many sons, the youngest of whom was David. David became the King of Israel, a man after God's own heart. Naomi discovered her purpose, years after it seemed she had nothing of significance to contribute.

Never doubt the power and influence of a holy woman. You may or may not have a child at your knee, but you have the opportunity to influence the next generation nevertheless. There are countless children who desperately need a loving, godly role model, someone who will take the time to know them, love them, and teach them about God. What are some ways that you can speak God's truth and love into the next generation? How can you pass on the baton of faith?

5. Who would have ever thought that the story would turn out so well? When we glimpsed Ruth and Naomi on the dusty road to Bethlehem, their prospects didn't seem very cheery. Ruth had many opportunities to take matters into her own hands and do the things that those around her felt made sense. But time and time again, she chose to trust God for the outcome. She kept her eyes on what God expected her to do, and she trusted Him with the results. Are you feeling responsible for something? So often we feel like it's all up to us. Many of us are walking around with our stomachs in knots because we feel like we've got to figure it all out and solve the problem. Let's learn an important lesson from Ruth. We are responsible for being obedient to what God has asked of us, but we are not responsible for the results. The "how" of where we need to get to is not up to us. That's God's territory. When we recognize this and relinquish control, we'll find that God can suddenly turn events in a way that we never would have expected. Is there an area of your life where you are feeling an overwhelming weight of responsibility? Write a short prayer to God asking Him to make clear to you what He wants you to do. Then affirm your trust in His ability to bring about the needed result.

Dear God,

Quiet your heart and enjoy His presence. . . . Bask in His smile as He delights in you.

Dear Lord,

I so often try to run my own life, doing things my way. I forget how important it is for me to trust You and give You control.

When I forget to do this, I feel the weight of burdens and I fear the future. I forget to stop and put everything into Your hands. I want to follow You and do things Your way, but the weight of responsibility can trick me into thinking that it's really all up to me.

Help me to remember that just because I can't see You at work doesn't mean that You aren't doing amazing things. Give me the humility to recognize my inability to see things as clearly as You do. Help me to remember that when You close a door, it's for my protection, and You'll open just the right one when the timing is perfect.

Help me to be thankful for all the times You've taken care of me in the past. Help me to obey You with the things You've asked me to do, and then leave the rest in Your capable hands. Amen.

Conclusion

"All my fellow townsmen know that you are a woman of worth" (Ruth 3:11).

Ruth was a woman of true worth, noble character, excellence, and virtue. Her life reminds us that no matter the bend in the road or change in life, nothing should keep us from making a difference in God's kingdom. Ruth's story reminds us that God doesn't expect women to sit on the sidelines. He has important work for us to do, and He considers our contributions to be significant. Just as the book of Job reveals that God takes a man's suffering seriously, the book of Ruth highlights struggles and heartaches that are unique to women. When we are able to persevere through difficulties, blessing and opportunity await.

Who was the true hero of the story? Who was the rescuer? A quick read might cause one to say it was Boaz. But the real hero is God Himself. He is the One who took the unraveled threads of two women's lives and began to weave a tapestry of strength and purpose. He chose two women—both without value in their culture's opinion, without sons, without protection, without rights—to protect the royal line that would birth the King of kings and Lord of lords. God's eye was always on His promise of redemption. He never lost sight of His purposes. Those were dark days when the judges ruled and "everyone did as he saw fit" (Judges 17:6). This generation "knew neither the Lord nor what he had done for Israel" (Judges 2:10). And God saw two women, His beloved daughters, trying to trust Him in the midst of confusion and grief. He chose to raise them up and give them a significant role to play in His plan.

God is *for* women. He loves to pour out His goodness on His daughters. He is thrilled to see us take our place in the battle and do our part to bring the message of redemption to our hurting world. He is counting on His daughters. Whether we are missionaries in Africa, sharing His truth and love with a child, doing business with integrity, or caring for an aging relative—no matter our circumstances, He needs us. He values us. He is for us. In the words of author Bill Hybels:

> Friends, in what other life are you going to go all out? We all have one shot and one shot only to leave a lasting legacy . . . a legacy that says, 'I have been trusted to carry God's message of hope to an aching, fractured world in need, and I refuse to rest until my role in that is fulfilled. When we get this stuff right, we show the rest of the world that the present state of affairs does not determine the possibilities life holds. We can finish differently than we started, friends. We can.[31]

My Resolution

In what specific way will I apply what I learned in this lesson?

Examples:

1. Who is an older person in my life who needs to feel unconditional love and loyalty? I'll make a phone call, write a letter, or visit to actively show my love and loyalty to him or her.

2. When I feel the overwhelming weight of a particular responsibility in my life, I'll go to adoration and leave my burden at the foot of the cross. I'll ask God to show me in which specific ways I need to obey, and then I will trust Him with the rest.

3. I will come up with a concrete way in which I can pass on my faith to someone in the next generation.

---

[31] Bill Hybels, *Holy Discontent* (Grand Rapids, MI: Zondervan, 2007), 136.

My Resolution:

Catechism Clips

CCC 321 Divine providence consists of the dispositions by which God guides all his creatures with wisdom and love to their ultimate end.

CCC 1949 Called to beatitude but wounded by sin, man stands in need of salvation from God. Divine help comes to him in Christ through the law that guides him and the grace that sustains him:

Work out your own salvation with fear and trembling; for God is at work in you, both to will and to work for his good pleasure (Philippians 2:12).

CCC 1963 According to Christian tradition, the Law is holy, spiritual, and good, yet still imperfect. Like a tutor it shows what must be done, but does not of itself give the strength, the grace of the Spirit, to fulfill it. Because of sin, which it cannot remove, it remains a law of bondage. According to St. Paul, its special function is to denounce and disclose sin, which constitutes a "law of concupiscence" in the human heart. However, the Law remains the first stage on the way to the kingdom. It prepares and disposes the chosen people and each Christian for conversion and faith in the Savior God. It provides a teaching which endures for ever, like the Word of God.

CCC 1972 The New Law is called a law of love because it makes us act out of the love infused by the Holy Spirit, rather than from fear; a law of grace, because it confers the strength of grace to act, by means of faith and the sacraments; a law of freedom, because it sets us free from the ritual and juridical observances of the Old Law, inclines us to act spontaneously by the prompting of charity and, finally, lets us pass from the condition of a servant who "does not know what his master is doing" to that of a friend of Christ—"For all that I have heard from my Father I have made known to you"—or even to the status of son and heir.

Verse Study

See Appendix 3 for instructions on how to complete a verse study.

Ruth 1:16–17

1. Verse:

2. Paraphrase:

3. Questions:

4. Cross-references:

5. Personal Application:

Lesson 10: Connect Coffee Talk

ABIGAIL – GOING IT ALONE

Accompanying DVD can be viewed at:
www.walkingwithpurpose.com/courses/videos
Select: *Discovering Our Dignity* – Talk 03 – Abigail – Going It Alone

Please read 1 Samuel 25:2–43 before watching the video. Lesson 11 will allow you to follow up with a deeper dive into Abigail's story.

1. **Abigail's Trials**

2. **Abigail's Choices**

   A. Worry and fear

   When we are tempted to give in to worry and fear, it's helpful to remember Psalm 91:1.

   The antidote to worry and fear is to dwell on _____ more than we dwell on the potential _____ _____.

   B. Anger

   Three criteria for righteous anger (taken from *Uprooting Anger*, by Robert Jones):

   1. Righteous anger reacts against _____.

2. Righteous anger focuses on _____ and _____ kingdom, rights, and concerns, not on _____ and _____ kingdom, rights, and concerns.

3. Righteous anger is accompanied by _____ _____ _____ and expresses itself in _____ _____.[32]

Ephesians 4:26–27

C. Self-pity

When we turn our gaze toward _____ and away from our _____, we are reminded of the role of suffering in our lives.

Instead of asking, "Why is this happening to me?" we can ask, _____?

Ephesians 6:13–17

2 Corinthians 4:16

The antidote to self-pity is _____ and _____.

3. **Abigail's Solution**

---

[32] Robert D. Jones, *Uprooting Anger* (Phillipsburg, NJ: P&R Publishing, 2005), 29–30.

Questions for Discussion

1. When difficult circumstances hit, we are always tempted to magnify potential negative outcomes and underestimate the difference that our loving God can make. What are some things we can do to help get a grip on our thoughts so that we dwell on God more than we dwell on our negative situations?

2. When we feel alone and helpless, it's easy to feel angry about our circumstances. Author Robert Jones gives three criteria for "righteous anger." Read below, and discuss whether your anger tends to reflect these criteria or something else.

   Righteous anger:
   - Reacts against actual sin
   - Focuses on God and His kingdom, rights, and concerns, not on me and my kingdom, rights, and concerns
   - Is accompanied by other godly qualities and expresses itself in godly ways[33]

3. Do you think you are more focused on having a perfect life or on growing in holiness?

---

[33] Ibid.

Lesson 11

ABIGAIL

Introduction

As we move from Deborah's and Ruth's stories, we enter another phase in Israel's history. There has been a transition from the Israelites being ruled by judges with God as their king to being ruled by earthly kings. The first of these kings was Saul, and he is described as "a handsome young man. There was no other Israelite handsomer than Saul; he stood head and shoulders above the people" (1 Samuel 9:2). God had given the people what they wanted, even though He knew that a human king would struggle with sin issues that would affect the Israelites. They were settling for less than God's best, but He was (and is) a gentleman, and didn't insist on being their king. Before anointing Saul, God said through the prophet Samuel, "Today you have rejected your God, who delivers you from all your evils and calamities, by saying to him, 'Not so, but you must appoint a king over us'" (1 Samuel 10:19).

King Saul sinned against God, and as a result, God removed His blessing from Saul. He sent Samuel to Saul with this message: "The Lord has sought out a man after his own heart and has appointed him commander of his people, because you broke the Lord's command" (1 Samuel 13:14). That man was David. Samuel anointed David, but David didn't take the throne for many years. During that time, he was on the run from King Saul, who wanted to kill him. There were opportunities during this time for David to kill King Saul and ascend the throne more quickly, but he never took them. He trusted God and His timing, and endeavored to live honorably.

It is during this season of running and hiding from King Saul that the story of Abigail takes place. The prophet Samuel had just died, and David was hiding in the Desert of Maon, near the home of Abigail.

Abigail had heard of David, but certainly never expected her life to intersect his. She was living in the midst of frustrating circumstances, stuck in a marriage that left much to be desired. A rescue was coming, but it was going to get worse before it got better.

A dear friend of my husband's often tells us, "Remember, the darkest hour is the hour before dawn." You may feel stuck in the midst of circumstances that feel a bit like Abigail's. If so, take heart. God is at work, even if you can't see the evidence around you. As you wait to see what He will do, Abigail serves as a wonderful example of how to live in the meantime. Three things stand out about Abigail: her faith, her loyalty, and her respect. She didn't despair, no matter how bad things looked, and she decisively and gracefully influenced those around her.

Day One
MISMATCHED MARRIAGE

Read 1 Samuel 25:2–3.

1. What words are used in this passage to describe Nabal?

2. What insight is gained from Matthew 6:24 regarding the interplay among these qualities?

3. A. Which principles do the following verses and Catechism clip reveal regarding our attachment to money?

   "The earth is the Lord's and all it holds, the world and those who live there" (Psalm 24:1).

   "God loves a cheerful giver" (2 Corinthians 9:7).

"There was a rich man whose land produced a bountiful harvest. He asked himself, 'What shall I do, for I do not have space to store my harvest?' And he said, 'This is what I shall do: I shall tear down my barns and build larger ones. There I shall store all my grain and other goods and I shall say to myself, 'Now as for you, you have so many good things stored up for many years, rest, eat, drink, be merry!' But God said to him, 'You fool, this night your life will be demanded of you; and the things you have prepared, to whom will they belong?' Thus will it be for the one who stores up treasure for himself but is not rich in what matters to God" (Luke 12:16–21).

CCC 2536 The tenth commandment forbids greed and the desire to amass earthly goods without limit. It forbids avarice arising from a passion for riches and their attendant power. It also forbids the desire to commit injustice by harming our neighbor in his temporal goods:

When the Law says, "You shall not covet," these words mean that we should banish our desires for whatever does not belong to us. Our thirst for another's goods is immense, infinite, never quenched. Thus it is written: "He who loves money never has money enough."

B. Which of these principles do you struggle with the most?

R. G. LeTourneau, a wealthy manufacturer, lived for years on 10 percent of his income and gave away 90 percent. "The question," LeTourneau said, "is not how much of my money I give to God, but rather how much of God's money I keep for myself."[34]

Unfortunately, this wasn't Nabal's attitude.

---

[34] Joe Plemon, "The Money Quiz: Do You Serve God or Money?" Personal Finance by the Book, February 5, 2010, http://personalfinancebythebook.com/the-money-quiz-do-you-serve-god-or-money/.

4. Nabal's wife, Abigail, was very different from him. She is described in 1 Samuel 25:3 as intelligent and beautiful. As this week's Bible passage will reveal, the two were mismatched on many levels. When a couple's differences result in frustration, arguments, and anger, the desire to try to change the other can be all-consuming. If you are married, have you ever thought about how much better things would be if your spouse would just stop doing things his way and start listening to you? Our temptation to control, manipulate, and complain grows quickly. But is that our only option? An alternative approach wives can take when they are spiritually mismatched with their husbands is presented in 1 Peter 3:1–4. Read the passage and describe this different approach.

This passage challenges us to win over our husbands with our inner transformations. As our spiritual lives deepen, we should be growing more like Christ. Our growth in love, joy, peace, patience, gentleness, kindness, and self-control should be something that is seen without our saying a single word. Genuine growth in this way will communicate that God is real, and that a relationship with Him makes a huge difference in life. This is so much more effective than leaving Christian books on his bedside table, nagging him to come to Mass, or comparing him to more spiritual men.

Gary Smalley and Ted Cunningham write about the difficulty of being spiritually mismatched in their book, *From Anger to Intimacy*. They describe three journeys at work within a marriage:

1. **Your spiritual journey.** You are 100 percent responsible for discovering your gifts and being a good steward of your walk with Christ. Your mate is 0 percent responsible for this journey.

2. **Your mate's spiritual journey.** You are 0 percent responsible for this journey, but your mate is 100 percent responsible for discovering his gifts and being a good steward of his walk with Christ.

3. **Your marital journey.** You are both to honor, encourage, and assist each other throughout a lifetime of commitment.[35]

---

[35] Dr. Gary Smalley and Ted Cunningham, *From Anger to Intimacy: How Forgiveness Can Transform Your Marriage* (Ventura, CA: Regal, 2009), 216.

Looking at the marriage journey from this perspective helps us to withstand the urge to control, and instead practice the principles found in 1 Peter 3.

Quiet your heart and enjoy His presence. . . . He is all you need.

In any relationship, whether it's with a spouse, a work colleague, a friend, or a relative, there are bound to be moments when the other's behavior drives us crazy. It can be appropriate to "speak the truth in love" (Ephesians 4:15), but there often comes a time when words aren't helpful. It's then that we need to remember that we can't control another person or make him or her do things a certain way, but we can always work on ourselves. Think of a person who consistently gets a rise out of you and annoys you like no other. Ask God to shed light on ways in which he or she is presenting you with opportunities for spiritual growth.

Day Two
WISDOM IN ACTION

Read 1 Samuel 25:4–19.

1. What service had David and his men been providing for Nabal? See 1 Samuel 25:7, 15–16.

2. How many men were with David? See 1 Samuel 25:13.

3. What was Nabal's response to David's request? See 1 Samuel 25:10–11. Was this an appropriate response? See 1 Samuel 17:49–54 for added insight.

4. Abigail's quick response to her husband's foolish reaction reveals her wisdom, which protected her family and exemplified Proverbs 4:5–6: "Get wisdom, get understanding! Do not forget or turn aside from the words I utter. Forsake her not, and she will preserve you; love her, and she will safeguard you." The book of Proverbs is full of applications regarding wisdom. Record your insights about the following verses below.

"When pride comes, disgrace comes; but with the humble is wisdom" (Proverbs 11:2).

"The prating of some men is like sword thrusts, but the tongue of the wise is healing" (Proverbs 12:18).

"The stupid man sows discord by his insolence, but with those who take counsel is wisdom" (Proverbs 13:10).

"The fool gives vent to all his anger; but by biding his time, the wise man calms it" (Proverbs 29:11).

As Dan Allender put it succinctly, "Here's a necessary irony: Those who are wise know they lack wisdom."[36]

---

[36] Allender, *How Children Raise Parents*, 38.

Quiet your heart and enjoy His presence. . . . You are precious in His sight.

The Bible tells us, *"Wisdom builds her house, but folly with her own hands tears it down"* (Proverbs 14:1). Tearing down our homes is easy. If we lack self-control, focus on ourselves, say whatever we think, and generally lack a servant's heart, it won't be long before our homes suffer. A wise woman chooses her words, her timing, and her priorities all with the overarching goal of building her home. She knows that it's not just about outward actions. The attitude of her heart is all-important. Take some time to reflect on your recent interactions within your home. Are your choices building your home or tearing it down? Do your words build up family members or tear them down? Ask the Holy Spirit to make clear any areas that need attention, and then ask Him to strengthen you to make the necessary changes.

Day Three
CAREFUL WORDS

Read 1 Samuel 25:20–35.

1. What was David planning to do when he arrived at Nabal's home?

2. How would you describe Abigail's entreaty to David?

3. When Abigail spoke the words in verse 26, had David already agreed not to carry out his plan?

Even though David hadn't said a single word about calling off his plan to kill all the males, Abigail decided to act as if he had. My mother wisely once told me that if you regularly show a man his failures, that is what he will become. But if you communicate to him who you believe he *could be* as if that is who he is *now*, he will do all he can to become the man he sees reflected in your words. Saying things like "You are a wonderful leader" builds confidence in him. If you tell him, "You are a fantastic provider; we have all that we need," this reassures him and keeps him from making decisions based on fear and worry. And the truth is, most of us do have all that we need; we just don't have all that we want. If you tell him, "I think you can do anything. These are your wonderful qualities . . ." this fills him with the determination to go out and face challenges with strength and tenacity.

Author Dan Allender tells the story of how his wife communicated with him so effectively in this manner. Someone had given him a free ski pass for his whole family. One of his sons was unquestionably the best skier in the family. But this particular day, the son got to the top of the hill and froze with fear, insisting that he couldn't go down. Dan began to say things to his son like, "Come on! You're the best skier—you've been on tougher hills than this. You can do it!" But no matter what he said, his son refused to try. Dan kept pushing him, and finally lost his patience. His wife intervened and asked him to let her handle it. He started to ski down the hill, but halfway down, he pulled off to the side and turned to watch her progress. She wasn't having any success, so seething inside, he laboriously went back up the hill on his skis. When he got to the top and started to ski over to them, his wife saw him coming and met him. She laid her hand on her husband's chest and said, "I know the way men hurt you when you were growing up. And I know you don't want to do that to your son." And she turned and skied down the hill. And something changed in that moment. She had seen in his heart the kind of father that he *wanted* to be, and even though he wasn't behaving that way, she brought attention to his pure desire. She had called out the good in him. Dan looked at his son and said simply, "I know you can do this. Come on down when you're ready." Then he headed down the hill and had a spectacular wipeout. Somehow *this* is what gave his son confidence, and he followed his dad down the hill.

4. Is there anyone with whom you could practice this principle of building up by communicating who he *could be* as if that is who he *is today*? Reflect on what kind of difference your words could make in this person's life.

5. Abigail used her skills to promote peace by preventing David from making a rash choice. By her actions, his anger was assuaged. This brings up some questions: Did David have a right to be angry? Is anger always a sin? Jesus displayed anger when He overturned the tables of the moneychangers in the temple, so does that make all anger OK?

We touched on this issue in Lesson 10. Author Robert D. Jones gives three criteria for righteous anger:

- It reacts against actual sin.
- It focuses on God and His kingdom, rights, and concerns, not on me and my kingdom, rights, and concerns.
- It's accompanied by other godly qualities and expresses itself in godly ways.[37]

A. Based on this criteria, was David's anger toward Nabal righteous?

B. How can you apply this to your own life? When you assess your motives and underlying concerns, do you think your anger is usually righteous or sinful?

Quiet your heart and enjoy His presence. . . . Bask in His smile as He delights in you.

Abigail's wise words and well-timed intervention saved many lives. No doubt, God was at work behind the scenes, moving David's heart to respond with grace and mercy. God's protection was evident. How many times has God protected you? How many times has He quietly intervened, preventing you from experiencing tragedy? Reflect on this, and thank Him for the many times He has kept you safe.

---

[37] Jones, *Uprooting Anger*, 29.

"O LORD, my rock, my fortress, my deliverer, my rock of refuge! My shield, the horn of my salvation, my stronghold, my refuge, my savior from violence, you keep me safe" (2 Samuel 22:2–3).

Day Four
JUSTICE AND MERCY

Read 1 Samuel 25:36–38.

1. Nabal had no idea of the disaster Abigail was averting as he drunkenly partied with his friends. She had just orchestrated a significant peace treaty, and he wasn't even able to listen to what had happened. How do you typically react when your sacrifice goes unnoticed and unappreciated?

2. Nabal might have gotten away with treating people horribly for most of his life, but the consequences of his actions finally caught up with him. Describe what happened.

3. God sees. God remembers. God is a just judge, and there will be consequences for the evils perpetrated by man. It may seem like He never steps in and makes things right. It may seem like people get away with doing horrible things, but one day, there will be a reckoning. God sees. God remembers. So why does He wait? Why does it often seem like judgment is such a long time coming? See 2 Peter 3:9.

anger would only harm her. It would eat at her from within. The following excerpt from the WWP talk "Loving like Him Through Forgiveness" sheds light on the process of forgiveness:

What does forgiveness *NOT* mean?

> It's important to remember that forgiving someone doesn't mean that you throw common sense out the door and continue in a relationship that is unhealthy. Forgiveness does not mean enabling. If the hurt has been caused by destructive behavior, it is essential that you set boundaries for the future that will protect you. You get to the root of anything that is unhealthy in the relationship and fix it. You make new rules. You have new parameters. You can forgive and demand that it never happen again.
>
> Forgiveness does not let the other person off the hook with God. God is a God of justice, and He will deal with the person who has hurt you. Choosing to forgive means that I am no longer the enforcer. God is. If a punishment needs to be doled out, God will do it. Each time I'm triggered and can feel the anger returning, I need to say, "Whoa—this no longer belongs to me. It belongs to God." Give it to Him again.
>
> Forgiveness is not the same as condoning what the person did to you, or allowing them unlimited access to you to do the same thing again. But just as you protect and guard yourself from a dangerous relationship or situation, you need to guard your physical, emotional and spiritual health by not allowing unresolved anger to rule your life.[38]

Is there someone in your life whom you need to forgive? Do these guidelines bring any clarity to that situation?

---

[38] Lisa Brenninkmeyer, Walking with Purpose, "Loving like Him Through Forgiveness" (2012).

5. What additional insight do you gain about forgiveness from CCC 2843?

Quiet your heart and enjoy His presence. . . . He longs to shower you with love.

You will be enabled to forgive as you focus on how much God has forgiven you. This truth is addressed in the book From Anger to Intimacy: How Forgiveness Can Transform Your Marriage. *The authors write, "No matter what has happened, you are invited to forgive just as God has wholly and fully forgiven you. Where do you find that kind of forgiveness? Through the person of Jesus Christ. Matthew 10:8 says, 'Freely you have received, freely give'. . . . If you are not a forgiving person, if you have unresolved anger, bitterness or resentment in your heart, and you do nothing to get rid of it, then you have not yet experienced or realized the forgiveness you have received."[39]*

Do you truly appreciate the forgiveness that Christ purchased for you? Or have you become callous to its reality? Do you take God's forgiveness for granted?

Day Five
FAITH AND HUMILITY

Read 1 Samuel 25:39–43.

1. What emotions might Abigail have felt when she received the news in verses 39 and 40?

---

[39] Smalley and Cunningham, *From Anger to Intimacy*, 137–8.

2. Abigail believed that one day David would be King of Israel, as seen by 1 Samuel 25:30: "When the LORD carries out for my lord the promise of success he has made concerning you, and appoints you as commander over Israel . . ." She had most likely heard the story of David slaying Goliath, and believed he was a man of courage. She perceived his proposal to be advantageous because of his character and his promising future, even though he was currently in the midst of difficult circumstances. She was willing to face trials by his side, filled with hope for what she believed would happen in the future. What virtue does this exemplify? See Hebrews 11:1.

3. In what way is our relationship with Christ similar to Abigail's relationship with David? See 2 Timothy 2:11–12.

4. What character trait did Abigail exemplify in verse 41?

5. Abigail's life was about to change drastically. Who gave a similar answer in response to an invitation to enter into a life-changing relationship? What did she say? See Luke 1:38.

Quiet your heart and enjoy His presence. . . . His love for you is unconditional.

Blessed Mother Teresa wisely said, "If you are humble nothing will touch you, neither praise nor disgrace, because you know what you are." This doesn't mean we consider ourselves worthless. True humility means seeing ourselves through the eyes of God. And how does He see you? He sees you as His beloved daughter. There is nothing you can do to make Him love you more or less. When you begin every day with your focus on this truth, all the events that come your way can be seen as having been filtered through His loving hands. He only allows circumstances to touch you that can be used for your good. He promises to be there for you always, giving His unconditional support, understanding, and protection. Take a few moments to bask in His love. Close your eyes and meditate on this truth: "I am God's beloved daughter." Thank Him for treating you not as a slave, but instead as His treasured child.

Conclusion

At first glance, it would seem that Abigail got her fairy tale ending. Her difficult marriage to a foolish man ended with her dignity still intact. The future King of Israel found her so desirable and appealing that he married her. She had gone from feeling alone in marriage to being far from it. She was finally yoked to a man who was described as "a man after God's own heart." But she was, in fact, headed for future heartache. Her marriage was to be shared with many other women—at least seven other wives and various concubines. Surely, Abigail learned that pinning her hopes for happiness and fulfillment on a man was a path to disappointment.

The God-shaped hole in each one of us results in a constant temptation to look to a person, someone we can see, hear, and touch, to fill it. But even the best people eventually disappoint. Only God will understand us fully and recognize the motives of our hearts. Only God will always think the best of us. Only God has the ability to measure our strength and match His expectations of us to what we are able to deliver. Isaiah 42:3 tells us that "a bruised reed [God] will not break, and a smoldering wick he shall not quench." When we feel broken, useless, and weary, God won't crush us. He recognizes when we need tenderness and mercy.

When we feel alone in life, we can cling to God. He is our rock and will never fail us.

"Fear not, for I have redeemed you;
I have called you by name: you are mine.
When you pass through the water, I will be with you;
In the rivers you shall not drown.
When you walk through fire, you shall not be burned; the flames shall not consume you. . . .
Because you are precious in my eyes and glorious and because I love you" (Isaiah 43:1–2, 4).

My Resolution

In what specific way will I apply what I learned in this lesson?

Examples:

1. Before I'm too quick to judge Nabal, I will recognize my own tendency to hoard stuff that I don't need. Because I want to be completely free from a love of money, I will go through a closet or a room in my house and give away the things I'm no longer using.

2. Because I have a tendency to try to control and manipulate people through my words, I want to change and live according to 2 Peter 3:1–4. I will meditate on this verse every morning and ask God to help me influence others through encouragement instead of trying to control them through my words.

3. I'm struggling to forgive someone. I'll take an hour this week and go to adoration in order to focus on all that Christ has forgiven in me. I'll pray that the mercy He's showered on me will fill my heart and help me to forgive the person who has hurt me.

My Resolution:

Catechism Clips

CCC 2536 The tenth commandment forbids greed and the desire to amass earthly goods without limit. It forbids avarice arising from a passion for riches and their attendant power. It also forbids the desire to commit injustice by harming our neighbor in his temporal goods:

When the Law says, "You shall not covet," these words mean that we should banish our desires for whatever does not belong to us. Our thirst for another's goods is immense, infinite, never quenched. Thus it is written: "He who loves money never has money enough."

CCC 2843 Thus the Lord's words on forgiveness, the love that loves to the end, become a living reality. The parable of the merciless servant, which crowns the Lord's teaching on ecclesial communion, ends with these words: "So also my heavenly Father will do to every one of you, if you do not forgive your brother from your heart." It is there, in fact, "in the depths of the heart," that everything is bound and loosed. It is not in our power not to feel or to forget an offense; but the heart that offers itself to the Holy Spirit turns injury into compassion and purifies the memory in transforming the hurt into intercession.

Verse Study

See Appendix 3 for instructions on how to complete a verse study.

Colossians 3:12–13

1. Verse:

2. Paraphrase:

3. Questions:

4. Cross-references:

5. Personal Application:

Lesson 12

BATHSHEBA

Introduction

Have you ever witnessed someone being misjudged because all the facts about his or her life haven't been presented? That's how I feel as I introduce this lesson on Bathsheba. King David is one of my favorite people in the Bible, and the three lessons in *Discovering Our Dignity* in which he plays a part (Abigail, Bathsheba, and Tamar) all paint him in a poor light. But this isn't the whole picture of who he was. So much of his life was spent delighting God and pursuing His purposes with a humble, worshipful spirit. He wrote many of the Psalms, such precious expressions of the way we feel today, thus giving us words to pray when we lack our own.

But he had weaknesses, as we all do, and he seemed to consistently falter in the area of his relationships with women. This week's lesson marks a turning point in the life of King David. Things began to go downhill from here in a cascade of decisions that led to future heartache. The early decisions were small ones—seemingly harmless choices. But these small poor choices led to big mistakes later.

Even good men and women fall. Often it begins with an unmet desire, which is played with in the mind until it grows in the heart. It can happen to any of us. We can be living lives of integrity and character when out of nowhere, temptation hits. The desire can become all-consuming. At this point, self-control and accountability become crucial.

Wouldn't it be wonderful if the story of David and Bathsheba were an unusual one? But, unfortunately, stories of adultery and betrayal are all too common. Before we let our minds wander in judgment, let's be reminded that any of us could fall. Small, seemingly harmless choices can leave even the most virtuous woman vulnerable. When we don't feel listened to or appreciated, when we are desperately longing for someone to value us, we can easily be led toward gratification of our desires. The early choices don't seem harmful—connecting with an old boyfriend on Facebook, inviting intimate conversation with men we can never have, indulging in fantasies. But all these are small steps that eventually lead to destructive decisions. May we instead run to God with our needs and feelings of loneliness. May we heed the wise words of Proverbs 4:23: "With all vigilance guard your heart, for in it are the sources of life."

Day One
SMALL COMPROMISES LEAD TO BIG MISTAKES

Read 2 Samuel 11.

1. A. What was the first bad decision that set King David on a path to serious sin?

    B. What are your primary responsibilities? Where do you feel tempted to ignore those duties and instead give your time to something more appealing but less important? What consequences have you experienced from these choices?

2. David's decision to commit the sin of adultery with Bathsheba was not an isolated decision. Two decisions preceded his fall. List them here.

Where was David's accountability? Where was the person who would love him enough to stand up to him and warn him of the consequences of this choice? David sent people to inquire about Bathsheba and then to go get her for him. No one questioned him. They just did what he asked. They were probably servants who would have been terrified of the consequences had they questioned their king. David surrounded himself with people who were there to do his bidding, not keep him on track. Do you do the same? Do you welcome constructive criticism from friends, or do you only surround yourself with people who tell you what you want to hear? Accountability is something we have to ask for. We need to give our friends permission to love us in this way.

3. David's descent into sin bears a striking similarity to Eve's. In Lesson 2, we learned that each of her mistakes led her farther down the path to sin. She started by conversing with temptation; she looked at the temptation, and then allowed her desires to drive her decision making. So often, when we are faced with temptation and fall into sin, the excuses we make about it later on sound like we were facing some unique, extra-difficult choice. We find a response to those excuses in 1 Corinthians 10:13. What wisdom can you glean from this verse to help you in times of temptation?

The passage doesn't make clear what part Bathsheba had to play in the adultery. Did she bathe in plain sight, knowing that people could see her? Did she invite attention? Or did she think she was enjoying a private bath, and had no choice but to go when the King of Israel summoned her? We don't know. But it serves as a reminder that we are not helping matters when we dress seductively and invite emotional intimacy with men. This doesn't mean we have to dress in sackcloth, quit styling our hair, or swear off makeup forever. There is such a thing as modest beauty. It also doesn't mean that it's all up to us, and that when men fall, women are always to blame. But we're wise to check our actions and motives. Why do we dress the way we do? Whose eye are we trying to catch? Are we making it easier or more difficult for men to stay faithful to their wives?

4. When David found out that Bathsheba was pregnant, he tried to cover his tracks, which ultimately revealed Uriah's character. What kind of a man was Bathsheba married to?

Quiet your heart and enjoy His presence. . . . He is all you need.

David wasn't the only one who felt that the normal duties of life were flagging in excitement and appeal. We all can be tempted to ignore our basic callings, our primary vocations, in order to spice up our lives with a little excitement. There's nothing wrong with adding some fresh, new fun to life, as long as it's not sinful. But we're wise to learn from David and to make sure that before we charge off after some new pursuit, we have given our best to our priorities in life. Take some time in prayer to reflect on your priorities, checking to see if you are giving the most important ones your best efforts or your leftovers. In the WWP course Opening Your Heart, *we suggest the following priorities (listed in order of importance): your relationship with God, your relationship with your spouse, your relationship with your children, and then outside activities.*

Day Two
A STORY MEANT TO PIERCE THE HEART

Read 2 Samuel 12:1–14.

No matter how much we may try to hide our sin, God sees everything, and He often allows other people to see it, too. About a year after the affair with Bathsheba, Nathan, a prophet, was sent by God to confront David. Nathan's role as a prophet was to confront sin and point people to the truth. He showed great wisdom in his choice of words. He knew using an analogy involving sheep would touch David's heart; he well remembered the great love a shepherd has for his sheep. David spent many years as a shepherd before being anointed king, and Nathan's story brought David's mind back to a purer time in his life.

1. What does David's reaction in 2 Samuel 12:5–6 reveal about his conscience?

When we don't confess our sin, our hearts become hardened and we become less sensitive to the promptings of the Holy Spirit. When nothing makes us feel convicted or guilty, it may be because we are living perfectly holy lives. Or it may be that our unconfessed sin has allowed our hearts to become callous, and nothing is penetrating. When we do a nightly examination of conscience, a wonderful verse to turn into a prayer is Psalm 139:23: "Probe me, God, know my heart; try me, know my thoughts. See if there is a wicked path in me; lead me along an ancient path." Regular confession keeps the heart tender.

2. A. What consequence did David think should be given to the rich man who took the poor man's ewe? See 2 Samuel 12:5–6.

Without realizing it, David pronounced a death sentence upon himself. When Nathan spoke the piercing words, "You are the man," David recognized that he deserved to die. This brought him face-to-face with his desperate need for God's mercy. There would be consequences for his sin, but God spared David's life. When the truth of David's sin began to sink into his soul, Nathan said to him, "The Lord has removed your sin. You shall not die" (2 Samuel 12:13). David knew what he deserved, but God gave him the undeserved gift of life—a taste of the Gospel.

B. What consequences did God say David would experience because of his sin?

3. CCC 2538 refers to the story Nathan told King David when he wanted to spur him to repent his sin. It identifies what was at the root of David's sin, and what can lead to the worst crimes then and now. What is this sin? Where do you see its destructive force today? Share an example.

4. What point was God making in verses 7–8 when He spoke to David through Nathan the prophet?

Quiet your heart and enjoy His presence. . . . His love for you is unconditional.

David wrote Psalm 51 after Nathan had pointed out his sin with Bathsheba. It was his prayer, begging for forgiveness, restoration, and the return of joy. Have you drifted from God? Is sin weighing heavy on your heart? Make David's words your prayer. Echo his words of sorrow, as well as his words of hope and trust in the surety of forgiveness.

> *Have mercy on me, God, in accord with your merciful love; in your abundant compassion blot out my transgressions.*
> *Thoroughly wash away my guilt; and from my sin cleanse me.*
> *For I know my transgressions; my sin is always before me.*
> *Against you, you alone have I sinned; I have done what is evil in your eyes so that you are just in your word, and without reproach in your judgment.*
> *Behold, I was born in guilt, in sin my mother conceived me.*
> *Behold, you desire true sincerity, and secretly you teach me wisdom.*
> *Cleanse me with hyssop, that I may be pure; wash me and I will be whiter than snow.*
> *You will let me hear gladness and joy; the bones you have crushed will rejoice.*
>
> *Turn away your face from my sins; blot out all my iniquities.*
> *A clean heart create for me, God, renew within me a steadfast spirit.*
> *Do not drive me from before your face, nor take from me your holy spirit.*
> *Restore to me the gladness of your salvation; uphold me with a willing spirit.*
> *I will teach the wicked your ways, that sinners may return to you.*
> *Rescue me from violent bloodshed, God, my saving God, and my tongue will sing joyfully of your justice.*
> *Lord you will open my lips; and my mouth will proclaim your praise.*
> *For you do not desire sacrifice or I would give it; a burnt offering you would not accept.*
> *My sacrifice, O God, is a contrite spirit; a contrite, humbled heart, O God, you will not scorn. (Psalm 51:1–19)*

Day Three
IRREVERSIBLE CONSEQUENCES

Read 2 Samuel 12:13–25.

David was genuinely sorry for what he had done, but his sorrow and repentance didn't erase the consequences of his actions.

1. How did David react when his son became ill?

2. A. What was the purpose of David's fast, and why do we fast today? See CCC 1434.

The glossary of the *Catechism of the Catholic Church* defines *penance* as follows: "*Interior* penance: a conversion of heart toward God and away from sin, which implies the intention to change one's life because of hope in divine mercy (1431). *External* acts of penance include fasting, prayer, and almsgiving (1434). The observance of certain penitential practices is obliged by the fourth precept of the Church (2043)."[40] Further explanation of the purpose of fasting is found in CCC 2043: "The fourth precept... ensures the times of ascesis and penance which prepare us for the liturgical feasts and help us acquire mastery over our instinct and freedom of heart."

B. Has your experience of fasting served this same purpose of expressing sorrow for sin and strengthening your will to help you "acquire mastery over [your] instinct and freedom of heart"? What has been your experience with fasting? Can you think of any ways to make it more meaningful and less of an obligation?

David fasted and prayed intensely for seven days, but still his little boy died. Was his time wasted? God had already spoken through Nathan. Was there any point in asking Him to reconsider? David knew his God, and knew that there had been times when God changed His mind in response to His people's prayers (Genesis 18:16–32; Exodus 33:3, 15–17; Isaiah 38:1–8), so he begged God not to take his child. Scripture doesn't reveal why, but this particular time, God said no.

---

[40] U.S. Catholic Church, *Catechism of the Catholic Church* (Washington, DC: United States Conference of Catholic Bishops, 2000), 892.

Was God unmoved by David's sorrow and grief? We can be assured that He certainly felt compassion for David. While God isn't ruled by feelings, He has a tender heart, and does not enjoy punishing His children. He aches when the only thing that will get through to us is something painful. God hears all our cries, and even as He disciplines us, He holds us and gives us the strength to endure it.

When we ignore the gentle prodding of the Holy Spirit encouraging us to turn from our sin, we risk experiencing far larger, more painful consequences. God sends these consequences in order to teach us and to remind us of our dependence on Him. When we think we are getting away with sin, we can mistakenly believe that we are the ones in charge. God will use painful circumstances to remind us of our need for Him. It's so important to remember that He wants us to learn in the least painful way possible. This is well said in the book *Trustful Surrender to Divine Providence*: "As a surgeon who has to operate on a person of great importance takes care to cause him as little suffering as possible and only what is strictly necessary for his recovery, or as a father unwillingly punishes a son he loves dearly only because he is obliged to do so for his son's good, so God treats us as noble beings for whom He has the highest regard, or as beloved children whom He chastises because He loves them."[41]

3. A. How did David react when he heard his son had died?

   B. When have you experienced an immediate response of worship after something painful has occurred, either in your own life or in the life of another person?

Responding with worship to painful circumstances, ones that God could have prevented, is rare. It comes from a heart that considers knowing God and becoming more and more like Jesus to be the most important things in life. It's the result of believing Hebrews 12:6: "For the Lord disciplines him whom he loves." It comes from standing on the foundation of faith instead of feelings. Faith says, "Even though I cannot see why God is allowing this terrible circumstance, I know the truth about who He is. He is loving. He is compassionate. He is in control. He

---

[41] Father Jean Baptiste Saint-Jure and Blessed Claude de la Colombière, *Trustful Surrender to Divine Providence* (Quebec: St. Raphael Editions, 1980), 22–3.

didn't stop being any of those things when this difficulty occurred. I will trust Him in spite of my pain, and in spite of the fact that I don't understand why He has allowed it." It pours out of a humble heart, one that embraces the truth of Saint Augustine's words: "Since it is God we are speaking of, you do not understand it. If you could understand it, it would not be God."

4. Grief is never easy and puts an incredible strain on a marriage. Men and women grieve differently, and this can make loss even more painful. The Scripture passage gives us insight into what David was feeling and how he reacted to his grief, but it says little about Bathsheba. Put yourself in her shoes. What might she have been feeling and experiencing?

Quiet your heart and enjoy His presence. . . . You are precious in His eyes.

Think of a follower of Christ whom you admire for his or her spiritual depth. More than likely, if you were to hear his or her life story, you'd find that many heartaches and difficulties had lined the path. Saint Teresa of Ávila reflected on this truth, saying, "We always find that those who walked closest to Christ were those who had to bear the greatest trials."[42] But it all has to do with our response to those trials. They can make us more compassionate toward others and more intimate with God, or they can make us bitter. It's up to us. What are our expectations? Do we expect life to be easy and to go our way? Or have we fully surrendered to God—are we willing to take the good and the bad, whatever He gives us, with a surrendered spirit?

"We are at Jesus' disposal. If He wants you to be sick in bed, if He wants you to proclaim His work in the street, if He wants you to clean the toilets all day, that's all right; everything is all right. We must say, 'I belong to you. You can do whatever you like.' And this . . . is our strength, and this is the joy of the Lord."[43] —Blessed Teresa of Calcutta

Can you turn Mother Teresa's words into a prayer?

---

[42] "Defend the Faith: Catholic Quotes," Angelfire, angelfire.com/nb/defendthefaith/quotes.html.
[43] Ibid.

"When shall it be that we shall taste the sweetness of the Divine Will in all that happens to us, considering in everything only His good pleasure, by whom it is certain that adversity is sent with as much love as prosperity, and as much for our good? When shall we cast ourselves undeservedly into the arms of our most loving Father in Heaven, leaving to Him the care of ourselves and of our affairs, and reserving only the desire of pleasing Him, and of serving Him well in all that we can?"[44] — *Saint Jane Frances de Chantal*

Day Four
PASSING THE CROWN AND THE BATON OF FAITH

Read 1 Kings 1.

Note: Adonijah was the oldest of David's surviving sons. He was David's fourth son, but the firstborn, Amnon, had been murdered by his brother Absalom; the second son, Daniel (Abigail's son), had probably died by this time; and the third son, Absalom, was killed when he tried to seize control of his father's throne.

1. Because David was still living and Adonijah hadn't been named his successor, it was presumptuous of him to boast, "I shall be king!" What were his bold moves recorded in 1 Kings 1:5–10? What qualities or circumstances made things look favorable for him?

2. What was David's response to Adonijah appointing himself as his successor?

[44] Ibid.

David's lack of authority in his family is shocking. He was King of Israel, yet he considered it antagonizing to even ask his son why he was making such a flagrant, presumptuous, dangerous claim to the throne. Perhaps Adonijah knew his father would do nothing, based on David's history. (We'll look at this in greater depth in the next lesson.) Unquestionably, David's decision not to "rock the boat" and instead to allow his children to make bad choices was foolish, and led to their ruin.

3. Why did Nathan give advice to Bathsheba in order to save her life and the life of her son Solomon (1 Kings 1:12)? Additional insight is gained from Bathsheba's words in 1 Kings 1:21 when she pleaded with David not to passively ignore what was going on.

4. Solomon was God's choice to succeed David, regardless of his place in the family line. God always looks at the heart, and He saw something in Solomon that He loved. Which of Solomon's godly qualities were revealed in 1 Kings 3:5–14?

Scripture doesn't reveal what led to Solomon having a tender heart toward God, but it certainly seems likely that David and Bathsheba had raised him to love the Lord. Passing the baton of faith to the next generation is not something that happens by chance. It comes from decisions and sacrifices, and a determination to not settle for merely good, but to be God's best. Disciplining a child effectively is a part of this process. If a child is undisciplined and consistently gets away with doing whatever he or she wants, something happens to his or her heart. It becomes callous and hardened. A callous heart is less receptive to God's truth. I'm challenged by award-winning writer Ginger Hubbard's words: "We are tools used by God to whittle away the calluses of the heart, keeping the heart tender and inclined to obedience. When we call our children to obey us we are preparing them to obey Jesus, which is our ultimate goal."[45]

---

[45] Ginger Hubbard, *Don't Make Me Count to Three!* (Wapwallopen, PA: Shepherd Press, 2003), 75.

What happens when we don't confess our sins? Our hearts grow hard and callused, and we become less sensitive to God and more prone to further sin. In the same way, if we don't address heart issues with our children and we allow them to get away with unacceptable behavior, we are allowing their hearts to grow callused. If we want to teach them spiritual truths, we want their hearts to be as soft and open as possible!

5. This process starts when children are small. What are some practical ways to pass on the faith to children? What obstacles stand in the way?

One of the greatest obstacles to this kind of focused parenting is being too busy. We settle for good instead of best. We are led by our culture instead of by God's priorities, and we spend our best time and energy on sports, music, and other extracurricular activities, leaving little time for passing on spiritual truth. Frankly, we're tired! Sometimes our own laziness gets in the way. We know what we should do, but it seems like so much effort, so we put it off for another day. Another obstacle is not knowing how to pass on the faith. If this is your obstacle, I encourage you to look at the Samaritan woman at the well (John 4). Follow her example. There was much she didn't know about Jesus, but she shared what she did know, and her whole town was changed. Take advantage of the many resources available to you at Christian bookstores and online; they can give you the words to communicate spiritual truths to children.

This kind of spiritual impact is not only imparted to children by their parents. In fact, if we want to avoid losing this next generation spiritually, it is critical that we all reach out and pour into children, drawing them closer to Jesus.

Quiet your heart and enjoy His presence. . . . He longs to shower you with love.

Think of the children who are most important to you. Take some time to call down God's power and blessing on them through prayer. Instead of asking God to give them things they desire, ask Him to give them what they most need: a heart for God. Use your own words or the following prayer, adapted from 1 Kings 3:7–9.

Dear Lord,

I lift up before Your throne this precious child, _____. He is young, and doesn't always know how to act. I pray that You would give him a listening heart and a teachable spirit so that he can discern between good and evil. As he grows, he'll be surrounded by friends and a culture that will often present evil as if it is good. Please, Holy Spirit, give him a sensitive heart that sees sin for what it is, and runs from it instead of playing around with it. When he makes the wrong choice, I pray he will get caught, so that he can be disciplined to keep his heart soft and not callous. Give me opportunities to talk about You naturally. Help me to see opportunities throughout the day to draw our attention to You.

Help me to not settle for second best, thinking that getting good grades, going to a great college, and being a financial success is the same as success in Your eyes. Help me to say no to the things that will drain my energy from passing on the baton of faith to this child whom I love so much.

Day Five
THE QUEEN MOTHER

Read 1 Kings 2:10–25.

1. Why do you think Adonijah chose to approach Bathsheba with his favor?

Adonijah was just following the custom of the times; he recognized who had power and the king's ear.

In the Davidic monarchy, as well as in other ancient kingdoms in the Near East, the king's mother held the most important office in his royal court. She influenced political, economic, and liturgical affairs in the kingdom, and she played a key part in the process of dynastic succession. What is most striking, however, is the fact that she even ruled as queen. It was not the king's wife who held the queenship, but his mother. . . . When we consider the fact that most ancient Near Eastern kings practiced polygamy and had large harems, the idea of a queen mother makes a lot of sense. Think of King Solomon, who had seventy wives. Imagine the chaos in the royal court if all the wives were awarded the queenship. . . . In the Davidic kingdom, when a new king assumed the throne, his mother was given the special title gebirah, which in Hebrew means "great lady" or "queen." As queen mother, she possessed the second most powerful position in the kingdom—second only to the king himself.[46]

2. A. When Bathsheba entered King David's presence in 1 Kings 1:16, what was her posture before him?

   B. When Bathsheba entered King Solomon's presence in 1 Kings 2:19, what was his posture toward her?

3. What was the significance of Bathsheba being given a throne at King Solomon's right hand in 1 Kings 2:19? See Matthew 20:21.

---

[46] Scott Hahn and Leon J. Suprenant Jr., eds., *Catholic for a Reason II: Scripture and the Mystery of the Mother of God* (Steubenville, OH: Emmaus Road Publishing, 2000), 85.

4. This was not a situation unique to King Solomon and Bathsheba. Almost every time a new king was introduced in 1 and 2 Kings, it mentioned the king's mother as well.[47] This wasn't just a way for the queen mother to be shown respect. She held a position of influence and power in the kingdom. How is this seen in the following verses?

2 Kings 24:12

Jeremiah 13:18, 20

5. Adonijah was asking Bathsheba to fulfill one of her primary roles within the kingdom: that of advocate for the people. In what way does this, and the preceding information about the queen mother, foreshadow the role that Mary plays in our lives today? See also Luke 1:31–33.

Quiet your heart and enjoy His presence. . . . Bask in His smile as He delights in you.

When Bathsheba sat with King Solomon, he said, "Ask it, my mother, for I will not refuse you" (1 Kings 2:20). But then he denied her request. Does this discredit the claim that the queen mother had influence? No. King Solomon wanted to do everything he could to please her, but he couldn't risk the safety of his kingdom for his mother's request. "Abishag had belonged to David's harem, which Solomon inherited. Adonijah's request could imply a challenge to Solomon's accession and so exposes Adonijah to the suspicion of insurrection that will cost him his life."[48] Our queen mother, Mary, intercedes on our behalf. Jesus listens to all our requests, but will only say yes to the things that will benefit His Kingdom and our hearts. Ask Mary to intercede on your behalf, trusting that Jesus will not refuse any request that is in keeping with His character and His will. He always gives what is best for us!

47 Ibid., 86.
48 Study note from 1 Kings 2, *Catholic Teen Bible, NAB* (Mesa, AZ: Life Teen, 2009), 337.

Conclusion

"But since you have utterly spurned the LORD *by this deed, the child born to you will surely die"* (2 Samuel 12:14).

We pause at the severity of these words. What kind of an ending is *that*? To take the life of a child? To let the guilty go free and the innocent son die? To force a mother to watch her child suffer and die, bidding, just to pay for the sins of . . . *wait*. We know this story. Jesus, another innocent son, died for our sins. The events of 2 Samuel foreshadow the cross.

"Then Nathan returned to his house. The LORD struck the child that the wife of Uriah had borne to David, and it became desperately ill" (2 Samuel 12:15).

Liz Curtis Higgs reflects on that verse in her book *Really Bad Girls of the Bible*:

> The child was not born sick. *The child was struck by God.* I know this is almost impossible to comprehend. And yet, when Christ went to the cross, the Scripture says, 'Yet it was the Lord's will to crush him and cause him to suffer.' [Isaiah 53:10] And it crushes me to read that. To think of almighty God pressing His own son against the cross, holding Him there until all the life went out of His body because He loves us so much. Sisters, don't turn away! See him hanging there—for David and Bathsheba, for you, for me, for all who have sinned and fallen short of the glory and goodness of God.[49]

Because He hung there with our sins upon Him, we can be forgiven. Even when our choices have ruined our reputations, even when we can't see any way out of the mess we have made, because of Jesus, beauty can come out of ashes. Redemption. A fresh start. A way to be good again. Where do we go to find it? To the One who promises, "Behold, I am making all things new!"[50]

---

[49] Liz Curtis Higgs, *Really Bad Girls of the Bible* (Colorado Springs: Waterbrook Press, 2007), 153.
[50] Revelation 21:5.

My Resolution

In what specific way will I apply what I learned in this lesson?

Examples:

1. I'll look at my primary responsibilities differently this week. I'll recognize that I need to give them my best. If I am feeling bored, lazy, or weary because of my vocation, I'll be especially aware that temptation is probably not far behind. I won't take my eye off my priorities. They will get my best, not my leftovers.

2. I recognize that I need a prophet Nathan in my life. I will choose two wise friends and invite them to love me enough to hold me accountable. I will invite their honest input into my life, and promise that I will not get defensive in response to their constructive criticism.

3. Instead of dwelling on my past sins and getting discouraged, I'll go to confession this week. In the words of Liz Curtis Higgs:

   > When we turn back to embrace the One who loves and forgives us, we are made new. The old sin is washed away and gone for good, like that sudsy water from your shower that disappears down the drain, never to be seen again. Some of us put in a drain stopper, though, and insist on bathing in that same polluted water every day, beating ourselves up for last week's dirt still swirling around us rather than letting God wash it off for good.[51]

   But not me. I'm not going to put in a drain stopper. I'm going to run to confession, and accept God's limitless mercy.

My Resolution:

---

[51] Higgs, 155.

Catechism Clips

CCC 1434 The interior penance of the Christian can be expressed in many and various ways. Scripture and the Fathers insist above all on three forms, *fasting, prayer,* and *almsgiving,* which express conversion in relation to oneself, to God, and to others. Alongside the radical purification brought about by Baptism or martyrdom they cite as means of obtaining forgiveness of sins: effort at reconciliation with one's neighbor, tears of repentance, concern for the salvation of one's neighbor, the intercession of the saints, and the practice of charity "which covers a multitude of sins."

CCC 2043 The fourth precept ("You shall observe the days of fasting and abstinence established by the Church") ensures the times of ascesis and penance which prepare us for the liturgical feasts and help us acquire mastery over our instincts and freedom of heart.

CCC 2538 The tenth commandment requires that envy be banished from the human heart. When the prophet Nathan wanted to spur King David to repentance, he told him the story about the poor man who had only one ewe lamb that he treats like his own daughter and the rich man who, despite the great number of his flocks, envied the poor man and ended by stealing his lamb. Envy can lead to the worst crimes. "Through the devil's envy death entered the world."

We fight one another, and envy arms us against one another.... If everyone strives to unsettle the Body of Christ, where shall we end up? We are engaged in making Christ's Body a corpse.... We declare ourselves members of one and the same organism, yet we devour one another like beasts.

Verse Study

See Appendix 3 for instructions on how to complete a verse study.

Proverbs 4:23

1. Verse:

2. Paraphrase:

3. Questions:

4. Cross-references:

5. Personal Application:

Lesson 13

TAMAR

Introduction

I have countless memories of things I was taught by my mother, over and over again. She'd repeat them to me whenever I needed encouragement. She would remind me who I was by saying, "You are a child of the King. Do you know what that makes you? You are a princess. Other people may not recognize that this is true, but in your heart, you can know every day—that is who you are." These words served as protection over my heart. Things that happened still hurt, words carelessly spoken still stung, but I always had this truth to go back to. It made an enormous difference in my self-esteem.

But what of the countless women who weren't taught this truth in childhood? Or what of the many who were taught their true identity and worth in Christ, but who have experienced such traumatizing events that the truth no longer penetrates their hearts?

So many dear friends, *too many* dear friends, have shared with me stories of heartache and abuse from their past. They would relate personally to the story of Tamar. People who should have respected and cherished them instead robbed them of their innocence. The consequences have been varied, but always they have involved a questioning of worth and a loss of self-esteem. Some became promiscuous afterward, figuring that their purity was gone, so why bother keeping their bodies for their husbands? They felt they were damaged goods. Some became so devastated that they never recovered, and have gone through life considering themselves worthless. Great potential has been lost, as they have defined themselves by what was taken from them. Yet some have experienced healing, and although it has remained a constant struggle, they have refused to let what was done to them determine their future.

It is God's desire to redeem even the most terrible hurts that His precious daughters have experienced. He promises that if we allow Him into our pain—into the deep recesses of our hearts that we don't want exposed—He will bring healing. In Joel 2:25, the prophet shares this promise from God: "I will restore to you the years that the locust has eaten." Wild locusts destroy everything in their path. And that is what the enemy of your soul wants to do with your hurts. He wants them to be so magnified in your life that they block the blessings of God. He wants them to eat away at your joy and freedom so that you can't see all the good that God surrounds you with. We must resist the enemy's work in our lives, and instead turn to the One who can make our futures utterly different from what we have previously experienced. We can finish differently than how we started. We serve a God of restoration. May our master Creator take the shreds of our dignity and weave them into a covering of beauty.

Day One
THE BATTLE STARTS IN THE MIND

Read 2 Samuel 13:1–2.

1. To set the stage for Tamar's story, fill in the following blanks, based on 1 Chronicles 3:1.

   _____ was David's firstborn son, from his wife _____. He married her at the same time he married Abigail.

   _____ was David's second son. His mother was Abigail. Many commentators believe that he was no longer living at this time, as he is only mentioned in 1 Chronicles 3:1, and was not a contender for his father's throne.

   _____ was David's third son, the son of Macaah, who was the daughter of _____, the _____ of _____. He had a sister named _____.

2. What two details do we learn about Tamar from these verses?

3. A. What behavior do we see in Amnon that he saw modeled by his father?

   B. Have you observed the passing of negative traits from parent to child in your own life experience?

Children learn by imitation. We can tell them how we want them to live, but they will reflect what they see us doing. The responsibility is enormous. Titus 2:6–8 says to "urge the younger men [and women] . . . to control themselves, showing yourself as a model of good deeds in every respect, with integrity in your teaching, dignity, and sound speech that cannot be criticized." It's a tall order, but well worth pursuing when you think that the future of the next generation is at stake.

4. Amnon's obsession had serious consequences. Whenever we decide that we should have every unfulfilled longing satisfied, we are in trouble. When have you obsessed over something you wanted but couldn't have? Explain.

5. Amnon's battle, and ours, begins in the mind. What are we to do when our thoughts run wild and out of control? Write down any insights the following verses give to help us in this common struggle.

   Colossians 3:2

   1 John 4:4

1 John 1:9

Philippians 4:8

Quiet your heart and enjoy His presence. . . . He is all you need.

"The One who is in you is greater than the one who is in the world" (1 John 4:4).

When we recognize that our hearts lack contentment or are actually obsessed with something we don't have, we can rest assured that God is capable of changing our hearts. No matter how severe the temptation or longing is, the Holy Spirit gives us the power to overcome. But we have the responsibility to guard our thoughts and to remove ourselves from situations that agitate us. This can mean being careful about whom we spend time with, what we watch on TV, the books we read, and the number of magazines and catalogs we thumb through. Take some time to reflect. Are you struggling with discontent? Ask God to reveal to you any faulty thinking or unwise uses of your time. Commit to Him to do your part so that nothing stands in the way of His transformative power in your life.

Day Two
THE POWER OF INFLUENCE

Read 2 Samuel 13:3–11.

1. It seems that Amnon needed a friend like Jonadab in the same way that I need a friend who encourages me to max out my credit cards when I'm feeling depressed. Jonadab may have been clever (verse 3), but his intellect was so dark that it encouraged depraved manipulation rather than moral behavior.

   What do the following verses teach us about friendship?

   Proverbs 13:20

Proverbs 27:17

Proverbs 15:2 and 2 Timothy 2:16

Proverbs 22:24

Jesus gave careful thought to the choosing of His friends. He spent all night in prayer before choosing His twelve disciples, asking God to help Him discern with whom He should surround Himself. He then chose three of the twelve (Peter, James, and John) to be the closest of all.

What is it that attracts you to a potential friend? Is it her style? Her vibrant personality? Her graciousness? Her kindness? Her obedience to God? Are the qualities you are drawn to superficial ones, or are they qualities that really matter in the long run?

It can be a costly mistake when your closest friends' spiritual or moral foundation is very different from yours. When the chips are down and you are in crisis, you need friends who can speak the truth in love. Too often, our friends will only tell us whatever makes us feel good, when they could have helped to mold us into women of wisdom and maturity.

2. Reflect on your circle of friends. Who are your three closest friends? Do they encourage you to grow in godliness, or do they negatively influence you? Is there a godly woman whom God has placed in your life who might grow into a wonderful friend?

3. Although Jonadab's advice was terrible, Amnon still had the choice to follow it or not. James 1:12–15 describes the progress from temptation to sin:

Blessed is the man who perseveres in temptation, for when he has been proved he will receive the crown of life that he promised to those who love him. No one experiencing temptation should say, 'I am being tempted by God'; for God is not subject to temptation to evil, and he himself tempts no one. Rather each person is tempted when he is lured and enticed by his own desire. Then desire conceives and brings forth sin, and when sin reaches maturity it gives birth to death.

That is what happened to Amnon. He started with thinking evil thoughts, which then turned to action. What warning do these verses give us about facing temptation?

Quiet your heart and enjoy His presence. . . . His love for you is unconditional.

Meditate on the following writings about temptation by Saint Francis de Sales. Read with a prayerful heart, asking God to strengthen you in any area in which you are feeling a pull toward sin.

The beginning of all temptation lies in a wavering mind and little trust in God, for as a rudderless ship is driven hither and yon by waves, so a careless and irresolute man is tempted in many ways. Fire tempers iron and temptation steels the just. Often we do not know what we can stand, but temptation shows us what we are. Above all, we must be especially alert against the beginnings of temptation, for the enemy is more easily conquered if he is refused admittance to the mind and is met beyond the threshold when he knocks.[52]

We should not despair, therefore, when we are tempted, but pray to God the more fervently that He may see fit to help us, for according to the word of Paul, He will make issue with temptation that we may be able to bear it. Let us humble our souls under the hand of God in every trial and temptation for He will save and exalt the humble in spirit. In temptations and trials the progress of a man is measured; in them opportunity for merit and virtue is made more manifest. When a man is not troubled, it is not hard for him to be fervent and devout, but if he bears up patiently in time of adversity, there is hope for great progress. Some, guarded against great temptations, are frequently overcome by small ones in order that, humbled by their weakness in small trials, they may not presume on their own strength in great ones.[53]

---

[52] "Temptation," WhiteLilyofTrinity.com, http://whitelilyoftrinity.com/saints_quotes_temptation.html.
[53] Ibid.

Day Three
AN ATTACK ON DIGNITY

Read 2 Samuel 13:11–22.

My heart aches as I read verse 14. In that moment, everything changed for Tamar. Her life from that point on would be divided into two parts: before and after. As we move into this sensitive topic, I'm very aware that you may have been affected personally or very closely by a tragedy like this one. Every 107 seconds, someone in the United States is sexually assaulted. Each year, there are about 293,000 victims of sexual assault.[54] Both are sobering statistics. May God protect our hearts as we move into this section of Scripture—it's so loaded with pain and devastation.

1. Why do you think Amnon's immediate reaction to Tamar was intense hatred? See 1 Corinthians 13:4–8 for added insight.

What Amnon had felt for Tamar in the first place was never love; it was lust. Lust is the opposite of love, as seen by 1 Corinthians 13:4–8. Love is patient; lust demands immediate gratification. Love is kind; lust is self-focused and selfish. Love and lust can be confused for each other at first, but they are utterly different. When love is given and received, it increases. When lust is gratified, the person often feels guilty and disgusted with him- or herself. Because of human nature's tendency to blame, the disgust is often projected onto the one who was lusted after. This victim blaming is undeniably wrong and incredibly destructive.

2. List the ways in which Amnon mistreated Tamar after the rape.

---

[54] "Statistics," RAINN, http://www.rainn.org/statistics.

3. What was Tamar wearing, and what did it represent? What did she do to her clothes? What does this suggest?

4. How was Tamar hurt by all three men in her life—Amnon, Absalom, and King David?

   Amnon:

   Absalom:

   David:

5. How did Tamar live out the rest of her life? See 2 Samuel 13:20.

Quiet your heart and enjoy His presence. . . . You are precious in His eyes.

Who was Tamar? She was a princess. She was King David's daughter and the granddaughter of the King of Geshur. She was a royal on both sides of her family tree. Nothing Amnon could do could take that away from her. But she apparently lived the rest of her life believing she could never be restored. The quality of our lives usually stems from what and who we believe we are. And who was Tamar in her own eyes? She believed she was damaged goods. She thought she was worthless. The Bible says she lived the rest of her life desolate. How heartbreaking.

Who are you in your own eyes? Have you been convinced that you are damaged, beyond redemption, impure, without worth? If you see yourself as anything less than a princess, the daughter of the King of kings, then you are looking at yourself through foggy glasses. Your identity as the beloved daughter of God, His precious princess, cannot ever be taken from you. Nothing someone does to you can take that away, and nothing that you do is beyond the scope of forgiveness and restoration. May God mend your torn tunic and help you to see yourself as He sees you. May He restore your dignity and give you hope.

Day Four
THE CHOICE: REVENGE OR FORGIVENESS

Read 2 Samuel 13:23–28.

1. How many years had passed since the rape of Tamar?

2. What might have the people involved been thinking at this point?

   Tamar:

   Amnon:

Absalom:

David:

3. When it appears that evil is victorious, we can be tempted to take matters into our own hands. What do we learn about taking revenge from the following Catechism clips?

   CCC 678

   CCC 1861

4. If we aren't supposed to take matters into our own hands and exact revenge, what are we supposed to do with our pain? See CCC 2842, making special note of *how* we are to follow this teaching. How is it possible?

Our forgiveness of another person is not dependent upon this person asking for forgiveness. If we want to break out of the cycle that unforgiveness creates, then we will very often have to forgive even if the person never apologizes.

Choosing to forgive is a matter of the will. This is not a onetime event. As new memories might surface or as new things come to light in terms of how the hurt is affecting us, we will have to forgive again. We can't forgive what we don't know; therefore, as the consequences develop, we have to forgive each time. This is not because the original forgiveness was insincere. It's simply because forgiveness is a process.

Forgiveness says, "I will no longer bring up the offense, play around with it in my mind, or throw it back in the person's face." This is not letting someone get away with what he or she has done. It's leaving the judgment and punishment to God.

When we forgive, we free ourselves from a future destroyed by bitterness. It allows us to take charge of our own stories. It give us the power to rewrite the ending.

Quiet your heart and enjoy His presence. . . . He longs to shower you with love.

We can't control what happens to us, but we can decide what we're going to allow our minds to dwell on. If we want to be free of bitterness and resentment, then we need to refuse to rehash or rehearse or replay the offense in our minds. Each time a memory of the hurt comes back, we must use it as an opportunity to remind ourselves of our own need for mercy and for God's constant, gracious forgiveness. Let's ask God to help us, through His Holy Spirit, to work in our hearts so that we can let go of bitterness and find freedom through forgiveness.

Day Five
THE FINAL COST

Read 2 Samuel 13:29–39.

1. What report was incorrectly relayed to King David?

2. Who gave him the correct report? Do you see any irony in this?

3. Whom did Absalom flee to? How long did he stay there?

4. How did David initially react to Amnon's death?

5. Eventually David allowed Absalom to come home. But no real healing had occurred. There is no evidence that Absalom sought forgiveness. He returned, but King David gave this stipulation: "Let him go off to his own house; he shall not appear before me" (2 Samuel 14:24). When bitterness, regret, anger, and resentment go unchecked, they only go deeper and grow stronger. This is what happened with Absalom. Eventually, David pardoned him, but it was too late. A root of bitterness had already grown strong and deep in Absalom's heart.

   A. What was the ultimate result of Absalom's disgust over his father's lack of leadership and intervention in his family problems? See 2 Samuel 15:10.

   B. What was the ultimate consequence for Absalom? See 2 Samuel 18:9–15.

Quiet your heart and enjoy His presence. . . . He brings beauty from ashes.

What was Tamar left with? A dead brother, life in the household of a proven traitor, and a niece who bore her name ("Absalom had three sons born to him, besides a daughter named Tamar, who was a beautiful woman" [2 Samuel 14:27]). She was left with the ashes of mourning and a glimmer of hope. Could things be different for her niece? Could their family experience redemption? To whom would they all turn in their grief and sadness?

God promised in Isaiah 61:3 that He would "provide for those who grieve in Zion—to bestow on them a crown of beauty instead of ashes, the oil of gladness instead of mourning." But they would have to choose to turn to Him instead of wallowing in sadness and regret.

The same is true for us today. Sometimes we are so overcome by the sadness and apparent hopelessness of our circumstances that our focus remains entirely on the problem. We fail to lift our eyes to the One who holds the solution. God stands at the ready, with the desire to bestow on His royal daughters a crown of beauty instead of ashes. Can we trade our sorrows and shame for His mercy and grace? Yes, we can, and we do so by laying them all down at the foot of the cross. Do this daily, for as long as it takes. Ask Him to heal you. "For however many are the promises of God, their Yes is in [Christ]" (2 Corinthians 1:20).

Conclusion

When we experience hurt, whether small or significant, we are tempted to take matters into our own hands and punish the one who wounded us. So often it seems that retribution will never come.

We have talked a great deal about God's love and mercy, and those qualities are an integral part of His character. But another aspect of His character is that of judge. God sees. He is fair. One day, all wrongs and injustices will be made right. This is the side of God's character that we see in Daniel 7:9–14.

Daniel was experiencing a vision in which he saw evil being judged and destroyed. God was referred to as the Ancient of Days. This is what Daniel saw:

> As I looked, thrones were placed and one that was Ancient of Days took his seat; his raiment was white as snow, and the hair of his head like pure wool; his throne was fiery flames, its wheels were burning fire. A stream of fire issued and came forth from before him; a thousand thousands served him, and ten thousand times ten thousand stood before him; the court sat in judgment, and the books were opened (Daniel 7:9–10, RSV).

The Ancient of Days, seen by Daniel, sat on His throne. He was sitting on His throne the day you were hurt. He will be sitting on His throne the day we must all account for the way we have lived. The person who hurt you will be held responsible. Even if it seems that justice will never be served, be assured: God knows. One day, He will make everything right.

But one day we, too, will stand before Him. When our life passes before our eyes, how will we feel, looking at our choices in His presence? Will we have chosen to trust Him and let go of anger, or will we have clung to bitterness, letting it burrow deep within our hearts, impeding our ability to love? Will we have allowed God to work within our pain, redeeming it, teaching us things that we wouldn't otherwise have learned? Will we have welcomed His Holy Spirit into our hearts, helping us to forgive?

God can bring beauty from ashes during our lifetimes, but our full restoration will take place in heaven. All will be purified there, and we'll be able to see ourselves and God with clarity. Saint Thérèse of Lisieux reminds us, "The prophet Isaiah says that God 'will have a new name for his own servants,' and in St. John we read that to the victor God will give 'a white stone, on which stone a new name is written, known to him only who receives it.' It is in heaven that we shall know our titles of nobility."[55] Our torn robes will be replaced with robes of righteousness. Our dignity will be restored. We will be healed, and every tear will be wiped from our eyes. One day. Can you trust Him as you wait?

My Resolution

In what specific way will I apply what I learned in this lesson?

Examples:

1. Thinking about what a poor friend Jonadab was to Amnon reminds me of the importance of having godly influences in my life. I'd like to widen my circle of closest friends to include a woman who will encourage me to become the person God wants me to be. I'll call a woman who I think would be this kind of friend to me, and make plans to get together with her. I'll recognize that it takes time to build a friendship, and I will begin making that investment.

2. I struggle with my sense of worth and value. I relate to Tamar in this way. To combat these destructive thoughts, I will go to adoration this week and sit in God's presence. I'll meditate on the cross and think about God's great love for me evidenced by His suffering and death for my sake. I'll remind myself that I am God's beloved daughter, a princess. Nothing and no one can take that away from me.

---

[55] Saint Thérèse of Lisieux, *Story of a Soul* (New York: Doubleday, 2001), 68.

3. I am struggling to forgive someone who has hurt me. Every day this week, I will make the decision to forgive, asking God to do this work in me. I will start every day by meditating on how much God has forgiven me, and I will try to keep that at the forefront of my mind whenever I think of hurts others have caused me.

My Resolution:

Catechism Clips

CCC 678 Following in the steps of the prophets and John the Baptist, Jesus announced the judgment of the Last Day in his preaching. Then will the conduct of each one and the secrets of the heart be brought to light. Then will the culpable unbelief that counted the offer of God's grace as nothing be condemned. Our attitude to our neighbor will disclose acceptance or refusal of grace and divine love. On the last day Jesus will say: "Truly I say to you, as you did it to one of the least of these my brethren, you did it to me."

CCC 1861 Mortal sin is a radical possibility of human freedom, as is love itself. It results in the loss of charity and the privation of sanctifying grace, that is, of the state of grace. If it is not redeemed by repentance and God's forgiveness, it causes exclusion from Christ's kingdom and the eternal death of hell, for our freedom has the power to make choices for ever, with no turning back. However, although we can judge that an act is in itself a grave offense, we must entrust judgment of persons to the justice and mercy of God.

. . . as we forgive those who trespass against us

CCC 2842 This "as" is not unique in Jesus' teaching: "You, therefore, must be perfect, as your heavenly Father is perfect"; "Be merciful, even as your Father is merciful"; "A new commandment I give to you, that you love one another, even as I have loved you, that you also love one another." It is impossible to keep the Lord's commandment by imitating the divine model from outside; there has to be a vital participation, coming from the depths of the heart, in the holiness and the mercy and the love of our God. Only the Spirit by whom we live can make "ours" the same mind that was in Christ Jesus. Then the unity of forgiveness becomes possible and we find ourselves "forgiving one another, as God in Christ forgave" us.

Verse Study

See Appendix 3 for instructions on how to complete a verse study.

Isaiah 61:3

1. Verse:

2. Paraphrase:

3. Questions:

4. Cross-references:

5. Personal Application:

Lesson 14: Connect Coffee Talk

ESTHER – THIS IS YOUR MOMENT

Accompanying DVD can be viewed at:
www.walkingwithpurpose.com/courses/videos
Select: *Discovering Our Dignity* – Talk 04 – Esther – This Is Your Moment

Please read Esther 1:10–22 and 2:1–10 before watching the video. Lesson 15 will allow you to follow up with a deeper dive into Esther's story.

1. **The Measure of Beauty**

   What was King Ahaseurus doing? He was _____ their _____.

   What does our King do? He _____ our _____.

   Isaiah 61:10

   Ephesians 5:25–27

   Colossians 2:10

What is God attracted to?

1 Corinthians 1:27

Isaiah 53:4–5

When, because of your faith, your life too becomes perceptibly different; when your reactions are quite opposite to what the situation seems to call for and your activities can no longer be explained in terms of your personality; that is when your neighborhood will sit up and take notice. In the eyes of the world, it is not our relationship with Jesus Christ that counts; it is our resemblance to Him.[56] — Ray Stedman

2. Royal Dignity Attained for Just This Moment

The news was received as the Jews celebrated _____.

Esther was placed in the royal family for a purpose, and so were you.

1 Peter 2:9

In order to put on our royal robes, we have to get rid of the rags we've been wearing.

---

[56] Ray C. Stedman, *The Queen and I* (Waco, TX: Word Publishing, 1977), 92.

Ephesians 4:22–24

3. Remember the Victory

Questions for Discussion

1. In what ways have you experienced your worth being measured by the world's standards of beauty?

2. Esther wasn't noticed only because of her outer beauty. Her inner qualities also made her stand out. We are to stand out for Christ because of the radical way that we love and the supernatural way we respond to difficult situations.

   Share a story of a woman whose reactions have been quite the opposite of what the situation seems to call for and whose activities can only be explained because of her faith.

3. Just like Esther, you have been placed on the earth for such a time as this. What does your heart beat for most passionately? What change would you like to see in our world today?

Lesson 15

ESTHER

Introduction

If you feel that you will never move beyond your past, that you are powerless to bring change to your circumstances, or that brokenness defines you, Esther's narrative is for you.

Her story is a reversal of destiny. It's a reminder that everything is used in our lives—all the beauty and all the brokenness, all the successes and the failures, the encouragement we've been given and the lies we've been told; nothing is wasted.

When God calls us to take our place in our generation, when He calls our hearts to join Him in making this world a better place, He uses all of it to form us into women of strength, dignity, purpose, and healing—even the things that you worry disqualify you from serving Him. Those are the very things that make you authentic, human, and someone others can relate to when they are overwhelmed by their own weaknesses.

God has promised never to leave you or forsake you. He has placed limitless beauty within you, and His presence is what allows that beauty to shine forth. When you invite Him into the tender places of your heart, He promises to make everything beautiful in its time. Perhaps if you could stop your striving and slow down, you'd hear His whisper, His still, small voice, beckoning you to a different path.

You are here for such a time as this. There is a holy destiny with your name on it. But it will take courage to take hold of it. It will require you to claim God's promise that the old things have passed away and all things are being made new in your life (2 Corinthians 5:17).

In the words of Amena Brown Owen and Ann Voskamp in their poem, *Esther Generation*:

Sometimes we imagine that God's voice is a disappointed hard lined teacher
Who is waiting to whack our knuckles with a ruler for any imperfections
But that isn't God's voice at all
That isn't God's heart at all
He speaks tenderly
He doesn't need to raise his voice
He speaks as if He's right next to us
Because He's right next to us
Because He goes before us
Because His Spirit lives inside us
He starts with love
And not because He is a hopeless romantic
But mostly because
He is ALL LOVE and HOPE and SECOND CHANCES.[57]

May the God of all hope soften us, strengthen us, and restore us. May we place our stories—our past, present, and future—into His hands. May all of it be used for His glory, for such a time as this.

Day One
NO LONGER AN ORPHAN

Read Esther 2:5–7.

1. A. Being orphaned as a child caused Esther enormous pain. What sorts of fears might she have struggled with as she dealt with the loss of her parents?

    B. Even those of us who haven't lost our parents can experience the pain of abandonment, loneliness, and isolation. This may come from an experience of rejection or conditional love. When we feel insecure, self-protection is often our default response. We may put up walls around our hearts, and then set out

---

57 Amena Brown Owen and Ann Voskamp, "This Is Us: The #Esther Generation [a Spoken Word Poem]," A Holy Experience, http://aholyexperience.com/2014/03/this-is-us-the-esthergeneration-a-spoken-word-poem/.

to create our own security. Underlying these behaviors is a fear that if we don't perform, if we don't control our circumstances, we will be left alone. Has this ever been your experience? Share your thoughts here.

2. What drives fear out of our hearts? See 1 John 4:18.

God's love for us is perfect because it is utterly selfless and pure. He proved His love on the cross. What more could He have offered? There is nothing He wouldn't do for us. Place His perfect love between you and your fear, and let it remind you that His presence makes all the difference.

3. Because of His love, what did God destine us for? See Ephesians 1:4–5.

The Amplified translation of the Bible (AMP) says, "He predestined and lovingly planned for us to be adopted to Himself [as His own] children through Jesus Christ, in accordance with the kind intention and good pleasure of his will." He chose this. He chose *you*. He has always wanted you.

4. No matter how many times people have mistreated and abandoned you, no matter how many mistakes you have made, what promise has God given you in John 14:18?

5. What a difference there is between a slave who earns her keep and a daughter who simply rests in her position in the family, confident that she belongs. What is our position in the family of God? See Romans 8:15.

Quiet your heart and enjoy His presence. . . . He is your Abba.

Holy Spirit, John 14:26 promises that You will teach me all I need to know. I ask You to teach me how to receive the love of my heavenly Father. I don't want to just exist. I know Scripture promises me an abundant life. Please break down any barriers I have built around my heart. Help me as I speak these words out loud:

> *Heavenly Father, I am Your daughter. I am not an orphan. I am beloved, and I don't need to perform in order to earn Your love. Help me to stop behaving like a performing orphan. That is not who I am. You have adopted me and made me Your own. I can call You Abba, just as Jesus did. I rest in this truth. Help me to enjoy the life of joy and fulfillment You offer to me simply because You love me.*

Day Two
WINNING THE FAVOR OF ALL

Read Esther 2:8–17.

1. What qualities do you believe caused Esther to win the favor of those around her? Think beyond her outer beauty and focus on her inner qualities.

2. Superficial beauty catches the eye, but a woman with inner beauty wins people's hearts. The literal translation of Esther 2:9 is, "She lifted up grace before his face." What might change in our world if women made that their goal? Think of a person with whom you have a close relationship. What is a practical way you can lift up grace before his or her face this week?

3. Read the following verses, and record the aspects of inner beauty that they describe. Share one practical way you could display that quality this week.

"She is clothed with strength and dignity and laughs at the days to come" (Proverbs 31:25).

"She opens her mouth in wisdom; kindly instruction is on her tongue" (Proverbs 31:26).

"Charm is deceptive and beauty is fleeting, but a woman who fears the Lord is to be praised" (Proverbs 31:30).

4. Few things are as winsome as a woman who is totally at home in her own skin. When a woman is truly authentic, who she is on the inside radiates on the outside. The result can be quite irresistible. Anne Morrow Lindbergh writes of this in her classic book, *Gift from the Sea*:

> I want, first of all . . . to be at peace with myself. I want a singleness of eye, a purity of intention, a central core to my life that will enable me to carry out these obligations and activities as well as I can. I want, in fact—to borrow from the language of the saints—to live "in grace" as much of the time as possible. I am not using this term in a strictly theological sense. By grace I mean an inner harmony, essentially spiritual, which can be translated into outward harmony. I am seeking perhaps what Socrates asked for in the prayer from the Phaedrus when he said, "May the outward and inward man be one." I would like to achieve a state of inner spiritual grace from which I could function and give as I was meant to in the eye of God.[58]

A. Do you feel at peace with yourself in the way Anne Morrow Lindbergh describes? Why or why not?

---

[58] Anne Morrow Lindbergh, *Gift from the Sea* (New York: Pantheon Books, 1955), 23–4.

B. Do you believe you would be better able to "function and give as [you were] meant to in the eye of God" if you were experiencing more inner harmony?

Quiet your heart and enjoy His presence. . . . Allow Him to transform you.

The royal eunuch Hegai was drawn to Esther by her authentic beauty, which went beyond the superficial. She "lifted up grace to his face," and the virtue within her radiated outward. Do you want to grow in the area of authentic inner beauty? Ask God to help. Ask Him to give you depth of character. Seek His guidance. Be teachable. You can do this right now by turning to Him in prayer and telling Him how much you want to achieve a state of spiritual grace that would allow you to "lift up grace" to the faces of those you meet.

Day Three
HAMAN'S HATRED

Read Esther 3:1–11.

1. What do you learn about Haman's genealogy from Esther 3:1?

2. What did Haman seek to do when he saw that Mordecai would not kneel and bow down to him? See Esther 3:6. How does Haman's response to that offense strike you?

We have to look back at the Israelites' history to understand why Haman had such a strong reaction to Mordecai's refusal to bow. In 1 Samuel, we see that the Israelite king Saul was told by God to kill *all* the Amalekites. (The Amalekites were a nation that had attacked the Israelites as they left Egypt under the leadership of Moses. There had been bad blood between these two nations for a long time.) But Saul felt that partial obedience was good enough. He killed most of the Amalekites, but spared their king, Agag. The prophet Samuel confronted Saul about his disobedience of God, and Saul did eventually kill Agag. The Agagites, descendants of the Amalekites, took their name from King Agag. They absolutely hated the Jews. From generation to generation, that hatred was passed down. Haman hadn't been *born* with prejudice for the Jews, but he had been well trained to hate from childhood.

3. How did Haman convince King Ahasuerus to agree to the extermination of all the Jewish people in his nation?

4. Who was helping to advise the king on such a critical decision?

This is a classic case of dire consequences resulting from a lack of accountability. There was no one to step in and suggest that this response was extreme, unwise, or going too far.

5. We all need people who hold us accountable. These are people we *invite* to speak truth into our lives. Surrounding ourselves with people who just tell us what we want to hear leaves us vulnerable to poor decision making. Who holds you accountable? Which family member or friend is willing to speak the truth in love to you, even if you don't want to hear it?

Quiet your heart and enjoy His presence. . . . May He dispel any hatred in your heart.

We are deeply disturbed by a man like Haman allowing his hatred to justify genocide. But before we end this day's study, let's look a little closer to home. Is there a grudge you have been nursing? Is there someone who has hurt you deeply and you are waiting for a time when you can pay this person back? Is that lack of forgiveness festering in your heart?

The truth is, hatred and anger can get out of control for any of us. Thank God we have the daily dose of the Holy Spirit to help us work through our issues of forgiveness. When we are running low on grace, when we feel that we must take matters into our own hands, the Holy Spirit fills us with the patience that we need. If we ask Him, His goodness will grow in our hearts, allowing us to trust that one day, God will make everything right. He is a just judge. We can let go of our desire for revenge—in fact, we must *do this if we want to live freely and with joy.*

Ask God to reveal to you any bitterness or desire for revenge in your heart. Ask Him for the grace to forgive and let the grudge go.

Day Four
WHEN GOD SEEMS SILENT

Read Esther 3:12–13, Chapter B, verses 14 and 15.

Note: There are two different versions of the book of Esther—an older, Hebrew version and a Greek one. While the Hebrew version makes no mention of God, the Greek version has many references to Him. Protestant Bibles contain the Hebrew version; Catholic Bibles have the Greek version. When you see references to Chapters A, B, C, D, E, and F, these are the additional passages found in the Greek version that are not found in the Hebrew one.

1. What specific order was contained in the decree from King Ahaseurus? What did the king and Haman do after sending out the decree? What was the reaction of the people in Susa?

As King Ahaseurus and Haman lifted up a toast to genocide, the city reeled from a decree that had come out of left field. The word translated as *confusion* in Esther 3:15 is used two other times in the Bible: in Joel 1:18 to describe cattle who were beside themselves because they couldn't find pasture, and in Exodus 14:3 to describe the Israelites as they faced the Red Sea with Pharaoh and his army in pursuit. The people of Susa were frantic, bewildered, and utterly perplexed as to why this edict had been sent out.

2. How did Mordecai and the Jews in the outlying provinces react to the decree? See Esther 4:1–3.

In the ancient Near East, grief was not a private matter. When a person put on sackcloth and sprinkled ashes on his or her head, it was a clear sign of suffering and anguish. The people were terrified and seemingly without hope. The edict had been signed with the king's signet ring, and according to the laws of the Persians and Medes, this edict could not be undone.

3. The Jewish people's circumstances could have tempted them to feel forgotten by God. Many probably asked, "Where is God? Does He care?" Their hearts would have echoed the words of the prophet Isaiah: "Truly you are a God who hides himself" (Isaiah 45:15).

Although God was hidden from their view, He did not take His eyes off of them for even one second. God isn't limited by time, and He had known that this threat was going to come. He had placed Esther in the perfect position to play her part in the rescue of her people. God was allowing an opportunity for the deepening of her faith and theirs while they waited for Him. When Mordecai asked Esther to go before the king to plead for their lives, she probably had to wrestle with her own feelings of abandonment and a fear that God wouldn't come through for her. What preparation process did she go through as she waited for the right time to act? How do you think that particular preparation would have helped her with her fears? See Esther 4:15–17.

4. We can understand Esther's fear and hesitation. When tragedy strikes or suffering comes, we often wonder where God is. The truth is, He has never been closer to us than in those moments. He is not indifferent; He is at work. According to a commentary on Esther, "God providentially allows adversity, through which you grow spiritually. God turns your adversity into His university."[59] God is at work, even now, teaching you something through your circumstances. But you get to

---

[59] Patterson and Kelley, *Women's Evangelical Commentary*, 805.

decide what kind of a student you will be. Will you be fearless or will you run away from the lessons? Is there an area of your life where God is trying to teach you something through adversity? If so, write it here. As you think about your reaction to your circumstances, are you more focused on self-protecting or on stepping into the lessons courageously?

5. When we are facing fear, it isn't enough to convince ourselves that God won't let our worst-case scenario happen. That is conditional faith. What we need to do is face our fear and trust that God's presence in our lives will make the unbearable bearable. We need to have Esther's attitude. She faced down her fear of death and moved forward courageously, step by step. The root of the word courage is *cor*, which is the Latin word for *heart*. Courage comes from a heart that knows it is loved. Read the following verses about God's love for you and write them out in your own words. Allow these truths to infuse you with courage.

Romans 8:31–32

Romans 8:38–39

1 John 4:18

Come to God purely through reason, expecting Him to explain everything, and you will find Him unfathomable. Come to God with faith and an open heart and you will find that He transforms you and sets you free through the very circumstances that you thought would destroy you.

Quiet your heart and enjoy His presence. . . . "For a sun and shield is the LORD *God . . . the* LORD *withholds no good things" (Psalm 84:12).*

Esther and her people had no choice but to hope in God and wait for Him to act on their behalf. That waiting can feel excruciating when God seems silent. The waiting can also be a time of enormous growth for us, if we cooperate. We are promised in Isaiah 40:31 that "those that hope in the LORD *will renew their strength, they will soar on eagles' wings; they will run and not grow weary, walk and not grow faint." Read the following stanza from the old hymn "Immortal, Invisible, God Only Wise." Allow the words to lead you to reflect on God's character and goodness. May it give you new perspective for the times when He is hidden from your sight.*

"Immortal, Invisible, God Only Wise"

Immortal, invisible, God only wise,
in light, inaccessible, hid from our eyes,
most blessed, most glorious, the Ancient of Days,
almighty, victorious, thy great name we praise.

Unresting, unhasting, and silent as light
nor wanting, nor wasting, thou rulest in might;
thy justice like mountains high soaring above
thy clouds which are fountains of goodness and love.

To all, thou life givest, to both great and small;
in all life thou livest, the true life of all;
we blossom and flourish as leaves on the tree,
and wither and perish, but naught changes thee.

Thou reignest in glory; thou dwellest in light;
thine angels adore thee, all veiling their sight;
all laud we would render: O help us to see
'tis only the splendor of light hideth thee.[60]

---

[60] *United Methodist Hymnal* No. 103. Text: Walter Chalmers Smith. Music: Welsh melody from John Roberts' *Canaidau y Cyssegr.*

Day Five
HIS ARM IS NOT TOO SHORT TO SAVE THEM

"Let us never give up: there are no situations which God cannot change."[61] —*Pope Francis*

1. As Esther prepared to go to the king to plead for her people, what thoughts might have been running through her mind? Go back to Esther 4:9–11 for insights into her fears.

Everything hinged on how King Ahaseurus would respond to Esther. And what did she have to count on? Had the king always been faithful, merciful, and compassionate to the women in his life? No. It must have felt as if he held the world in his hands. His power seemed limitless.

2. Why had Mordecai refused to bow to Haman? See Esther Chapter C, verses 1–7.

So there they were, Esther and Mordecai. Both were in tenuous, dangerous situations because they considered doing the right thing to be more important than self-preservation. It would be so much easier if God's people were always rewarded here on earth for putting Him and His purposes first. But that's not how it goes. In fact, there will always be someone in your life who resents your devotion to God. Sometimes, this will be the person closest to you, the one whose opinion matters so very much. When this is the case, the ache in the heart that it causes goes really deep. It can tempt us to hopelessness. It can tempt us to compromise—to hide our faith. Maybe you are in this situation, and you're wondering if you should take a step back spiritually. Are you debating slowing down to match the pace of your loved one? If I could cup your face in my hands, I would, and I would say to you, *Please don't. Please don't stop running your race because someone close to you resents it. Run hard after God. Continue to give Him your whole heart. Trust Him with the heart of the one you love.*

---

[61] Pope Francis, "Easter Vigil: Homily of Pope Francis," The Holy See, March 30, 2013, http://w2.vatican.va/content/francesco/en/homilies/2013/documents/papa-francesco_20130330_veglia-pasquale.html

Running hard after God doesn't mean you take it on yourself to be the teacher of everyone in your path. You are running your race; they are on their own journey. Your transformed life will speak far louder than your instructions or book recommendations.

3. A. How is a king's heart described in Proverbs 21:1?

Please go back and reread that verse. It is so loaded with hope! It flies in the face of the despair we feel when we look at a hardened heart and want to give up. Are you looking at your current situation and thinking it will never change? If a powerful king's heart is just like channeled water in God's hands, then make no mistake, there is no heart that God cannot budge. He can open the most closed heart. There is nothing and no one beyond His reach. *Do not give up.*

B. Read CCC 269, and list each phrase or word that reminds you of God's power to bring change.

Note: Although God is all-powerful, He always respects human freedom. He doesn't force anyone to love Him. But what He *does* do is create opportunity after opportunity for people to see His goodness. He orchestrates people's paths to cross so that His children can share about the difference He makes. He softens hearts. He breaks down barriers. God's heart and arm are moved toward these actions in response to our prayers.

4. An important principle: You will have the greatest influence on people when they know that you love them. When they can rest in your unconditional love, when they trust that you are for them, when they don't feel like a "project," when they don't feel that you will love them if they change—then, and only then, will barriers come down. And don't doubt the power of the unspoken word. We may pat ourselves on the back, saying we love unconditionally because we bite our tongues and don't say what we are thinking. Oh, friends, *they know.* They sense the judgment. They see the disappointment in our eyes. We *earn* the right to be heard. We earn the right to speak truth into our loved ones' hearts. We earn it when we learn how to love without conditions and then put into practice what we know.

It's as we do this that we truly reflect the heart of God to those who desperately need to know His love. Is there a relationship in your life in which you want to grow in your ability to love unconditionally? Journal about it here. You might want to write a prayer, asking God to help you to love in this way.

Esther was filled with courage. Despite the risk, she approached the king. His heart was like channeled water in God's hand, and he gave Esther what she requested. Because the edicts of the Medes and Persians couldn't be overturned, the best Esther could do was write an additional edict that allowed the Jewish people to defend themselves. This proved to be enough. Esther's boldness set events in motion that resulted in the rescue of her people. Evil Haman's motives were revealed and he was executed. There was never a moment when God was not in control, even if He seemed absent in the midst of dire circumstances.

5. According to author Michelle McClain-Walters, "Esther would not have had the boldness to speak to the king about her people if she had not prayed and fasted, been filled with the heart of God for her people, and then been emboldened with righteous indignation to risk death to see them through to their deliverance."[62] And we are no different. If we want to step out in faith—to run our race in such a way that our faith is caught more than taught—we have got to be women of prayer. Friends, this is where the rubber meets the road. Read CCC 2732. What does it say is the most common yet most hidden temptation in prayer? What truth do we need to grasp in the depths of our hearts if we're going to be humble and full of faith?

---

[62] Michelle McClain-Walters, *The Esther Anointing* (Lake Mary, FL: Charisma House Book Group, 2014), 96–7.

Quiet your heart and enjoy His presence. . . . "Surely the arm of the LORD is not too short to save" (Isaiah 59:1).

God can handle anyone.

The same cannot be said about us. No amount of manipulation, or orchestration of circumstances, or perfect words, or even the perfect example of godliness is going to open and change the hearts of our loved ones. Some of those things help, and some of them hinder. But at the end of the day, apart from God, we can do nothing. When a heart softens and breaks open, that is the work of God. It is only He who can reach into the secret places of the heart, bringing healing, comfort, and a quenching of thirst.

Not only is God's arm not too short to reach into your loved one's heart, He has limitless patience and matchless love. Are you desperate for your loved one to know Christ? Be assured, God is even more desperate to be known. *Go to the Lord in prayer for your loved one. Storm heaven. Don't give up. Never, ever, ever give up. God wants this even more than you do, and He will not cease drawing hearts to Him. Your loved one is not the exception to the rule. God has not given up.*

"Ah, my Lord God! You made the heavens and the earth with your great power and your outstretched arm; nothing is too difficult for you" (Jeremiah 32:17).

Conclusion

"The most deadly poison of our time is indifference." —Saint Maximilian Kolbe

One woman decided it was worth the risk. She could see all the reasons why she should stay silent, but her determination to do the right thing—to stand in the gap, to do her part—propelled her to action. This was the pivotal moment of Esther's life. She had come to the royal throne "for such a time as this" (Esther 4:14).

God is looking for women today who are willing to stand in the gap of our generation. Are you willing to bridge the distance between what is and what could be? Are you willing to do what it takes to impact your current sphere of influence? It begins with a heart that is wholly devoted to Christ. We read in 2 Chronicles 16:9 that "the eyes of the Lord move to and fro throughout the earth that He may strongly support those whose heart is completely His." God is searching among us, looking for women who are willing to be taken through a preparation process. While Esther's preparation to go before the king involved outer beauty treatments, our preparation is on the inside. God asks us to allow Him to cleanse us of our impurities—pride, selfishness, bitterness—so that we can be pliable in His hands. It's only after we have gone through this cleansing that we are ready to be used by God—to follow His lead to pursue His purposes for us in our generation.

So often we shrink back because we wonder what difference one woman can make. We're disheartened when we see the enormity of the issues in our world. But the truth is, God created you for a purpose. He doesn't ask you to solve the greatest problems—just to do your part. I like the way Edward Everett Hale, historian in the 1800s, responds to our tendency to underestimate the power of one:

> I am only one,
> But still I am one.
> I cannot do everything;
> but still I can do something;
> and because I cannot do everything
> I will not refuse to do the something that I can do.[63]

A woman who follows in the footsteps of Esther places her influence, her wisdom, her favor, and her femininity in the hands of God. She offers God all that she has, and asks Him to do in and through her whatever He wills. "Who is this coming up from the wilderness leaning [and depending] upon her beloved?" (Song of Solomon 8:5) It's a woman motivated by her love of God and leaning on His strength, one who steps out courageously, because she knows she is here for such a time as this.

My Resolution

In what specific way will I apply what I learned in this lesson?

Examples:

1. Esther didn't achieve mastery just over her enemies; she achieved mastery over herself. I will choose one habit that I know is holding me back from stepping out in boldness. I will ask God to help me grow in self-control in this area, and I will do my part to change.

---

[63] John Bartlett, *Bartlett's Familiar Quotations*, ed. Emily Morison Beck (Boston: Little, Brown and Co., 1980), 590.

2. I will commit to praying daily for my loved one who is far from God. I will not lose heart, and I will remember that "a king's heart is like channeled water in the hand of the LORD" (Proverbs 21:1).

3. A key component of Esther's victory was her preparation. Her fasting released spiritual blessings she desperately needed. Fasting can strengthen us spiritually (Luke 4:14, 18), unlock wisdom and direction for decision making (Judges 20:26–28), and humble us and help us to pray (Ezra 8:21). I will fast one day this week to be strengthened in this way.

My Resolution:

Catechism Clips

CCC 269 The Holy Scriptures repeatedly confess the universal power of God. He is called the "Mighty One of Jacob," the "LORD of host," the "strong and mighty" one. If God is almighty "in heaven and on earth," it is because he made them. Nothing is impossible with God, who disposes his works according to his will. He is the Lord of the universe, whose order he established and which remains wholly subject to him and at his disposal. He is master of history, governing hearts and events in keeping with his will: "It is always in your power to show great strength, and who can withstand the strength of your arm?"

CCC 2732 The most common yet most hidden temptation is our *lack of faith*. It expresses itself less by declared incredulity than by our actual preferences. When we begin to pray, a thousand labors or cares thought to be urgent vie for priority; once again, it is the moment of truth for the heart: what is its real love? Sometimes we turn to the Lord as a last resort, but do we really believe he is? Sometimes we enlist the Lord as an ally, but our heart remains presumptuous. In each case, our lack of faith reveals that we do not yet share in the disposition of a humble heart: "Apart from me, you can do *nothing*."

Verse Study

See Appendix 3 for instructions on how to complete a verse study.

Deuteronomy 4:29

1. Verse:

2. Paraphrase:

3. Questions:

4. Cross-references:

5. Personal Application:

Lesson 16

MARY, THE BLESSED MOTHER

Introduction

We all need a mother. No matter how old we are, we long to be nurtured, protected, and loved. Yet many of us, for various reasons, are not receiving this tender care. Without even realizing it, we can end up living like orphans. We may feel like a motherless daughter because our mother has died. Or perhaps our earthly mother wasn't able or willing to love us in a way that really satisfied our needs. We might be caring for our mothers as they age, and our roles have been reversed. Whatever the reason, we can end up in a place where we're doing all that we can just to hold it together. And needing to be strong all the time only intensifies the desire to find a place where we can arrive broken and needy and receive comfort.

The good news is: We have parents. We are not orphans. We are beloved daughters. We have a heavenly Father who is always there to heal, forgive, restore, and redeem us. We have a heavenly Mother who longs to spread a blanket (her mantle of protection) over us, to comfort us, to come alongside us in our times of need, to pray for us when we need strength, to help us stay on a path that leads us closer and closer to Jesus.

Who needs Mary?
Those who don't feel known.
Those who are harsh.
Those who don't feel loved.
Those who are afraid that if they do too much, they'll be taken advantage of.
Those who are afraid of what obedience to God might cost.
Those who take care of everybody else and need someone to take care of them.
We all need a mother.

When Mary was asked to collaborate with God, she was given no guarantees—just the opportunity to love. The first thing the angel said to her was, "Do not be afraid." These were Jesus' first words to His disciples after His resurrection. They are Mary's words to us, as well. She led by example, showing total confidence in God when she said, "Let it be to me according to your word." She showed total confidence in Jesus when she turned to the servants at the wedding at Cana and said, "Do whatever He tells you." She gives us the same message: "Do whatever He tells you." But we hesitate, wondering how much pain or sorrow that obedience might cause us.

Mary didn't know what suffering her yes—her fiat—might bring. And we don't know, either. But we do know that we don't walk that path alone. And we know that obedience, though costly, pays eternal, joyful, fulfilling dividends that make any sacrifice worth it.

Behold your heavenly Mother. Let her teach you how to love. May her example and intercession draw you to a place where you want what God wants, when He wants it, how He wants it. May your will become totally united with His.

Day One
MARY, EVER VIRGIN

Read Matthew 1:18–25.

1. At what point in Mary and Joseph's relationship did the conception of Jesus take place?

2. For the Israelites, the betrothal period meant more than a modern engagement does. A betrothal was a binding commitment; ending a betrothal required a divorce. We see this in Deuteronomy 22:24, in which a betrothed virgin is referred to as a "wife," not a "fiancée." What might people have expected Joseph to do when he realized Mary was pregnant? What caused him to marry her despite her circumstances? See Matthew 1:23.

3. Why was it important that Jesus be born of a virgin? See CCC 503 and John 3:16.

The Catholic Church teaches that Mary was not only a virgin when Christ was born; she remained a virgin her entire life. Many objections are raised to this teaching. One of the most common comes from Matthew 13:55, in which James and Joseph are referred to as Jesus' "brothers" (*adelphoi* in Greek). It's important to note that the Greek word *adelphoi* can also be used to refer to a cousin or a close relative. This word is found in the Greek Old Testament in Genesis 13:8 and 14:16 and is translated as *kinsman*. If Jesus had had brothers and sisters at the time, the giving of His mother, Mary, to the apostle John would have been unthinkable; it would have been their responsibility to care for their mother.

Additional insight comes from the fact that it was not unusual at the time of Jesus' birth for married couples to take vows of celibacy. Mary's response to the angel's announcement that she would have a son ("How can this be?") suggests that she and Joseph had taken such a vow. At this point, the angel simply said that she would conceive and give birth to a child. If she had been planning on marrying and having sexual relations with Joseph, she would have known exactly "how this could be." Since the angel hadn't given her any kind of a timetable, Mary logically would have interpreted his words to mean sometime in the future. Her response, "How shall this be, since I know not man?" (Luke 1:34), only makes sense in light of a vow of perpetual virginity. If she had planned to consummate the marriage after the betrothal period was over, the angel's words would have simply seemed prophetic, something that was yet to happen down the road.

4. Because of Jesus' death and resurrection, we are offered a new relationship with God. Describe that relationship according to John 1:13. Do you see any connection between this verse and Mary's virginal motherhood? See CCC 505.

5. We are God's daughters. As members of the Church, the Bride of Christ, we also have a spousal relationship with Jesus. This, of course, is not a sexual union. Saint Paul writes of this spousal relationship in 2 Corinthians 11:2: "For I am jealous of you with the jealousy of God, since I betrothed you to one husband to present you as a chaste virgin to Christ." When Saint Paul writes of God's jealousy, he is revealing God's desire that our hearts belong entirely to Him. He longs for us. In the words of Blessed Mother Teresa of Calcutta, "He thirsts for us." She explains this in a letter written to her Missionaries of Charity:

> [Our Lady] was the first person to hear Jesus' cry "I thirst" with St. John, and I am sure Mary Magdalen. Because Our Lady was there on Calvary, she knows how real, how deep is His longing for you and for the poor. Do we know? Do we feel as she? Ask her to teach. . . . Her role is to bring you face to face, as John and Magdalen, with the love in the Heart of Jesus crucified. Before it was Our Lady pleading with Mother, now it is Mother in her name pleading with you—"Listen to Jesus' thirst." "For I am jealous of you with the jealousy of God, since I betrothed you to one husband to present you as a chaste virgin to Christ."[64]

Jesus thirsts for you. Are you thirsty for Him? Sometimes we aren't thirsty for God because we've been drinking something else. We know it isn't totally satisfying, but it takes the edge off. Can you identify anything in your life that you are substituting for the refreshment that Christ is offering you through His presence?

Quiet your heart and enjoy His presence. . . . He thirsts for you.

Blessed Mother Teresa's letter continues:

> *How do you approach the thirst of Jesus? Only one secret—the closer you come to Jesus, the better you will know His thirst. "Repent and believe," Jesus tells us. What are we to repent? Our indifference, our hardness of heart. What are we to believe? Jesus thirsts even now, in your heart and in the poor—He knows your weakness, He wants only your love, wants only the chance to love you. He is not bound by time. Whenever we come close to Him—we become*

---

[64] Michael E. Gaitley, *33 Days to Morning Glory: A Do-It-Yourself Retreat in Preparation for Marian Consecration* (Stockbridge, MA: Marian Press, 2012), 74.

partners of Our Lady, St. John, Magdalen. Hear Him. Hear your own name. Make my joy and yours complete.[65]

Day Two
MARY, THE ARK OF THE NEW COVENANT

1. The Ark of the Covenant was a wooden chest covered in gold, which God commanded Moses to build and house in the holy of holies, the Tabernacle. "The ark was the mark of the Lord's intimate presence among his people,"[66] and was carried before the Israelite army in battle. What was contained in the Ark of the Covenant? See Hebrews 9:3–4.

Manna was the bread that God sent from heaven to feed the Israelites when they were wandering in the wilderness during the Exodus. Aaron was Moses' brother, the first high priest of Israel. His sprouted staff symbolized the priesthood. The tablets of the covenant were the Ten Commandments—God's words to the Israelites, carved into stone by His own hand.

2. How are the three objects found in the ark similar to the three descriptions of Jesus in John 6:35, Hebrews 4:14, and John 1:1, 14? Can you see the parallels?

---

[65] Ibid., 72.
[66] Scott Hahn, *Catholic Bible Dictionary* (New York: Doubleday, 2009), 69.

3. We read in 2 Maccabees 2 that in anticipation of the invasion of Israel by the Babylonians, the prophet Jeremiah took the Ark of the Covenant and hid it on Mount Nebo. When he realized that the people were wondering where he had hidden it, he said that the place would remain unknown for a period of time. When did Jeremiah say that God would reveal the Ark of the Covenant again? See 2 Maccabees 2:7–8.

4. The glory cloud mentioned in 2 Maccabees 2:8 is significant throughout the Old Testament. What did it do in Exodus 40:34–35?

Shekinah is a Hebrew word meaning "the dwelling place of God. It is any visible manifestation of God's presence, several times alluded to in the Bible. It corresponds to God's glory in Isaiah 60:2, His glory in Romans 9:4, and the cloud that directed the Israelites on their way to the Promised Land (Exodus 14:19)."[67] It was the Shekinah glory that appeared in the form of a cloud, and overshadowed the Ark of the Covenant within the Tabernacle.

5. What similarities do you see between the manifestation of God's presence in the cloud in Exodus 40 and the action of the Holy Spirit in Luke 1:35?

Many connections can be found between the story of King David bringing the Ark of the Covenant to Jerusalem (2 Samuel 6:2–16) and Mary's visit to Elizabeth (the visitation, Luke 1:35–56).

- King David "arose and went" to Judah to bring up the Ark of the Covenant; Mary "arose and went" to Judah to visit her cousin Elizabeth (2 Samuel 6:2, Luke 1:39).

---

[67] CatholicCulture.org, "Catholic Dictionary: Shekinah," Trinity Communications, https://www.catholicculture.org/culture/library/dictionary/index.cfm?id=36453.

- David expressed humility in God's presence by asking, "How can the ark of the Lord come to me?" Elizabeth expressed humility in God's presence within Mary by asking, "And why is this granted to me, that the mother of my Lord should come to me?" (2 Samuel 6:9, Luke 1:43)

- David "brought up the ark of the Lord with shouting" and leapt in front of it. John leapt in Elizabeth's womb when he heard Mary's voice, and Elizabeth "exclaimed with a loud cry, 'Blessed are you among women, and blessed is the fruit of your womb!'" (2 Samuel 6:15–16, Luke 1:41–42)

- David left the ark in the hill country, in the house of Obed-Edom, for three months; Mary stayed in the hill country, in Elizabeth's house, for three months (2 Samuel 6:11, Luke 1:56).

Quiet your heart and enjoy His presence. . . . Wait patiently for Him.

"The place [of the Ark of the Covenant] shall be unknown until God gathers his people together again and shows his mercy. And then the Lord will disclose these things, and the glory of the LORD and the cloud will appear." (2 Maccabees 2:7–8)

When Jeremiah spoke those words, the Israelite people were being deported to Babylon. The temple was destroyed. Their hope lay in shreds. But years later, God gathered His people together again and they were able to return to Israel. They were home, although still ruled and oppressed by foreign powers. They called out to God, asking Him to show His compassion, and God put skin on, becoming incarnate of the Virgin Mary. Why? In order to show His mercy. The cloud of the Holy Spirit overshadowed Mary and the glory of the Lord took up residence within her womb.

Did everyone realize the significance of what was happening? No. The wait had been long, and God's answer was so surprising, so unexpected, so unlike the way they would have planned it. God came quietly, but faithfully.

Isn't this how God so often answers our prayers? We come to Him with our petitions, and really have the best plan of action already in mind. "Please, Lord, help me with [abc] . . . and this is exactly how I'd like you to do it." But God comes quietly, meeting our unspoken need rather than the "want" that is our focus. If He is currently asking for you to wait, be patient. "They who wait for the LORD shall renew their strength, they shall mount up with wings like eagles, they shall run and not be weary, they shall walk and not faint" (Isaiah 40:31).

Day Three
MARY, THE QUEEN OF HEAVEN

The honor we give Mary as the Queen of Heaven is drawn from Scripture. We first see the significance of the role of the queen mother (mother of the king) in the Old Testament. Polygamy was accepted in the ancient Near East, and kings had many wives. This created a difficulty: Whom should the people honor as the queen? And how would the succession work? Whose son would be the next king?

Read 1 Kings 1:15–16 and 2:19–20.

1. Describe the way in which Bathsheba, King David's wife, approached him in 1 Kings 1:15–16.

2. In contrast, how did Bathsheba approach King Solomon (her son) when she became the mother of the king, or the queen mother? See 1 Kings 2:19.

The problem caused by a king having many wives was alleviated by honoring the mother of the king as queen. The Hebrew word for "queen mother," *gebirah*, means "great lady." The *gebirah* had influence with the king. This is seen through the background story that preceded Bathsheba's request of her son King Solomon in 1 Kings 2:19. Bathsheba had been approached by Adonijah, King Solomon's half brother. Adonijah was the son of King David by a woman named Haggith. Bathsheba must have raised an eyebrow at his approach, because before King David's death, Adonijah had boasted, "'I shall be king!' and he provided himself with chariots, horses, and a retinue of fifty to go before him" (1 Kings 1:5). His ambition was shut down after King David made it clear that Solomon, his son with Bathsheba, was to succeed him on the throne.

At the end of King David's life, he had been kept warm by a young woman named Abishag.[68] After his death, beautiful Abishag was available. Adonijah wanted to marry her, but he knew he needed special permission, because such a move could have been perceived as a challenge to the throne. It's very telling that Adonijah approached the queen mother, Bathsheba, to ask her to appeal to the king on his behalf.

3. What kind of honor and authority was given to the queen mother? See 1 Kings 2:20.

4. To understand the significance of the role of the queen mother as it pertains to Mary, we need to remember that King Solomon was a part of the Davidic kingdom. A very important prophecy had been given to his father, King David. Read it in 2 Samuel 7:12–14, 16. How long would King David's royal throne last?

This meant that a descendant of David was to sit on a throne that was to last throughout eternity. But the Israelites disobeyed God, and His hand of blessing was removed. The kingdom of Israel split in two, and outside nations conquered the land. It seemed that the prophecy would never be fulfilled. But God always keeps His promises. . . .

5. Skim Jesus' genealogy in Matthew 1:1–17. What is the significance of his ancestry as it pertains to the prophecy of 2 Samuel 7? And what impact does this have on Mary's role?

[68] "When King David was old and advanced in years, though they covered him with blankets he could not get warm. His servants therefore said to him, 'Let a young virgin be sought to attend my lord the king, and to nurse him. If she sleeps with you, my lord the king will be warm.' So they sought for a beautiful girl . . . and found Abishag . . . so they brought her to the king" (1 Kings 1:1–3).

Quiet your heart and enjoy His presence. . . . Approach Him with the confidence of a beloved daughter.

What a gift it is that we can approach the King of the Universe with confidence! "So let us confidently approach the throne of grace to receive mercy and to find grace for timely help" (Hebrews 4:16). We can revel in the joy of being able to approach God directly, and also ask the Queen of Heaven to intercede on our behalf. Both are available to us! God loves us lavishly. Go before His throne, in the spirit of Psalm 100:

Enter his gates with thanksgiving, his courts with praise.
Give thanks to him, bless his name;
God indeed is the LORD,
His mercy endures forever,
His faithfulness lasts through every generation.

Day Four
MARY, OUR ADVOCATE

Read John 2:1–12.

1. What similarities do you see in the interaction between Jesus and Mary at the wedding at Cana and Bathsheba and King Solomon in 1 Kings 2:19–20?

2. What insight do you gain from CCC 969 in terms of Mary's role as our advocate today?

3. Many people struggle with certain titles for Mary, one of them being "mediatrix." Why would we need her mediation? Isn't Jesus enough? They might refer to 1 Timothy 2:5, which states that Jesus is the "one mediator between God and man." How did Saint Paul reconcile this concern in 1 Corinthians 3:9 and Colossians 1:24?

The cross is the unique sacrifice of Christ, the "one mediator between God and men." But because in His incarnate divine person He has in some way united Himself to every man, "The possibility of being made partners, in a way known to God, in the paschal mystery" is offered to all men. He calls His disciples to "take up [their] cross and follow [Him]." In fact Jesus desires to associate with His redeeming sacrifice those who were to be its first beneficiaries. *This is achieved supremely in the case of His mother, who was associated more intimately than any other person in the mystery of His redemptive suffering.* "Apart from the cross, there is no other ladder by which we may get to heaven" (CCC 618).

4. Mary is an observant mother. Oftentimes, just as at the wedding at Cana, she sees needs even before we do. Have you ever asked for Mary's intercession for a special need? Or have you found it difficult to ask for it? Some find it helpful to remember that we freely ask people on earth to pray for us. We believe that saints are fully alive in heaven. When we ask them to pray for us, we are not consulting the dead. We aren't asking for secret information to be revealed (as would be the case in a séance). We are asking someone in heaven who is beholding the face of God to appeal to God on our behalf—to pray for us. What has your experience been in terms of praying to Mary and the saints?

5. What "hour" was Jesus referring to in John 2:5? Was He being rude to His mother, or was there a deeper message that He was communicating to her? See John 12:23–26.

Jesus referring to Mary as "woman" sounds a bit harsh to our ears. His choice of this word was significant, but not in a negative way. Before the fall, Eve was called "woman" (cf. Genesis 2:22–23; 3:2, 4). This was when Eve was still full of grace. The Greek word translated as *woman* also means "my lady," a respectful address.

Quiet your heart and enjoy His presence. . . . That's always where Mary will point you.

Mary will never direct us away from her son. She never takes the place of Jesus. She lives to glorify God. She lives to point us to Jesus. Her words to the servants at the wedding are her words to us: "Do whatever He tells you." Is there something in your life that Jesus is asking you to change? Is He inviting you to step out and take a risk? Get rid of a habit that's hurting you? Forgive an offense? Reach out to offer love to someone in need? Spend some time in His presence, asking Him to speak to you. Then do whatever He tells you.

Day Five
MARY, OUR MOTHER

"There is a secret in our culture, and it's not that childbirth is painful, it's that women are strong."
—Laurie Stavoe Harm

The Blessed Mother is our beautiful example of inner beauty, purity, trust, faith—and strength. And isn't this what we want in a mother? Don't we long for someone who has the strength to stand up for what is right and to fight for those who have no voice?

Read Genesis 3:14–19.

1. Our first glimpse of the Blessed Mother is in Genesis 3:14–19. In this passage, God was spelling out the consequences of Adam and Eve's sin. It was full of bad news for all involved, but tucked in the middle of His words was a glimmer of hope. What was it? Which wound is worse—a heel or a head injury? Who could the woman be in this passage? See Genesis 3:15.

Read Revelation 11:19–12:17.[69]

The book of Revelation is full of spectacular imagery, but we won't be doing a verse-by-verse analysis of this passage. We're reading it in order to draw attention to the interplay among the three key players in the drama of Revelation 12. Don't get too bogged down trying to interpret every detail.

2. Identify the three key players in this passage. Whom do they represent?

It's helpful to note that the chapter and verse markings that we find in Scripture were added later, in order to aid in the study and location of portions of the Bible. Especially after our study on Day Two, it's interesting that as Saint John took in the vision of the Ark of the Covenant in heaven (Revelation 11:19), he immediately saw the woman clothed with the sun, with the moon under her feet, and on her head a crown of twelve stars. He saw the Ark of the Covenant from the Old Testament and the new Ark of the Covenant: Mary.

3. Read Revelation 12:4 and meditate on Jesus' birth. What insight do you gain into Mary's strength?

---

[69] The book of Revelation has multiple layers and many rich meanings. For the purpose of our study, we are interpreting the woman of Revelation 12 to be a representation of Mary. This is a common interpretation, as seen by the fact that this passage is one of the readings for the Feast of the Assumption of the Blessed Virgin Mary (August 15). This interpretation of Revelation 12 is certainly not the only valid one. The woman adorned with the sun, moon, and stars can also symbolize the Church and the nation of Israel.

As Mary was giving birth, Satan watched, desiring nothing more than to devour Jesus. Mary rose as her child's protector. Nothing would get in the way of God's plan being fulfilled in her child's life. If it meant everyone whispering behind her back, she'd keep her eyes fixed on God and what *He* thought of her. Loss of reputation? A gift to her Lord. If it meant giving birth in wretched circumstances, she wouldn't flinch. If it meant fleeing in the middle of the night to Egypt, so be it. Let the dragon raise his talons. Let the serpent slither around her feet. She wouldn't back down.

4. Make no mistake about it. Satan absolutely hates Mary. There was enmity between him and Mary from the very beginning (Genesis 3:15). He stood before her as she was about to give birth, just waiting to devour her child (Revelation 12:4). His stance before Mary was one of fury. Why is this? We find the answer in Revelation 12:12: "The devil has come down to you in great fury, for he knows he has but a short time." He knows he's a defeated foe but he's hell-bent on fighting to the bitter end. He's angry with Mary, and he's angry with Mary's children. Who is considered Mary's offspring according to Revelation 12:17? Whom did the dragon go off to wage war against?

5. Picture Jesus on the cross. Then look below to those who stayed close to Him throughout His passion. Mary was there. What kind of strength did it take for her to remain at the foot of the cross as Christ suffered? Think of the movie *The Passion of the Christ*, and how difficult it is for us to watch the scenes of the flogging and the crucifixion. How much harder would it have been for Mary, watching her own child being hurt?

Mary at the foot of the cross is a picture of the strongest of mothers. There is nothing worse than watching your child suffer. The urge to turn away, to run home and sob into her pillow must have been so strong as Mary looked on in horror as the depths of human cruelty were unleashed on her son. But she stayed. Mary's steady strength served as a visual reminder to Jesus that His mission was worth the pain.

Quiet your heart and enjoy His presence. . . . All strength comes from Him.

If Mary's "spiritual motherhood extends to all men [and women] whom indeed [Jesus] came to save,"[70] then each one of us has a very strong mother just waiting to come to our aid. This is a woman with the strength and courage to face a serpent and slam her foot on its head. This is a woman who can face down a dragon bent on the destruction of her child at the same time that she is giving birth. This is a woman unafraid of evil, because she knows and keeps her eyes on the One who has triumphed over the most heinous depravity. She is a warrior. Where is Satan rearing his head in your life? Ask Mary to intercede for you, and to step on the head of anything that is taking away the peace, joy, and contentment that God wants you to experience as His beloved daughter.

Conclusion

"Why do you Catholics make such a big deal of Mary? Why do you worship her?"

This is a question posed to many Catholics, and we often don't know how to respond. The question, usually well meant, comes from a misunderstanding of the way that we relate to the Blessed Mother. *Latria* is the Latin word meaning "adoration." This form of worship is given to God alone. *Dulia* is the Latin word meaning "honor," or "devotion." We offer this to the saints. They've gone before us, and remained faithful to God. We honor that and seek to follow their example. *Hyperdulia* is the devotion we offer to Mary, recognizing that she is different from all the saints. She is special—not divine, but deserving of special honor. We offer *hyperdulia* to Mary, never *latria*.

Where does this devotion to Mary come from? Much of it flows from a deep understanding of Scripture. There is much in the Old Testament that pulls back the curtain on the New Testament. We see foreshadowing, prophecies, and typology,[71] all of which remind us that God's plan of redemption through Christ was in place from the very beginning. God's hand has been in the big picture, and in every detail that is contained within it. This is the Catholic way of reading the Scriptures, whereby we allow the Old Testament to enlighten our understanding of the New, and vice versa. As we read the Scriptures through Jewish eyes, we see countless titles, devotions, and doctrines flowing out of the Bible.

---

[70] CCC 501: "Jesus is Mary's only son, but her spiritual motherhood extends to all men whom indeed he came to save: 'The Son whom she brought forth is he whom God placed as the first-born among many brethren, that is, the faithful in whose generation and formulation she cooperates with a mother's love.'"

[71] According to *The Merriam-Webster Dictionary*, typology is "a doctrine of theological types; especially: one holding that things in Christian belief are prefigured or symbolized by things in the Old Testament."

In no way does Mary's role as our mother diminish the importance of Jesus. It actually showcases His power. Everything that Mary has done in the past and will do in the future has flowed from "the superabundance of the merits of Christ, rests on his mediation, depends entirely on it, and draws all its power from it" (CCC 970).

As we turn our attention to Jesus' Blessed Mother, we follow His example. Jesus certainly would have followed the Ten Commandments, which means that He always honored His mother (Exodus 20:12). The more we understand her, the more we can love her. The more we love her, the more we'll be drawn to her son. When we turn our eyes to Mary, we don't take our focus off of Christ. She just helps us to see Him better.

There will be days when we will feel the heat of battle. We'll get weary and discouraged. This is inevitable, because the "dragon became angry with the woman and went off to wage war against the rest of her offspring [and that's us]" (Revelation 12:17). When this happens, be assured, it makes our heavenly Mother rise up to come to our aid.

My Resolution

In what specific way will I apply what I learned in this lesson?

Examples:

1. Reflecting on Day One, I'll respond to Christ's thirst for me. He longs for my love for Him to be pure. So much in my life makes it hard for me to focus on loving Him. This week, I'll spend time in adoration, meditating on Christ on the cross. I'll remember that thirst for me kept Him there until the price for my redemption was paid.

2. I'll approach the throne of grace with confidence, knowing that my King receives me as His beloved daughter. I'll also accept the gift offered by the Queen of Heaven to intercede for me. I'll pray the Rosary, visualizing myself in the throne room of God.

3. I'll bring a special intention to Mary, asking her to step on the head of any serpent in my life that seeks to draw my focus away from Christ.

My Resolution:

Catechism Clips

CCC 501 Jesus is Mary's only son, but her spiritual motherhood extends to all men whom indeed he came to save: "The Son whom she brought forth is he whom God placed as the first-born among many brethren, that is, the faithful in whose generation and formulation she co-operates with a mother's love."

CCC 503 Mary's virginity manifests God's absolute initiative in the Incarnation. Jesus has only God as Father. "He was never estranged from the Father because of the human nature which he assumed. . . . He is naturally Son of the Father as to his divinity and naturally son of his mother as to his humanity, but properly Son of the Father in both natures."

CCC 505 By his virginal conception, Jesus, the New Adam, ushers in the new birth of children adopted in the Holy Spirit through faith. "How can this be?" Participation in the divine life arises "not of blood nor of the will of the flesh nor of the will of man, but of God." The acceptance of this life is virginal because it is entirely the Spirit's gift to man. The spousal character of the human vocation in relation to God is fulfilled perfectly in Mary's virginal motherhood.

CCC 618 The cross is the unique sacrifice of Christ, the "one mediator between God and men." But because in his incarnate divine person he has in some way united himself to every man, "The possibility of being made partners, in a way known to God, in the paschal mystery" is offered to all men. He calls his disciples to "take up [their] cross and follow [him]" . . . In fact Jesus desires to associate with his redeeming sacrifice those who were to be its first beneficiaries. This is achieved supremely in the case of his mother, who was associated more intimately than any other person in the mystery of his redemptive suffering. "Apart from the cross, there is no other ladder by which we may get to heaven."

CCC 969 "This motherhood of Mary in the order of grace continues uninterruptedly from the consent which she loyally gave at the Annunciation and which she sustained without wavering beneath the cross, until the eternal fulfillment of all the elect. Taken up to heaven she did not lay aside this saving office but by her manifold intercession continues to bring us the gifts of eternal salvation. . . . Therefore the Blessed Virgin is invoked in the Church under the titles of Advocate, Helper, Benefactress, and Mediatrix.

Verse Study

See Appendix 3 for instructions on how to complete a verse study.

Luke 1:41–42

1. Verse:

2. Paraphrase:

3. Questions:

4. Cross-references:

5. Personal Application:

Lesson 17

THE POOR WIDOW

Introduction

Excess. My life is saturated with it. I sometimes wonder how long my family could live on the food in our pantry. The supply never seems to go down. There's always a stockpile, yet we still manage to say we're hungry and can't find anything to eat. Dinner is served and too much of it ends up in the garbage. My closet is full of clothes but there are times when I can't find anything to wear—at least not the right thing to wear, and to me, the two seem the same. We can barely move around in our storage room in the basement because it's loaded with stuff that I might need at some point and had better keep, just in case.

I read Jesus' words in the Gospel telling the rich young man to go and sell everything he has and give it to the poor, and I make myself feel better by saying that He didn't say that to *everyone*, so He must not mean me. "Please," I whisper, "may that not mean me."

Why do I pad my life with excess? Why do I panic at the thought of letting it go?

Where is my security found? A convicting thought, one that has been niggling at my heart for some time.

And ladies, most of us are in this boat. Most of us are wealthy by the world's standards. Do you make $35,000 a year? Then you are in the top 4 percent of wealth in the world. Fifty thousand? Top 1 percent.

In the words of Jen Hatmaker:

> Excess has impaired perspective in America; we are the richest people on earth, praying to get richer. We're tangled in unmanageable debt while feeding the machine, because we feel entitled to more. What does it communicate when half the global population lives on less than $2 a day, and we can't manage a

fulfilling life on twenty-five thousand times that amount? Fifty thousand times that amount? It says we have too much, and it is ruining us.[72]

The poor widow of Mark 12 shines as an example of an utterly different approach to life. Holding nothing back, generous to the point of personal sacrifice, she points the way to freedom.

Day One
REMARKABLE GENEROSITY

Read Mark 12:41–44.

1. The poor widow could certainly have justified keeping her money for herself, especially after seeing rich people putting large sums of money into the treasury. What character qualities did she exemplify through her generosity?

2. How close did Jesus need to be to the treasury box in order to take notice of the wealthy people giving large amounts, and the exact amount that the poor widow gave? What might this indicate about the interest Jesus takes in the way we handle our money?

3. What are some ways we justify our decisions to keep money for ourselves that could be given away instead? Name some emotions that block our desire to be generous.

---

[72] Jen Hatmaker, *7: An Experimental Mutiny Against Excess* (Nashville, TN: B&H Publishing Group, 2012), 3.

Very often, we resist the call to give generously because we are afraid that our own needs won't be met. Fear gets in the way of generosity. Greed is another real deterrent to radical giving, as we struggle to resist the urge to continually buy more and more, confusing needs with wants. Indifference is possibly the scariest emotion blocking generosity, as we don't even notice that it's within us. We're too busy paying attention to other things. When we don't see the poor up close, it's very easy to ignore their needs.

4. Agree or disagree with the following statement: "Our generosity isn't measured by how much we give, but by how much we keep." If you agree, why? If not, how would you rephrase the statement?

When we hear of large financial donations, our first reaction is often to elevate those gifts above all others. Large dollar amounts impress us because we can see the great good these financial gifts can accomplish. But as God measures our generosity, He is well aware of what we have held back for our own comfort. True sacrificial giving comes at a cost.

5. What does it mean to live out Jesus' command in Mark 12:31 to "love your neighbor as yourself"?

Quiet your heart and enjoy His presence. . . . God will never be outdone in generosity.

Certainly poverty isn't only an issue of finances. There is the poverty of food and water, but there is also the poverty of love, as well as deep loneliness. As Christians, we are called to alleviate both types of suffering. May our hearts stay tender to all the needs around us.

God, please free us from numbness, complacency, and indifference. All we have is Yours. May we seek to honor You with all we possess. Help us to differentiate between our wants and our needs. Help us to have the strength to forgo luxuries for the sake of those who don't have their most basic needs met.

Day Two
RADICAL DEPENDENCE

Reread Mark 12:43–44, and read Matthew 6:25–33.

1. How much did the widow give?

2. When the poor widow gave all that she had, she had no choice but to depend on God to provide for her needs. Can you identify something in your life that you are clinging to for security? Is it getting in the way of your dependence on God?

3. What are the specific areas of our lives that Jesus told us not to worry about in Matthew 6:25–33? Why did He say we shouldn't worry about them? Which of those areas causes you the most concern or anxiety?

4. We are surrounded by an ethos that celebrates self-sufficiency, personal advancement, the accumulation of possessions, and a perpetual move up the social ladder. The hard work it takes us to get there encourages the belief that all we achieve is due to our own blood, sweat, and tears. Do you believe that the "American dream" can get in the way of dependence on God? See also CCC 2547.

5. In John 15:5, Jesus reminds us of the importance of our dependence on God: "I am the vine, you are the branches. Whoever remains in me and I in him will bear much fruit, because without me you can do nothing." What are ways in which we can live out true dependence on God?

Quiet your heart and enjoy His presence. . . . Do not worry about tomorrow.

There is a blessing that can come when the rug is pulled out from under us, when what we previously thought would make us secure is suddenly gone. This is because it is when we are at the end of our resources that God can show us that He is truly enough. This blessing can *come, but it isn't guaranteed to come, because it depends on how we respond. Do we become bitter? Do we give in to fear? Does worry take over and rule our hearts? Or do we "cast all [our] worries upon [Jesus] because he cares for [us]"?[73] God wants us to depend on Him for our benefit, not for the sake of His ego. He loves us, and knows that only He will truly satisfy our longing and needs.*

Day Three
REFRESHING DETACHMENT

Read Matthew 19:16–22.

1. Contrast and compare the poor widow and the rich young man.

---

[73] 1 Peter 5:7.

2. Does God require that every person renounce all of his or her possessions and riches in order to be considered His follower or disciple? See Matthew 27:57.

3. If renouncing all our possessions and wealth (voluntary poverty) is not required of everyone, what lesson *can* we all learn from the story of the rich young ruler?

4. One way to practice a healthy detachment from possessions is to resist the urge to always buy the biggest or the best. Whether the sacrifice is made in order to give the monetary difference away or simply to strengthen the will, the benefits are many. If we aren't careful, we'll be enslaved by materialism. Saint Paul reminds us, "For freedom Christ has set us free; stand firm, therefore, and do not submit again to a yoke of slavery" (Galatians 5:1). What are some practical ways you can practice a healthy detachment from possessions this week and experience freedom from the slavery of materialism?

Quiet your heart and enjoy His presence. . . . Attachment to Him will satisfy the deepest needs of your soul.

Whenever we experience growth in the spiritual life, we are tempted to respond with pride. Practicing a healthy detachment from possessions is a radical choice in our culture today, and it's easy to look down on those who are trapped in the snare of materialism. The beautiful thing about making sacrifices in order to be truly free from the allure of riches is that we can do it quietly. There's no need for us to tell anyone what we've given up. It can be just between us and God. "When you give alms, do not let your left hand know what your right is doing, so that your almsgiving may be secret. And your Father who sees in secret will repay you" (Matthew 6:3–4).

Day Four
RARE FOCUS

Read Matthew 6:19–20.

Note: Ah . . . the irony of these verses. I'm writing this section as I grieve the fact that thieves *do* break in and steal—in fact, *did* break in and steal my favorite sunglasses from my car. And as I write, I am pining for those sunglasses like nobody's business. So all of this detachment is a journey. But if we don't even try, then where will we end up?

1. The poor widow had a rare focus. Instead of investing in the here and now, she stored up treasure in heaven. Why does Jesus say we should store up treasure in heaven instead of on earth?

2. What we value most will determine how we spend our money. Which things do you value that tempt you to invest here on earth instead of in heaven?

3. It's hard to store up treasure in heaven when our focus is simply on saying no to our desires. That often just makes us want things more. When we switch our focus to people who can be helped because of our sacrifice, and when those people go from being statistics to having faces, we get a bit more motivated to give. If you could help someone, who would it be? What sacrifices (time, money, talent) could you make today in order to help this person or group of people?

4. Do you live in a "bubble world," where you rarely encounter people in poverty? Is most of your time spent with people who have a similar lifestyle to yours, or a better one? If so, what could you do to "pop the bubble" in order to get face-to-face with people outside your comfort zone—training yourself and your heart to be aware of the needs of those around you?

5. According to 1 Chronicles 29:14, where does all we have come from? How should that affect our attitude toward earthly possessions?

Quiet your heart and enjoy His presence. . . . You are the treasure of God's heart.

All the good things that God gives us here are just a taste of what He has prepared for us in heaven. "What eye has not seen, and ear has not heard, and what has not entered the human heart, what God has prepared for those who love him" (1 Corinthians 2:9). When we share what we have with others, we are giving them a taste of God's goodness. As Saint John reminds us, "This is how all will know that you are my disciples, if you have love for one another" (John 13:35). Ask God to open your eyes so you can see those around you who need to feel His love in a practical way. Ask Him where you are blind to need. Trust that He'll reveal to you the places where He wants you to be His hands and feet.

"Living Holy Week, following Jesus, means learning to come out of ourselves—as I said last Sunday—in order to go to meet others, to go towards the outskirts of existence, to be the first to take a step towards our brothers and our sisters, especially those who are the most distant, those who are forgotten, those who are most in need of understanding, comfort and help. There is such a great need to bring the living presence of Jesus, merciful and full of love!"[74] —Pope Francis

---

[74] Pope Francis, "General Audience," The Holy See, March 27, 2013, http://www.vatican.va/holy_father/francesco/audiences/2013/documents/papa-francesco_20130327_udienza-generale_en.html.

Day Five
REAL LIFE

Read 1 Timothy 6:17–19.

1. According to 1 Timothy 6:17–19, what can riches lead to if we value them more than we value God?

2. What are we robbed of when we are caught in the snare of materialism? See Ecclesiastes 5:12.

3. In 1 Timothy 6:17–19, instructions are given for how the rich are to handle their wealth. What insights do you gain from these verses? Remember that most of us are wealthier than we realize. See also CCC 2404.

4. In John 10:10, Jesus tells us, "I have come that [you] might have life and have it more abundantly." How would you describe a truly abundant life? What should we do "to win the life that is true life"?

5. Practicing generosity also causes us to feel grateful and more aware of all that we have. If tomorrow you only had the things that you gave thanks for today, what would remain?

Quiet your heart and enjoy His presence. . . . Choose real abundance.

How different our lives would be if they were characterized by generosity and gratitude! Just imagine a life in which comparison simply makes you more aware of all that you have, rather than what you lack. What if we choose to really believe Jesus when He said, "He that loses his life for my sake will find it" (Matthew 10:39)? We often complain that we are stuck in the rat race, but the truth is, we have so many choices before us each day, and it's up to us to choose well. Spend a few moments asking God to give you wisdom in this area of life. He wants nothing more than for us to experience true abundance and real life.

"If we wish to follow Christ closely we cannot choose an easy, quiet life. It will be a demanding life, but full of joy."[75] —Pope Francis

Conclusion

God got ahold of Jen Hatmaker's heart, and real living began. It led to a radical change in the way she and her family are following the command in Scripture to "love your neighbor as yourself." They decided to adopt two children from Ethiopia. As they waited for the children's arrival, Jen wrote a book called *7*, based on a seven-month experiment in which she fasted from one thing each month. During the month when she focused on food, she made a commitment to eat only seven foods and fast from the rest. One particular night, she had made dinner for herself, and then fried up some fish for her kids. These were her three biological children, because she was still waiting for the adoptions to go through; two of her children were in Ethiopia that night. She went upstairs to do laundry while the kids ate. When she came back down, they were done with dinner and watching television.

---

[75] Pope Francis, Twitter post, July 10, 2013, 2:10 a.m., https://twitter.com/pontifex/status/354890430216810497.

She asked, "Did you finish eating already?"

"Yes."

"Did you eat everything?"

Long pause. "Pretty much."

She went to the trash can and saw five of the six fish fillets uneaten, not even bitten. When the kids saw her face, they mumbled, "We didn't have any ketchup."[76]

She writes:

> And tonight, my kids here with me in the land of plenty threw away a pound of food because they didn't have ketchup. . . . I wept for all my children tonight, my Ethiopian children orphaned by disease or hunger or poverty who will go to bed with no mother tonight and my biological children who will battle American complacency and overindulgence for the rest of their lives. I don't know who I feel worse for.[77]

God has convicted my heart about this. And honestly, I don't know exactly what to do about it. I don't know what the solution is. But step one for me is calling it what it is and asking for God's forgiveness. Step two is going on right now. I'm daily praying with my husband that God will show us what needs to change so that we are seeking *His* glory with our possessions instead of our glory and security.

He hasn't yet given us the answer, but I know that He will. I also know that although letting go is hard, what God places in our hands in exchange is always better.

But even if I knew specifically what God is calling my family to, I don't know that I would share it here. Not because I don't trust you. It's more because I think we love formulas, and it would just be too tempting for everyone to assume that what God is asking of me is what He's asking of you. And that's not how it works. It isn't cookie cutter. Each one of us is unique, and God has a special plan and a purpose for each of His children.

One thing I do know: He wants every one of us to want Him more than we want anything else. Matthew 6:21 says, "For where your treasure is, there your heart will be also." And I want my heart to belong to Him.

---

[76] Hatmaker, 7, 21.
[77] Ibid., 22.

My Resolution

In what specific way will I apply what I learned in this lesson?

Examples:

1. Instead of always choosing the biggest or the best, I'll choose less, and give the money saved to someone in need.

2. I'll find a concrete way to "pop the bubble," getting out of my comfort zone and into the presence of people who (on the surface) seem different from me.

3. I'll daily ask God to connect me with the people who need what I have. I'll break the habit of hoarding and instead give something that involves personal sacrifice.

My Resolution:

Catechism Clips

CCC 2404 "In his use of things man should regard the external goods he legitimately owns not merely as exclusive to himself but common to others also, in the sense that they can benefit others as well as himself." The ownership of any property makes its holder a steward of Providence, with the task of making it fruitful and communicating its benefits to others, first of all his family.

CCC 2547 The Lord grieves over the rich, because they find their consolation in the abundance of goods. "Let the proud seek and love earthly kingdoms, but blessed are the poor in spirit for theirs is the Kingdom of heaven." Abandonment to the providence of the Father in heaven frees us from anxiety about tomorrow. Trust in God is a preparation for the blessedness of the poor. They shall see God.

Verse Study

See Appendix 3 for instructions on how to complete a verse study.

Deuteronomy 6:38

1. Verse:

2. Paraphrase:

3. Questions:

4. Cross-references:

5. Personal Application:

Lesson 18: Connect Coffee Talk
MARTHA – DOES WHAT I DO MATTER?

Accompanying DVD can be viewed at:
www.walkingwithpurpose.com/courses/videos
Select: *Discovering Our Dignity* – Talk 05 – Martha – Does What I Do Matter?

Please read Luke 10:38–42 before watching the video. Lesson 19 will allow you to follow up with a deeper dive into Martha's story.

1. The Struggle

A. It's hard to serve with no recognition.

_____ we serve is as important as _____ we serve.

Jan Johnson, author of *Living a Purpose-Full Life*, suggests asking the following questions to help us check our motives in service:

Am I serving to impress anyone?
Am I serving to receive external rewards?
Is my service affected by my moods and whims?
Am I using my service to feel good about myself?
Am I using my service to muffle God's voice demanding I change?[78]

Matthew 20:26

---

[78] Jan Johnson, *Living a Purpose-Full Life* (Colorado Springs: Waterbrook Press, 1999), 151–2.

B. It's hard to serve when the needs are never ending.

Margin is the opposite of _____.

It means that we have a buffer of _____, _____, and
_____.

To experience margin, we need to develop the virtues of _____
and _____.

"To Americans usually tragedy is wanting something very badly and not getting it. Many people have had to learn in their private lives, and nations have had to learn in their historical experience, that perhaps the worst form of tragedy is wanting something badly, getting it, and finding it empty."[79] —Henry Kissinger

Matthew 6:19–21

2. The Turning

A. It's hard to serve with no recognition.

Psalm 17:4

Matthew 6:3

Ephesians 6:7

---

[79] L. S. Stavrianos, *The Promise of the Coming Dark Age* (San Francisco: W. H. Freeman and Company, 1976), 165.

B. It's hard to serve when the needs are never ending.

Isaiah 58:11

2 Corinthians 9:8

"Give yourself fully to God. He will use you to accomplish great things on the condition that you believe much more in his love than in your own weakness." — Blessed Mother Teresa

Questions for Discussion

1. Do you relate to Martha? Do you find it hard to say no to requests for help? Do you find yourself committed to many areas of serving and then skate close to burnout as a result?

2. Being surrounded by genuine needs makes it hard not to get stretched too thin. But we need to pay attention to the balance in our lives, or those closest to us will suffer. Dr. Richard Swenson encourages us to create margin in our lives. If we want to live in this way, it's essential that we grow in contentment and simplicity. What are concrete ways you can grow in the areas of contentment and simplicity?

3. In the excerpt read from the book *The Invisible Woman*, by Nicole Johnson, mothers are compared to cathedral builders. How are they alike, and how is the end result of their hard work similar?

Lesson 19

MARTHA OF BETHANY

Introduction

Does the thought of growing in intimacy with Christ ever feel like adding one more thing to an already overwhelmed schedule?

How many of us rush around with a constant inner dialogue of thoughts like these:

I'm never going to pull this off.
I'm the only one who can do this.
This isn't fair. I think I'm the only person working this hard.
Lord, don't you care?
I'm so tired.
I'm sick of living like this.

We get glimpses of other people's wholehearted living, and we recognize that there is something missing in our own lives. We wonder if we just need a vacation. Or less on our plate. Or a different job. Or more money.

I think Martha maybe felt a little bit that way when she peeked into the living room at Mary settled in at Jesus' feet. But that longing in her heart quickly turned to irritation. "What is wrong with her?" she must have thought. Everyone knew that a woman's place was not in the middle of a religious gathering of men. Her next thought might have been, "Who does she thinks she is?"

Make no mistake—anytime a person ventures out of safety and decides to live life with exuberance and joy, there will be someone who says, "Who does she think she is?" If it isn't a voice from outside, our own thoughts chime in. "Who do you think you are? Temper your expectations. This is just life. Stop expecting it to feel great. Just keep trucking. Just do the next thing on the list." The next thing on the list. And the next. And the next. And we trudge through life, halfheartedly and a little bit resentfully.

What if choosing the better part wasn't about something *more* being required of us? What if the key to wholehearted living was a trading of our current lists for the one Jesus offers us?

Here's an alternative to-do list for this week:

1. Explore who I am in Christ.
2. Worry less.
3. Be teachable.
4. Taste freedom.
5. Work with joy.

Let's see what Martha has to teach us.

Day One
IDENTITY

Read Luke 10:38–42.

1. What was Martha doing right?

2. What question did Martha ask Jesus in verse 40? How did He respond?

Martha asked, "Lord, do you not care?" Mary's unwillingness to help seemed like such a selfish choice. The injustice appeared obvious. When Jesus responded by *defending* Mary's choice, Martha must have been taken aback. No matter how gently He said it, exhausted Martha must have been incredulous that somehow she was the one being criticized. Well, at least that's the way I think I would have felt. "You mean there's something *more* I'm supposed to be doing?"

How easy it is to misunderstand the Lord when He gently corrects us.

Jesus didn't side with Mary because He didn't care about Martha; He pointed to a different choice precisely because He cared about Martha *so much*. It was clear to Jesus that Martha defined her worth by her productivity. Every time her burst of energy and hard work resulted in a successful event or a sense of accomplishment, she felt like she mattered. She measured her worth by her performance.

Jesus was inviting Martha to sit at His feet, because that is the best place to learn *who we really are*. When we are in productivity mode, we remember *what we can do*. Those are two very different things.

We produce a lot and then we're likely to fall into the traps of self-sufficiency and pride. Or we don't produce enough and we feel like failures. Both responses leave us vulnerable to believing the wrong messages about who we are and what we're worth.

3. The world is constantly sending us messages about who we are. "You are what you produce." "You are what you eat." "You are what you wear." "You are what you make of yourself." Jesus invites us to sit at His feet and fill up our minds with His perspective. Read the following messages that we hear day in and day out. Then look up the corresponding verse and write down what God's voice says.

    The world's message: Do more! Be more!
    God's message: Psalm 46:11, NAB.

    The world's message: Get your pre-baby body back and you'll be you again!
    God's message: 1 Samuel 16:7.

    The world's message: Your worth is tied to your bank balance.
    God's message: Luke 12:33–34.

4. Sometimes all our best efforts still don't seem to be enough. **Read Appendix 4, "Who I Am in Christ,"** and write down the verses that resonate most with you. May they remind you that because of Jesus dwelling within you, you are enough. Let the truth crowd out the lies.

Quiet your heart and enjoy His presence. . . . Sit at His feet and remember who you are.

Dear Lord,

I'm slowing down, taking some deep breaths, and sitting at Your feet. This isn't an easy place for me to be. I'm used to hopping up and getting something done. Sometimes it feels a little selfish to just stop and soak up Your love for me. I struggle to feel worthy of that love. Help me to remember that You love me because I belong to You, not because I'm perfect or because of the things I do. Give me the mind of Christ so that I will live out the truth that I cannot earn Your love; it is unconditional. Help me to lift my eyes to Your face and see reflected back all the warmth, compassion, mercy, and grace that radiates from Your heart. Who am I? I am Your beloved daughter. When I fail, You fill in the gaps. When I see all I lack, You remind me that You, within me, are enough. When I'm tempted to beat myself up, You remind me that You took the beating so that I could rest in grace. Help me to do that. May I cease my striving, because my worth was defined and settled when You died for me on the cross.

Day Two
WORRY

"Martha, Martha, you are anxious and worried about many things" (Luke 10:41).

"Wait a minute, Lord," Martha must have wanted to say. "You think that the problem is my worrying? Well, thank heavens I do worry about things. If I didn't, then what would everyone be eating for supper? If I don't stay ahead of the game, figuring out what the people around me need and then making sure those needs are met, none of it will get done. It's practically my job to worry. What's on my to-do list today? Oh, right—*everything*."

Of course, that's not what she said, because, after all, it was Jesus who was making the point. But just because she didn't *say* it doesn't mean she wasn't *thinking* it and justifying her actions. Because isn't that what we so often do? When someone tells us not to worry, it can almost make us more anxious, because we think we're the only people paying enough attention to realize what is at stake. When we feel that level of responsibility, the weight of it all can be paralyzing.

Do we need to wait until there's nothing left to worry about in order to experience inner calm? Or is it possible to lay down our worries and pick up trust, right in the midst of it all?

1. A. Would you describe yourself as a worrier? If so, what do you worry about most, and why?

    B. Have you ever seen evidence of worry taking a toll on your health, your relationships, or what you're able to get done in a day?

2. A soul at rest is a soul free from worry. According to Psalm 62:6–9, NAB, our souls should rest in God alone. Write down descriptions of God from this passage, circling the one that means the most to you. Do any of these aspects of His character help free you from worry? If so, why?

3. According to 2 Thessalonians 3:16 and 1 Peter 5:6–7, how do we get peace?

We receive peace when the Lord of peace gives it to us. We can't conjure it up, or just determine to be peaceful. It's a gift that comes when we humble ourselves and ask for it. The problem is that all too often we are unwilling to admit that we can't do it ourselves. We might throw out a prayer, asking for help, but then every other ounce of our energy is spent trying to gain control of the situation. A part of humbling ourselves is taking a step back and asking for God's perspective on the situation.

Are things not going according to your plan? Could it be that they are going *exactly* according to His, and He knows something that you do not? Could it be that He even desires that you fail at something so that a significant lesson is learned? Might He be saying no to one prayer in order to say yes to a far more important one?

As Pastor Todd Wagner says, "Worry is believing God won't get it right." Peace comes when we trust God and say, "I don't have a clue what to do about this, but I am going to live free and light because God is in control, and He knows what He's doing."

4. What does Jesus tell us to do when we feel burdened? See Matthew 11:28–30.

When we put on Jesus' yoke, it doesn't mean that we sit down and abdicate all responsibility. We still need to move forward and do our part. The critical thing is to determine what we are responsible for and what part is out of our hands. We must trust God with what we cannot control.

5. Sometimes the things we are worried about concern people we love. It's hard to know how involved we should become in others' problems. We're called to be compassionate and to help. But can there come a point when we are worried and burdened about something that God wants us to release? Let's look at Galatians 6:2–5 to gain insight into this:

> **Carry each other's burdens**, and in this way you will fulfill the law of Christ. If anyone thinks he is something when he is nothing, he deceives himself. Each one should test his own actions. Then he can take pride in himself, without comparing himself to somebody else, **for each one should carry his own load**.

At first glance, these verses seem to contradict each other. We're to carry each other's burdens, but each one should carry his own load? They key to understanding this passage is to recognize the difference between a burden and a load. A burden is something so heavy, it's impossible for someone to carry it without assistance. A load is something that can be handled without assistance. The problem comes when people we love don't want to carry their own load, or we don't want to see them carrying it. Often we step in, taking on responsibility that God never intended for us to. This leads to overload, worry, and anxiety.

Is there a load you are carrying for a loved one that you need to lay down? If so, list it here.

Quiet your heart and enjoy His presence. . . . Lay the worries down.

Jesus never said that the things Martha was worrying about didn't matter. But His comment suggests that He didn't think the best response to them was anxiety. He spoke of this in Luke 12:25: "Can any of you by worrying add one moment to your life-span?" As the saying goes, worry is like a rocking chair: It gives you something to do but gets you nowhere.

"Worry is carrying tomorrow's load with today's strength—carrying two days at once. It is moving into tomorrow ahead of time. Worry does not empty tomorrow of its sorrow. It empties today of its strength."[80] —Corrie ten Boom

Instead of emptying today of its strength by worrying, write out your main concerns in the space that follows. Ask the Lord to help you to see what He is asking you to do, and then take responsibility for that part. Everything that's left, all the aspects of the situation that fall outside your control, cast those worries on the Lord. I promise you, He can handle it, and He will handle it. His ways are better than ours. "And let the peace of Christ control your hearts" (Colossians 3:15).

---

[80] Corrie ten Boom, *Clippings from My Notebook* (Nashville, TN: Thomas Nelson, 1982).

Day Three
TEACHABILITY

Martha was at a crossroads. Jesus had spoken truth into her life that was hard to hear. How would she respond? Would she conclude that He clearly didn't understand her unique situation and feel resentful, or would she change? Would she choose to root her identity not in her productivity, but in God's love for her? Would she let go of worry and trust that God is always in control?

The next time we see Martha is in John 11:1–44. Martha and Mary's beloved brother, Lazarus, was terribly sick. The sisters sent word to Jesus saying, "Master, the one you love is ill" (John 11:3). They knew that Jesus could heal Lazarus, and they knew He loved Lazarus. So they waited expectantly. And waited a little longer. They did the calculations. He should have been there by now. Doubt crept in. Many days later than they'd expected, Jesus arrived. But by then, Lazarus had died. Grief washed over the sisters like a tidal wave. Mary couldn't even come out and see Jesus when He arrived.

And what about Martha? This would be a defining moment for her. Would she crumple under the weight of doubt, questioning Jesus' love for her because He hadn't answered her request as she'd expected? Or would she remain rooted in the truth that Jesus loved her more than she could ever imagine, and that He was in control even if all circumstances suggested otherwise?

1. Read John 11:20–27. What did Martha say that revealed her faith in Jesus?

In Luke 10, Jesus had seen that Martha's identity was wrapped up in what she produced. Her worth was determined by her productivity. How did Martha respond to Jesus' correction? She *learned*. She *changed*. It's one thing to be humble in a general sense ("I'm such a hot mess"; "I'm flawed and broken"), but when something specific is pointed out in our lives, that's when we reveal whether or not we are truly teachable. Martha proved that she was.

In the midst of heartrending grief, Martha was able to say: "Yes, Lord. I have come to believe that you are the Messiah, the Son of God, the one who is coming into the world." It's interesting that this powerhouse statement of faith came not from contemplative Mary, but from recovering workaholic Martha. Because that's what an encounter with Jesus can do—*if* we are teachable.

2. One of the first steps toward teachability is described in Proverbs 2:1–5. What is it?

3. Another critical step in becoming teachable is described in James 1:22. Summarize the key takeaway from that passage.

In 2 Timothy 3:7 we read about people who are "always trying to learn but never able to reach a knowledge of the truth." This isn't intended to discourage us from learning. It's actually warning us about ineffective or pointless learning. There's nothing admirable about being a perpetual student who never takes the step of putting what she's learned into practice.

4. In Proverbs 1:23, NAB, God asks, "How long will you turn away at my reproof?" This reveals another critical component of being teachable: the ability to respond to correction. Are you teachable? Read the following questions and reflect on your level of teachability.

    Am I defensive when corrected?

    Do I invite feedback? Do people feel free to give me input?

    When I think of character traits that I've known for some time that I need to work on, can I see myself making progress?

To be teachable, we need to *listen*, *act on what we hear*, and *respond to correction*. "A single reprimand does more for a discerning person than a hundred lashes for a fool" (Proverbs 17:10).

Quiet your heart and enjoy His presence. . . . Responding to the truth will set you free.

"If you hold to my teaching, you are really my disciples. Then you will know the truth, and the truth will set you free" (John 8:31–32).

There is no greater key to freedom than being teachable. It will allow you to progress in the spiritual life by leaps and bounds. While others will be learning the same lesson over and over, you will be scaling new heights of holiness.

The alternative to being teachable is spiritual stagnation. When we don't respond to the correction God has given us, we don't progress. We remain stuck, sluggish, stale.

Spend some time in prayer talking to God about how teachable you are. Ask Him to reveal to you any area where He has been trying to teach you something but you have either not listened or not acted on what you have heard. Quiet your heart. Try not to rush through this. Taking time to do this today could be life changing for you. It could be that what God is going to reveal to you will unlock something that has left you feeling at a spiritual impasse for some time.

Day Four
FREEDOM

After declaring her faith in Jesus as the Messiah, Martha went back to the house and got her sister, Mary. The two (and all their fellow mourners) joined Jesus at Lazarus' tomb.

Read John 11:38–44.

1. What was Martha's concern in John 11:39? What did Jesus promise her in John 11:40 if she would believe?

2. What did it take for Jesus to raise Lazarus from the dead? See John 11:43.

3. Describe what Lazarus looked like when he emerged from the tomb. What were Jesus' instructions to the people watching? See John 11:44.

4. When Lazarus came out of the tomb, he was alive, but he wasn't free. He could move forward in a halting way, but he couldn't see, run, or dance. His grave clothes had to be removed in order for him to really live. In the same way, we can be given new life in Christ but still live in bondage.

One of the things that can keep us in bondage is a poor understanding of the magnitude of what happened in John 11:43–44 and when Jesus Himself rose from the dead. In both cases, we see that Jesus has power over death. Critical observation: In neither the raising of Lazarus nor His own resurrection did Jesus need the assistance of a few good men (or women). Our sins were placed on Jesus, and He received the punishment due us. When He died on the cross, it meant that the debt we owed was *paid in full.*

We remain in bondage when we have a faulty understanding of what purchased that freedom. It wasn't Christ *plus* our efforts. It was Christ, and Christ alone.

We must learn the same lesson Martha learned in Luke 10: Our identity isn't found in our productivity. But we must take it one step further and recognize that our salvation—our freedom—isn't found in our productivity either. Our salvation isn't something we *earn.* It has everything to do with what Christ already accomplished on the cross.

When we recognize this, we can follow Mary's example and rest at the feet of Jesus. We can ask Him to strip us of our burial clothes and to help us run in freedom.

Do you ever feel bound up by expectations that seem unattainable? What burial clothes need to be removed in your life so that you can experience the freedom Christ purchased for you?

For additional explanation of the freedom Christ offers each of us, **read Appendix 5, "Conversion of Heart."**

Quiet your heart and enjoy His presence. . . . Clothe yourself with Christ.

"For all of you who were baptized into Christ have clothed yourselves with Christ" (Galatians 3:27).

Once those burial clothes come off, we need to replace them with something less constricting. Being clothed with Christ is so much better than moving through life bound up. Ephesians 4:22 tells us to "put away the old self" and "put on the new self, created to be like God in true righteousness and holiness." That's the right response to our freedom. We don't want to wear those old clothes that represent all the things that keep us tied to our old ways of doing things. We want to put on Christ's righteousness instead.

Spend some time asking God to untie your burial clothes. Ask Him to help you to discern which thoughts are keeping you from resting in His grace and then running in freedom.

Day Five
WORK

Read John 12:1–2.

1. What was Martha doing in verse 2?

Martha was back to serving dinner. She had learned a life-changing lesson from Jesus, she had been transformed, and she had seen God's glory show up and exceed her wildest expectations when her brother was raised from the dead. And then she went back to her normal tasks, serving others.

Although Martha needed to avoid falling into the pit of rooting her identity in her productivity, that didn't mean she'd spend the rest of her life in contemplative prayer. Work was still required.

The same is true for us. We can experience spiritual awakening that makes us long to just stay in that place of worship and joy. But at some point, we need to go back to everyday life and do what is required. So how do we work in a way that pleases God?

2. What should our motive be when we are working? See 1 Corinthians 10:31.

3. According to Brother Lawrence, being made holy "does not depend upon changing our works, but in doing that for God's sake which we commonly do for our own."[81] Does your daily work look different when seen from that perspective?

4. Read the description of human work found in CCC 2427. Then read the following excerpts from that Catechism clip and give an example of how that teaching can be lived out in the day-to-day.

   "Work honors the Creator's gifts and the talents received from him."

---

[81]Brother Lawrence, *The Practice of the Presence of God* (Virginia Beach, VA: Whitaker Distribution, 1982).

"[Work] can also be redemptive. By enduring the hardship of work in union with Jesus . . . man collaborates in a certain fashion with the Son of God in his redemptive work."

"Work can be a means of sanctification and a way of animating earthly realities with the Spirit of Christ."

5. Work is a critical component of our growth in holiness. Without work, we would lack self-discipline and become lazy. But our work must be balanced with worship. *Both* are needed. Which comes first? Read the following quote by Christian author Joanna Weaver, and comment on how you have seen this play out in your own life:

> When we put work before worship, we put the cart before the horse. The cart is important; and so is the horse. But the horse must come first, or we end up pulling the cart ourselves. Frustrated and weary, we can nearly break under the pressure of service, for there is always something that needs to be done.[82]

---

[82] Joanna Weaver, *Having a Mary Heart in a Martha World* (Colorado Springs: Waterbrook Press, 2002), 10.

Quiet your heart and enjoy His presence. . . . Come to Him when the work piles up.

Even with all the best attempts to lead balanced lives, there are times when our work gets overwhelming. When days like that start to get the best of us, it's helpful to stop and ask a very important question:

What does God want?

God, more than anything, wants our hearts.

When we do nothing but work, we become production machines. When this happens, without intending to, we live detached from our hearts. We become robotic, simply going through the motions. We're on the treadmill of productivity, and there's no time to step off and rest or worship or play. All the while, we know God wants something from us, so we offer Him our good deeds—all the results of our productivity—instead of our hearts. But that's not what He's after.

Our work most glorifies God when our heart is in it, not detached from it. Our heart is where our joy lives. It's where our motives come from. God wants your work to be infused with joy. That doesn't mean that every single second of it is exciting and fun. Redemptive work is one way we carry the cross and follow Jesus, and that is difficult. But all of our work should not feel that way. Life should not feel that way. Take some time to meditate on what brings you joy. When was the last time you felt pure joy? Make sure your work is balanced with those times. Build them into your schedule. Put them on your calendar. Offer it all to the Lord as your worship. It's an offering of a full life well lived and saturated with gratitude.

Conclusion

The story is told of a young man in China who asked an older teacher if he would teach him. The older man invited the younger one to sit down and have tea. As the teacher spoke, he was continually interrupted by the student. "Oh, I already know that." "Oh, yes—that happened to me before and this is what I did." "Oh, I don't have that problem."

The teacher stopped talking, and began to pour tea into the teacup. He poured and poured until the liquid began to run over the sides of the cup. "Stop! It's enough! My cup is full!" said the student.

"I see that," said the teacher. "Your cup is very full. And I cannot teach you anything until you empty your cup."

If we were to apply only one part of this lesson, I pray that it would be in the area that we studied on Day Three: teachability. Without teachability, truth and wisdom become like the tea being poured into the already full cup. They run all over, without actually doing any good.

If we are to become more than workhorses—if we are going to take hold of our lives and live with joy and exuberance—we must be open to change. We must open our hearts wide and embrace new thoughts and new ways of doing things. We must empty our cups of old habits that aren't serving us well anymore. Old habits die hard, but they can die. And on the other side of that death is freedom and joy. It is possible to change and to experience the wholehearted living that has been elusive. In nineteenth-century author George Eliot's words, "It's never too late to be what you might have been."

But this change doesn't come from gritting our teeth, tensing our shoulders, and charging forward. It comes when we invite the Holy Spirit into the process. He is the One who whispers in our hearts who we are in Christ. He is the One who softens our hearts and makes us receptive to teaching. He is the One who redeems our work. C. S. Lewis says it well: "It is not trying that is ever going to bring us home. All this trying leads up to the vital moment at which you turn to God and say, 'You must do this. I can't.'"

We can't do it alone, but thank God, we are never alone. He is with us—behind us, before us, beneath us, ahead of us. And He beckons us forward, toward a life of freedom and joy.

My Resolution

In what specific way will I apply what I learned in this lesson?

Examples:

1. I will put it on my calendar to sit at Jesus' feet this week. If sitting there makes me feel like something isn't going to get done and as a result I might fail, I will accept the truth that failure might be God's plan for me in that particular area. Could it be that what I deem the worst-case scenario is something God is going to allow in order to teach me a critical lesson? I will meditate on these things, and ask God to help me let go of worry and instead trust that He is in control.

2. I will ask someone close to me if there is an area of my life where I am not teachable. I will invite that trusted person to speak truth into my heart. I will listen without being defensive, and then I will resolve to act on what I hear.

3. I will make a list of times that I have experienced pure joy. That list will serve as a springboard for me as I come up with something to put on my calendar *every day* this week that brings me delight. I won't consider this a waste of time, but instead will think of it as a way in which I can connect with my heart and offer it all to God in gratitude.

My Resolution:

Catechism Clip

CCC 2427 Human work proceeds directly from persons created in the image of God and called to prolong the work of creation by subduing the earth, both with and for one another. Hence work is a duty: "If any one will not work, let him not eat." Work honors the Creator's gifts and the talents received from him. It can also be redemptive. By enduring the hardship of work in union with Jesus, the carpenter of Nazareth and the one crucified on Calvary, man collaborates in a certain fashion with the Son of God in his redemptive work. He shows himself to be a disciple of Christ by carrying the cross, daily, in the work he is called to accomplish. Work can be a means of sanctification and a way of animating earthly realities with the Spirit of Christ.

Verse Study

See Appendix 3 for instructions on how to complete a verse study.

Colossians 3:23

1. Verse:

2. Paraphrase:

3. Questions:

4. Cross-references:

5. Personal Application:

Lesson 20

MARY OF BETHANY

Introduction

Are you feeling unsettled, wishing that you were farther down the path of spiritual maturity than you are today? Do you wish you could just hit a button and be finished with the hard work of becoming more like Jesus?

There are times when loving Jesus with your whole heart comes easily. The music around you is beautiful, the people near you aren't irritating, the teachings you are receiving are right on the mark, and you feel your spirit soar a little. Then there are the times when it all just seems like so much work. Giving up and eating a bag of Twizzlers while watching some Netflix seems like the preferable course of action.

We're going to take a closer look this week at Mary of Bethany. Certain things appear to have come easily to her. She sat at Jesus' feet and chose the better part when He taught. But there were also times in her life when faith didn't come so easily. She knew what it felt like to be unsettled, to be undone, and to wish that hitting a button would make all the hard stuff just go away.

It's a strange way to look at things, but when our hearts are unsettled, it's actually a gift from God. It's a little reminder from Him that there is greater freedom ahead. There is something we are missing—something that isn't right—and He is inviting us onto the road to find it. In the words of Joanna Weaver, "He only stirs us when He wants to change us. He only makes us feel uneasy with where we are so we're willing to do whatever it takes to get where He is."[83]

Are you willing to do whatever it takes to get to where He wants you to be? Make no mistake, that's the place of freedom and joy that you are longing for. And you are never on that journey alone. He is right there by your side.

---

[83] Joanna Weaver, *Having a Mary Spirit* (Colorado Springs: Waterbrook Press 2006), 9.

Day One
HE INVITES US TO SIT DOWN

Read Luke 10:38–42.

1. What was Mary doing in Luke 10:39? How did Jesus describe her choice?

2. Jesus commended Mary for her two actions: sitting and listening. This is a hard truth for me to swallow when my favorite activities are crossing things off my to-do list and talking. In the very moment when Jesus is inviting me to "come away to a deserted place and rest awhile" (Mark 6:31), I'm telling Him all the reasons why I just can't slow down. While it helps me to remember that my worth is not defined by my accomplishments, it also motivates me to sit at His feet when I recognize *all that is being accomplished* when I do. It's counterintuitive, but we actually become most productive when we just sit in His presence.

   Read the following verses, and list what God is accomplishing when we rest at His feet.

   Exodus 14:14

   Isaiah 30:15

   2 Corinthians 3:18

   So which item on our to-do lists is more important than:

   God fighting on our behalf,
   our hearts being infused with His strength so we can serve Him better,
   our hearts becoming more like His?

   Aren't these the things that we want *most?*

3. Maybe our busyness and unwillingness to sit down are a part of a bigger issue, one we're very anxious to ignore. In the words of cartoonist and essayist Tim Kreider, "Busyness serves as a kind of existential reassurance, a hedge against emptiness. Obviously your life cannot possibly be silly or trivial or meaningless if you are so busy, completely booked, or in demand every hour of the day."[84]

We avoid slowing down and sitting at the Lord's feet because we're afraid of what we'll hear when it all gets quiet. There's nothing like people and tasks to distract us from acknowledging inner emptiness and pain.

And here I have to pause. Because this is so my deal. The minute I start to feel pain, I begin to brainstorm how to fix what's hurting me. If I can't come up with a solution, then all too often, I determine to distract myself and stop thinking about what's wrong. But when I do this, when I kick my emotions and pain away from me and just get busy keeping the balls up in the air, I am leaving the One with the solutions out of the picture. I don't have the solution, but God does. Slowing down and acknowledging that there is something wrong inside me doesn't mean I am a failure. It means I'm human, I'm real, and that sometimes life really, really hurts.

Do you ever use busyness as a way of distracting yourself from what is going on inside? When you think about slowing down, what are you most afraid of?

4. We don't have all the solutions. Instead of distracting ourselves and ignoring this reality, we can chose to follow Mary of Bethany's example. Not only did she sit down at Jesus' feet, she *listened* to Him. Listening to Jesus is an essential part of our spiritual lives. As Blessed Teresa of Calcutta said, "God speaks in the silence of the heart. Listening is the beginning of prayer."

Listening to Jesus isn't something that necessarily comes naturally to us. It is something we learn to do by doing it, not by reading about it. That being said, perhaps these two steps will help:

---

[84] Tim Kreider, "The 'Busy' Trap," *New York Times*, June 30, 2012.

Step 1: What to say (see 1 Samuel 3:10):

Step 2: What to do (see Job 33:31–33):

The story is told of a man who was known as a prayer warrior. His name was John Nelson Hyde, and people referred to him as Praying Hyde. Dr. J. Wilbur Chapman shared an experience of prayer with Praying Hyde that gives us a glimpse of what it looks like when someone listens to God:

> Dr. Wilbur Chapman . . . asked, "Mr. Hyde, I want you to pray for me." Then he continued: "He came to my room, turned the key in the door, and dropped on his knees, and waited five minutes without a single syllable coming from his lips. I could hear my own heart thumping and beating. I felt hot tears running down my face. I knew I was with God. Then, with upturned face, down which tears were streaming, he said, 'O God.' Then for five minutes at least, he was still again; and then, when he knew that he was talking with God, there came from the depths of his heart such petitions for me as I had never heard before. I rose from my knees to know what real prayer is."[85]

Most of us will read this and think, "That sure doesn't describe me. I'll never pray that powerfully." Instead of measuring ourselves against this man, let's just be inspired for a moment. Let's picture going into a room, locking the door, and kneeling in silence for five minutes. This may be out of our comfort zones, but surely it isn't beyond our *abilities*. What might happen if we committed just to trying this for five minutes a day for two weeks?

---

[85] Dorothy C. Haskin, *A Practical Guide to Prayer* (Chicago: Moody Bible Institute, 1951), 73.

5. Sitting at the feet of Jesus means we are in a posture of humility and openness before Him. We open our hearts and offer Him access to the deep, hidden corners. These are the parts of us that are aching, rebelling, justifying, and desperately needing His healing. These are the places that we know are holding us back, but we don't know what we're supposed to do about it. These are the things we are stumbling over when we so desperately want to run with abandon. Take some time to sit at Jesus' feet and look with Him at your heart as you answer the questions in the following section. And it'll take some time. This question is for you, not for group discussion. This may be the greatest gift you can give yourself—taking the time to get real in God's presence. We can't experience freedom until we identify the things that are keeping us tethered to the ground.

Prayerfully identify:

The part of your heart that is aching:

The part of your heart that is rebelling:

The part of your heart that is justifying:

The part of your heart that desperately needs His healing:

Quiet your heart and enjoy His presence. . . . Come and rest at His feet.

"'Come,' says my heart, 'seek His face'" (Psalm 27:8).

When you sit at the feet of Jesus and gaze up at His face, you are reflected in His eyes. Make no mistake, He is not looking at you with disappointment. Lean in and look a little closer. What is reflected in His eyes is the you He had in mind when He created you. He not only sees you—the wrinkles, the wounds, the scars—He sees your potential. He sees who you can become.

It's hard to see ourselves through Jesus' eyes, so let's echo author Charlie Shedd's prayer: "Lord, help me understand what you had in mind when you made the original me."[86]

Day Two
HE DOESN'T ALWAYS SHOW UP THE WAY WE THINK HE SHOULD

Read John 11:17–37.

1. How do you think Mary felt when Jesus didn't come in time? Note John 11:20. Although Mary was at the feet of Jesus in John 11:32, how was this time different from the one in Luke 10:39?

2. Mary's heart—her raw grief—spilled out at Jesus' feet. What was His reaction to her pain? See John 11:33–35.

---

[86] Tim Hansel, *Holy Sweat* (Waco, TX: Word, 1987), 79.

3. How did the other mourners react to Jesus' tears? See John 11:36–37.

4. We've all experienced a time when Jesus hasn't shown up in the way that we felt He should. Perhaps something happened in your past that you feel He should have prevented. Maybe you are in the midst of a crisis right now, and you can't figure out why Jesus isn't stepping in and stopping the madness. It could be that you have an area of sin in your life that you have begged God to free you from, and yet you fall, time and time again. Take a look back at your answer to Day One, question 5, and you'll see parts of your heart where you desperately want to see a miracle. If the wait feels too long, perhaps you've asked, *Where are you, God?*

It's *there*, right there in that place, that He is meeting you. He may not have shown up in the way that you think He should, but I promise you, He is there. Just as He met Mary in her place of grief, He meets you, and weeps over what has hurt you. He grieves over all that sin has robbed from you.

He never encounters you with indifference. Never. He comes with tenderness. He looks into your heart and recognizes that you have blocked some corners of it because you are desperately afraid of being hurt or out of control again. He understands, but He doesn't want you to stay in that place.

He knows why you have rolled a big stone in front of that part of your heart. When you, like Martha, say, "That stone cannot be removed! There'll be a stench," He understands why you are self-protecting. But He also knows that you can't self-protect and love at the same time. And when you can't love, you are held back from experiencing the full life He created you for.

So here is what He's asking. He's asking if you will let Him roll back that stone and place His healing hands over each area that is causing you pain. He's asking you to surrender those areas to Him, one at a time, step by step. This is the path to freedom.

Write an honest prayer below, talking to the Lord as you process what you've just read.

Dear Lord,

5. When you were baptized, the Holy Spirit penetrated your soul and took up residence. And this makes all the difference in the world. It's because of the indwelling Holy Spirit that you can "have life and have it more abundantly" (John 10:10).

We are promised that "where the Spirit of the Lord is, there is freedom" (2 Corinthians 3:17). But the abundant life—the life of true freedom—only comes as we surrender each area of our hearts to the Lord. This is because although the Holy Spirit lives in our souls, *we need to invite Him to invade each area or relationship in our lives and become Lord over it.* This is the journey of spiritual maturity. Sometimes we hand over control entirely, but often this is something that happens step by step. For example, we can trust God and give Him control over one area of our lives, such as relinquishing control over our children's future, and still hold on to control in another area (like what we eat or what we watch on TV). The beautiful thing about God is He knows our limitations. He knows what we can handle. So this process of giving each area over to God is a lifelong journey. He is patient with us, but will always challenge us to move forward in trust, holding nothing back from Him. Every area we continue to control ourselves is an area where we aren't experiencing the freedom He wants us to have.

In which area of your life would you like to invite God to come in and take control?

Quiet your heart and enjoy His presence. . . . He shows up with victory in His wake.

Just as Mary wanted Jesus to come in time to prevent Lazarus from dying, we want Jesus to show up in the way that we expect. When we are struggling with sin, we want Him to wave a magic wand and release us from its temptation. We want the pain to stop. We want the crisis to end. When we've been praying for something for ages, we want the answer to come—now.

Never doubt it—Jesus always comes. And He always has the ability to fix things. But His timing is rarely the same as ours. While we wait, we must never forget that He weeps with us. He never intended for sin to invade our lives and destroy what He created and loves.

But Jesus doesn't weep because He is powerless. He always is victorious in the end, and if we allow Him to be in control of all areas of our lives, there isn't a single place where He won't win freedom for us.

Take some time to pray, asking God to bring victory in a specific area of your life where up until now you have only known defeat.

Claim Philippians 1:6 by praying God's words back to Him: "Lord, I am confident of this, that the one who began a good work in me will continue to complete it until the day of Christ Jesus!"

Day Three
GUARDING THE WEAK SPOTS

On the flip side of our strengths we often find our fault lines—our weak spots. A visionary leader's weakness may be the temptation to be all about the organization's goals and not enough about the people being led. A person with the gift of encouragement may be unwilling to speak truth even when that's what needs to be heard. The gift of mercy can become a tendency to enable.

Mary's strength was her contemplative spirit. Jesus called this "choosing the better part" and commended her for it. But a contemplative person doesn't just experience the spiritual high; her lows are also intense. A woman with a contemplative spirit feels deeply, which can make her prone to despair. Mary was devastated, perhaps in despair, after Lazarus' death. Jesus knew this, and didn't leave her there. He called her to come to Him, even though He knew how hard it was for her to even stand up and move.

Jesus longs to minister to you in the same way. He sees your strengths and weaknesses, and seeks to empower you to become the woman He had in mind when He created the original you. He wants to see you soar in your areas of strength and be shored up in your weak spots.

Let's explore how to identify where we are vulnerable and then how to become stronger in those areas of our lives.

1. How is the activity of the devil described in 1 Peter 5:8?

Our enemy prowls around, looking for a breach in the wall. He's looking for the chink in our armor, that place where we are at our weakest. And that's exactly where he attacks and tempts us. We are completely vulnerable if we have no idea where those breaches are. This is why self-knowledge is so valuable. We don't dwell on ourselves in a self-centered, selfish way; rather, we explore our hearts and minds as a means of knowing what parts of our lives need to be "shored up."

2. Identifying your areas of vulnerability isn't a quick process. Making a general confession and then looking for patterns among the sins is one helpful way to notice key weaknesses. Another is to look for repeat problems in your closest relationships. A third would be identifying your default behavior when you are coping with adversity.

    Are you prone to a critical spirit or a desire to control? Are you competitive? Discontented? Argumentative? Do you always need to be right? Do you hunger for approval? What do you think might be your core area of weakness?

3. Read the following, "How to Guard the Weak Spots," and write out the corresponding Bible verse below each point.

HOW TO GUARD THE WEAK SPOTS

Go to confession regularly, preferably to the same confessor. Recognize that when you don't want to talk about something, chances are *that is the very area holding you back* from a life of freedom and joy. When you want to keep something hidden, it retains power over you. Once you speak it out loud, its power over you will be reduced. The minute you realize that you are trying to cover something up or are unwilling to talk about it, there's a good chance you've recognized a weak spot. This is something to celebrate! This is progress.

Psalm 32:3–5:

Ask someone to stand guard at that spot. Let this person know that this is an area of weakness for you, and invite him or her to speak truth into your life when you start down that path. This accountability can make all the difference in the world. We all tend to distract ourselves from the interior things that need our attention or to justify our own actions when what we see in the mirror is unpleasant. An honest, good friend is a priceless treasure.

Proverbs 27:6:

Be alert to warning signs that all is not well. Before we fall into sinful behavior, we're probably experiencing negative thinking, an unsettled stomach, tension in relationships, or some other stress. These feelings and circumstances alert us to the fact that something isn't right. When this happens, we have a choice. We can either turn to God for refuge and shelter or fall into default behavior to create a false sense of safety. That default behavior often leads to sin, because we step away from dependence on God and toward self-sufficiency.

Psalm 61:2–5, NAB:

Give God permission to get to the bottom of the weakness. This means going to those hard places emotionally, not to navel-gaze, but to get to the root of the problem. It requires taking a few steps back in order to move forward. This often involves counseling, which is best done by a professional who recognizes that true healing must involve Jesus, the great physician.

Psalm 139:23:

4. Whom could you ask to hold you accountable in your area of weakness? Who could stand guard at that spot for you?

Quiet your heart and enjoy His presence. . . . You are loved in your weakness.

You are loved in your weakness. God doesn't wait until your vulnerabilities have been mastered. He steps into the darkness and fear, and He Himself *keeps watch at your weak spots. He strengthens you when you are weak. He whispers truth to your heart when lies are keeping you strangled. He reaches into the hurting places and heals the fault lines in your soul. But for Him to do this, you have to give Him access. He is a gentleman. He waits for your invitation.*

Pray this adaptation of Psalm 46 and invite the Lord to shore up the weak spots in your life:

Dear Lord,

You are my refuge and strength, an ever-present help in distress. I won't fear, even if everything in my life starts to shift and shake. If the earth is shaken and the mountains quake to the depths of the sea, if its waters rage and foam and mountains totter at its surging, I will stand firm. When You stand with me, I will not be shaken. You are my stronghold.

Help me, Lord, to be brave enough to speak my weakness out loud. Release me from its power. Bring me a trusted friend who can hold me accountable. Alert me to the warning signs that I'm about to create my own version of safety and security. Help me to break the patterns of behavior that are holding me back from true safety and security. Give me just a little more courage than fear so that I can invite You to get to the bottom of my weakness and struggle.

Day Four
BROKEN AT HIS FEET

Read John 12:1–8.

1. A. When was this dinner party given? See John 12:1.

   B. What was about to happen during Passover? See John 19:13–16.

   C. Did Jesus know this was going to happen? See Matthew 26:1–2.

2. Describe the perfume that Mary used to anoint Jesus' feet. See John 12:3.

The perfumed oil Mary poured over Jesus was worth a year's wages; it was an extravagant, sacrificial gift.

3. How did Judas respond to her actions? How did Jesus respond? See John 12:4–8 and Mark 14:6–9.

4. Did Mary know that this truly was the final anointing before Jesus' death? We can't know for sure, but she had observed the way Jesus pushed aside social conventions and loved the people on the margins; she had been allowed to learn theology along with the men; she had seen a man who touched the unclean leper, who ate with the tax collectors and sinners; and she had thought, "Our world just isn't going to accept someone who risks it all to love like that."

She had just seen Him bring her brother back from the dead. His resurrection power was utterly beyond her wildest imaginings. This was a man who could bring things back to life. When she pondered this, Mary concluded, "What is Jesus worth to me? He is worth *everything*." So she broke her jar, and poured out all she had. She knelt at Jesus' feet and poured out her future, her hopes, her dreams.

What is He worth to you? When you kneel at His feet, what kind of offering, what type of sacrifice do you pour out? Read Psalm 51:17, and describe the sacrifice that God welcomes.

Just as Mary broke her alabaster jar and a beautiful fragrance filled the room, when we break our hearts open before the Lord, the aroma of our humility, the scent of healing, permeates everything.

The broken and contrite heart offers honest, raw confession. It offers vulnerable authenticity, devoid of self-deception. It's a heart that longs for transformation and is willing to change.

Jesus is drawn to brokenness. As He said in Mark 2:17, "It is not the healthy who need a doctor, but the sick. I have not come to call the righteous, but sinners." He came for us in the midst of our mess and in the middle of the struggle. He doesn't ask us to get cleaned up and only then draw close. He only asks that we recognize our need. Weakness isn't our barrier; self-sufficiency is.

5. What do you need to lay down at Jesus' feet? What offering can you pour out for Him? Is it a dream that would be better tended in His hands than yours? Is it something you need to confess? Is it your discontent? Is it your need for control?

Quiet your heart and enjoy His presence. . . . Lay it down and let go.

When Mary let down her hair and used it to dry Jesus' feet, she defied social conventions. No woman let her hair down in public—it was scandalous to do so. We don't know why she made this choice, only that her love for Jesus was greater than any desire to preserve her reputation. When Jesus approved of her actions, that was all that mattered.

May we get to this place.

Oh Lord, please free us from the endless litany of things that we feel we should do or must do—the things our culture says matter so much. Help us to wipe the slate clean in our heads and start afresh, asking You, "What offering pleases You?"

(Ask Him this question now, and then allow silence to follow. You might want to lay your hands on your lap, palms up, in a posture of openness to His will. Or maybe you'll want to kneel or lie prostrate. This is a part of what we do as Catholics—we worship with our senses and our bodies. What we do automatically in Mass doesn't feel odd, but in our homes it can feel a little strange. But maybe we can venture out like Mary, and stop calculating in terms of what makes sense, what's weird, what's conventional, and instead let go.)

Day Five
BESTOWING DIGNITY

"Amen, I say to you, wherever the gospel is proclaimed to the whole world, what she has done will be told in memory of her" (Mark 14:9).

I just love this about Jesus. He appreciated and elevated the importance of an act of love that could have easily been noticed at that moment but forgotten later. He saw Mary's sacrifice and extravagant worship and promised that she would be honored for it forever.

1. Mary, Martha, and Lazarus had given Jesus a home—a soft place to land. The unique way in which they ministered to Him through hospitality and friendship had great significance. The ministry *we* do in our homes has dignity and is deeply valuable to God, too. What insight does Hebrews 6:10 shed on this truth?

He sees it all and remembers. When something we do goes unnoticed and unappreciated by others, Jesus receives it as an offering to Him.

2. How is a woman's dignity described in CCC 369 and 2334?

3. Far from treating women as "less than" men, Jesus went beyond the social and religious barriers of the time to restore them to their full dignity. The Catholic Church not only acknowledges a woman's innate dignity; she sees the important and integral role that women play in the Church. Read the following quote by

Saint John Paul and comment on how he described the woman's mission in the Church.

> The presence and the role of women in the life and mission of the Church, although not linked to the ministerial priesthood, remain absolutely necessary and irreplaceable. As the declaration Inter Insigniores points out, "the Church desires that Christian women should become fully aware of the greatness of their mission: today their role is of capital importance both for the renewal and humanization of society and for the rediscovery by believers of the true face of the Church."[87] —Pope John Paul II

My favorite portion of that quote is the part that women play in the "rediscovery by believers of the true face of the Church." What is the true face of the Church? It's faithfulness, mercy, compassion, courage, and goodness—it's a reflection to the world of Jesus' love. A woman's intuition helps her to gauge a situation—most important, to gauge a person's heart—and know what is most needed. Is it mercy? Is it tough love? Is it courageous words? Is it gentleness? Insight into what is going on below the surface is critical if we are going to effectively reach out and invite people closer to Christ.

Times have changed. We no longer live in a Christian culture, but in a postmodern one. In a postmodern society, truth is relative, not absolute. People are less likely to have a problem with Jesus and more likely to have a problem with the Church. Postmoderns have a rather pessimistic view of authority. This means that we as laywomen have a unique opportunity (and from a certain perspective, an *advantage* over a priest or a religious brother or sister) when we step into a world hungry for Christ.

Shouting the truth from the mountaintops (or via social media) is not going to draw people to the Lord. People want to be seen, heard, and loved before they are willing to listen to what we believe. We earn the right to be heard. Relationships need to be built before faith can be shared. As women, we are uniquely equipped for this kind of ministry. We can go to the margins; reach out in our families; impact the workplace, neighborhoods, and schools; and do it all with a sensitive, listening, humble approach.

---

[87] Pope John Paul II, "Apostolic Letter: *Ordinatio Sacerdotalis*," The Holy See, 1994, https://w2.vatican.va/content/john-paul-ii/en/apost_letters/1994/documents/hf_jp-ii_apl_19940522_ordinatio-sacerdotalis.html.

4. God treats us with dignity, and we in turn should treat others in that same way. Never is this more true than when we are sharing our faith. A postmodern culture places a high value on community, relationships, authenticity, and evidence that faith truly makes a difference in life—that it helps life to work better. Narratives are important; the value of a story cannot be underestimated. But the first step isn't us sharing *our* story; it's inviting the other person to share his or hers. Is there someone in your life whom you would like to see draw closer to Christ? Who is it? Can you apply anything from these thoughts on the postmodern culture to help you treat him or her with dignity as you share your faith?

Quiet your heart and enjoy His presence. . . . He gives dignity to His beloved.

"She is clothed with strength and dignity, and laughs at the days to come" (Proverbs 31:25).

A woman clothed in dignity can laugh at the days to come because she knows that the One in charge has got it all under control. We can't laugh at the future when we think it's all up to us. That perspective leaves us full of pride or full of fear or somewhere in between.

A woman of dignity doesn't need to grasp at titles or accolades in order to feel she matters. She can take the humblest position, pour all of her abilities and gifts at the feet of others, and know that not only is it enough, it matters throughout eternity. This isn't to say that a woman shouldn't have positions of honor. It does mean that our dignity doesn't come from those things. It comes from a far deeper source. It comes from God Himself.

Saint John Paul wrote, "A woman can only find herself by giving love to others." This is the way we find fulfillment, dignity, and purpose. This is the measuring stick of success—not our bank account, or degrees, or awards.

Spend some time talking to Jesus about your dignity and times when you grasp and scramble in order to hustle for your worth. Ask Him to help you see yourself through His eyes.

Conclusion

"In all these things, we conquer overwhelmingly through him who loved us" (Romans 8:37).

One of the favorite tactics of the enemy of our soul is to constantly preoccupy us with what we are not, so that we never fully encounter and embrace who God is. The more we focus on our inadequacies in a spirit of defeat, the less we appropriate the grace that God wants to pour into us.

When we sit at the feet of Jesus, He invites us to see ourselves through His eyes. He wants us to experience the mercy and unconditional love that He feels for us. But He also hopes our time together isn't all about what we feel. His desire is that we gaze on Him and see His greatness and power. He hungers for us to recognize that when we are honest about our weak spots, He comes with strength to fill in the gaps. He wants us to see that the only way we can conquer the things that hold us back from freedom and fullness in Him is to let Him do the work within us. Our strength alone is no match for hardwiring and patterns of sin. But with Christ? We conquer overwhelmingly through Him.

This posture of humility is the secret of the saints. They struggled with the same things we do. But moment by moment, they asked God to transform their natural tendencies into virtue. Even as we are inspired by the wonderful example of Mary of Bethany, we need to be patient with ourselves, knowing that it takes time to grow in these ways. God is always patient. He doesn't expect us to be "finished" today. He just asks that we depend on Him and keep putting one foot in front of the other on the journey. Missionary Amy Carmichael gives good perspective on this pilgrimage toward spiritual maturity:

> Sometimes when we read the words of those who have been more than conquerors, we feel almost despondent. I feel that I shall never be like that. But they won through step by step, by little bits of wills, little denials of self, little inward victories. By faithfulness in very little things, they became what they are. No one sees those little hidden steps. They only see the accomplishment, but even so, those small steps were taken. There is no sudden triumph no [sudden] spiritual maturity. That is the work of the moment.[88]

The people around us don't necessarily see the little hidden steps, but God does. He and the saints in heaven are cheering us on, encouraging us to keep going—to never give up. "Since we are surrounded by so great a cloud of witnesses, let us rid ourselves

---

[88] Hansel, *Holy Sweat*, 130.

of every burden and sin that clings to us and persevere in running the race that lies before us while keeping our eyes fixed on Jesus, the leader and perfecter of faith" (Hebrews 12:1–2).

My Resolution

In what specific way will I apply what I learned in this lesson?

Examples:

1. I identified a weak spot in my life this week. In order to put a "guard" on that spot, I will ask a friend to hold me accountable in that area. I will give him or her permission to call me out when I am starting to slip and fall.

2. I have rolled a stone in front of my heart, and I don't know how to move it. While I continue to pray for God to heal my hurts, I will also seek help from a Christian counselor.

3. There is someone I have wanted to share my faith with. I will get together with him or her for coffee or lunch, and instead of saying everything that I think, I will listen. I will ask questions. I will begin the process of earning the right to be heard.

My Resolution:

Catechism Clips

CCC 369 Man and woman have been created, which is to say, willed by God: on the one hand, in perfect equality as human persons; on the other, in their respective beings as man and woman. "Being man" or "being woman" is a reality which is good and willed by God: man and woman possess an inalienable dignity which comes to them immediately from God their Creator. Man and woman are both with one and the same dignity "in the image of God." In their "being-man" and "being-woman," they reflect the Creator's wisdom and goodness.

CCC 2334 "In creating men 'male and female,' God gives man and woman an equal personal dignity." "Man is a person, man and woman equally so, since both were created in the image and likeness of the personal God."

Verse Study

See Appendix 3 for instructions on how to complete a verse study.

2 Corinthians 3:18

1. Verse:

2. Paraphrase:

3. Questions:

4. Cross-references:

5. Personal Application:

Lesson 21

MARY, THE NEW EVE

Introduction

"The knot of Eve's disobedience was untied by Mary's obedience: What the virgin Eve bound through her disbelief, Mary loosened by her faith."[89] —*Saint Irenaeus*

I really couldn't help it. It was the perfect storm. I'd been up the night before with a sick and crying baby. Throughout the day, the only thing that made me feel better was the thought of an early night to bed. And in my defense, I'd made it through the day without any meltdowns. My daughter Amy had been home for just a few hours, a short break from her summer job as a camp counselor. We were chatting, but my pajamas were on. She was driving back to camp that night, and my bed was beckoning. But when her keys went missing, it became clear that the only solution was for me to get in the car and drive her to camp regardless of the fact that it was eleven p.m. and the drive would take three hours. It was all I could do not to scream, but off we went. I was still getting gold stars as the mother of the year (in my humble opinion), but when I took a wrong turn and found headlights coming toward me, I realized that I was traveling down an exit ramp in the wrong direction. And what erupted from my mouth widened my children's eyes and broadened their vocabulary. Who was to blame? I couldn't help it! Maybe I should've blamed Eve. If she hadn't eaten that forbidden fruit, wouldn't it be easier for me to make the right choices?

The good news is that the story didn't stop with Eve. Original sin doesn't get the last word. In the very moment that God explained the consequence of Eve's sin, He promised that hope was coming. Addressing the serpent, God said, "I will put enmity between you and the woman, and between your offspring and hers; He will strike at your head, while you strike at his heel" (Genesis 3:15).

Who was this woman? Mary was the extraordinary woman whose fiat—her yes—would put God's rescue plan in motion. And because of that rescue, we all get a fresh

---

[89] CCC 494.

start. Even though there are times when it seems like sin will always have the upper hand in our lives, Mary reminds us that things are different now. We have a new Eve, and because of her son,[90] "if anyone is in Christ he is a new creation. The old is gone, and the new has come" (2 Corinthians 5:17).

As we near the end of *Discovering Our Dignity*, we'll return to the same topics we addressed in Lesson 2: Eve. At the start of the course, we looked at dignity, temptation, contentment, hiding, and consequences through the eyes of Eve. This week, we'll see them through the life of Mary.

Day One
DIGNITY

Read Luke 1:26–28.

1. What words did the angel Gabriel use to greet Mary? See Luke 1:28.

The Greek words found in Luke 1:28, *chaire kecharitomene*, are often mistranslated as "Greetings, favored one." The word *chaire* is also found in John 19:3: "Hail, King of the Jews." It's a royal greeting, followed by a title.

Kecharitomene is very difficult to translate into English; our words don't adequately capture it. The root of the word means "to endow with grace." It describes a completed past action, which has effects that continue into the future. It's also a passive participle, meaning the person being described by *kecharitomene* is the passive recipient of the "endowing." In the lecture series Mother of the Messiah, Dr. Brant Pitre, professor of sacred Scripture at Notre Dame Seminary, offered the following literal translation: "Hail, She Who Has Been Perfected by/Filled with Grace."

---

[90] Saint Paul wrote of Jesus as the "last Adam" in 1 Corinthians 15:21–22, 25–29, and of Adam as a type of Christ in Romans 5:14.

2. The Catholic Church has always taught that Mary was conceived without sin. This belief, called the dogma of the Immaculate Conception, does not refer to Mary's conception of Jesus. It refers to the conception of Mary, in the womb of her mother, Saint Anne. According to CCC 492, how was Mary redeemed? Was Christ her Savior or did she save herself?

Jesus redeemed Mary. He saved her, not from the pit of sin; rather, before she fell into it. She was saved not through her own merits, but through the merits of Jesus. How is this possible, you might ask, since Jesus hadn't yet died on the cross or risen from the dead at the time of Mary's conception? We ask this because of our finite understanding of time. The Old Testament saints were saved by looking forward to the cross. They didn't have a perfect understanding of how their salvation would be won. They didn't have perfect sight, but they believed anyway. This is a description of faith. We look back at the cross. They looked forward. And in God's perfect plan, He saves in the timetable and manner that He chooses.

3. Does Romans 3:23 contradict the dogma of the Immaculate Conception?

4. Have you ever thought, "It was easier for Mary to be obedient to God than it is for me. She was given the gift of being full of grace from birth. She never had to deal with the effects of original sin." Meditating on Mary's dignity and holiness can inspire us, but if we don't have a clear understanding of our own dignity, it can cause us to feel discouraged, or to wonder if we can relate to Mary at all. To help avoid this pattern of thought, focus on your own dignity. Being "full of grace" is possible for us today! What are some ways in which God has filled us with grace, and continues to do so? See CCC 1997 and CCC 2003.

5. We read Ephesians 1:3–5 within CCC 492, applying the words to Mary. Reread Ephesians 1:3–5, making note of all the phrases that point to our dignity as daughters of God.

Quiet your heart and enjoy His presence. . . . Within you is an inherent dignity—God's gift to you.

You have an inherent dignity.
You share in the grace that God bestowed on Mary.
What radiance. What a privilege. What unmerited favor.
Oh, how He loves you!

Meditate on the following song, "How He Loves," by the David Crowder Band. Listen to it, if possible, and let the words draw you in to a time of praise as you thank God for His grace-filled love.

He is jealous for me,
Loves like a hurricane, I am a tree,
Bending beneath the weight of his wind and mercy.
When all of a sudden, I am unaware of these afflictions eclipsed by glory,
And I realize just how beautiful You are,
And how great Your affections are for me.

And oh, how He loves us oh,
Oh how He loves us,
How He loves us all

And we are His portion and He is our prize,
Drawn to redemption by the grace in His eyes,
If His grace is an ocean, we're all sinking.

And heaven meets earth like an unforeseen kiss,

And my heart turns violently inside of my chest,
I don't have time to maintain these regrets,
When I think about, the way . . .

Oh, how He loves us oh,
Oh how He loves us,
How He loves us all
How He loves.[91]

Day Two
TEMPTATION

Read Luke 1:26–38.

Real love is something chosen, not something forced on us. God could have made people robot-like, men and women who had no choice but to follow and obey Him, but that was never what He was after. God has always wanted authentic relationships with His children. He wants us to choose Him, even if there is risk involved. He wants us to trust Him, even when His plan seems risky and sometimes even scary.

When the angel Gabriel came to present Mary with a choice, she had the option to reject God's plan of redemption. Just like Eve, Mary had the freedom to distrust God's plan or to choose love. Nothing was forced on Mary. God asked her to decide, and as she pondered, she knew there was no guarantee that accepting this invitation would mean the path ahead would be easy. Did all of heaven hold its breath as the angels waited for her response?

Both Mary and Eve were created without original sin. This gave them the best start possible, but where they'd go from there would depend on their choices. Both women encountered temptation—sent by the enemy of their souls to draw them away from God's plan.

1. Satan began his temptation of Eve with the question, "Did God really tell you . . . ?" Underlying that question was the same one that is whispered in our ears: "Is God holding out on you? Does He really want what's best for you?" How might these same questions have tempted Mary to say no to God's plan?

---

[91] The David Crowder Band, "How He Loves," *Passion: Awakening* (Sparrow Records, 2010).

Remember that being tempted is not sin (sin results when we give in to temptation).

Don't forget that Satan is subtle. When he sees a woman who loves God, he knows better than to tempt her to outright rebellion. Instead, he plants seeds of doubt and mixes lies with truth. It's a plan as old as time, but unfortunately, it's just as effective today as it was in the Garden of Eden.

2. Eve's downfall came in stages. It began with her conversing with temptation, then being careless with God's Word, followed by looking at the temptation, and finally allowing her desires to drive her decision making (see Lesson 2, Day Two). By contrast, what drove Mary's decision making? See Luke 1:38.

3. Mary had a true understanding of who she was. She didn't doubt her dignity or worth in God's eyes. This is genuine humility, because humility is seeing ourselves as God sees us. While she was certainly amazed that God would choose her (she recognized that He had "regarded the low estate of his handmaiden"), she didn't question His choice. When God calls us to step forward and take our place in His plan, we can be tempted to respond with false humility. "Me?" we might say. "Why would you pick me? I'm not good enough. How can you use me? Can't you see how much I've messed up in the past?" But true humility is seeing ourselves as God sees us. Yes, God used Mary in all her beautiful perfection. But our all-powerful God can also use us in all our broken imperfection.

    A. What does God want each of His daughters to do with the gifts He has placed within them? See 1 Peter 4:10.

B. How does 1 Corinthians 12:7 respond to the temptation for us to say, "God may have given gifts to a lot of His daughters, but I think He skipped me"?

4. God is delighted when we realize that we would be nothing without Him (John 15:5). But He wants us to always remember that with Him, all things are possible (Luke 1:37)! Skim Jesus' genealogy in Matthew 1:2–16. Not many women are mentioned, but we studied three of them during our course this year. Were they likely choices for Jesus' ancestry? Why or why not? What does this tell us about whom God can use to bring about His purposes in the world?

5. God needs each of us to answer His call and to take our place in the spiritual battle that rages around us. If we want to see change in the world, if we want to leave it a better place for the generation that follows, we must resist the temptation to write ourselves off, saying that God only uses the beautiful, the smart, the pure, or the powerful. He uses ordinary, broken women who are willing to echo Mary's words: "I am the handmaiden of the Lord. May it be done to me according to thy word" (Luke 1:38).

Write out the following verses, choosing one to be your special focus this week. Write it on an index card, carry it with you, and read it whenever you're tempted to give up.

Jeremiah 29:11

Romans 8:37–39

Galatians 6:9

Quiet your heart and enjoy His presence. . . . You are not alone.

"Therefore, since we are surrounded by so great a cloud of witnesses, let us rid ourselves of every burden and sin that clings to us and persevere in running the race that lies before us while keeping our eyes fixed on Jesus, the leader and perfecter of faith" (Hebrews 12:1–2).

Ladies, we do not battle alone. We are surrounded by sisters in Christ whose hearts beat for the same things as our own. We are stronger together than alone. We also are surrounded by a cloud of heavenly sisters (and brothers) who are cheering us on. Mary and the saints in heaven are praying that we will persevere, that we'll continually choose to follow Christ in both our little and big choices each day.

How do we do it?

We learn what not to do from Eve. She took her eyes off God and placed them on the forbidden fruit. This made the temptation irresistible.

We learn what to do from Mary. She kept trust and love high by remembering who she was. She knew she was God's beloved daughter and that no matter how risky His plan seemed, He could use her to help carry it out for the world.

Throw off the burden of sin. Take a deep breath and keep running. Keep your eyes fixed on Jesus, and just watch what He can do. His specialties? Restoration. Transformation. Miracles.

Day Three
CONTENTMENT

Read Luke 1:46–55.

In Lesson 2: Eve, we learned that Satan tempted Eve to sin to gain something that she already had. She was already made in God's image, but was deceived into believing that eating the forbidden fruit would give her dignity and wisdom. Satan managed to get Eve to take her focus off of all that she had and instead zero in on the one thing that she couldn't have. Her longing for something more turned into discontent, which led her down the path of compromise and sin.

What about Mary? How did the new Eve respond differently? And what about us? How are we responding to our unfulfilled longings?

1. Meditating on Mary's life, at what points do you think choosing contentment would have been a challenge for her? How did she consistently respond to her circumstances? Remember, discontent rears its head whenever we focus on if-onlys and what-ifs.

2. When the circumstances around us are utterly contrary to what we want, we have to become extra-disciplined about where we allow our thoughts to dwell. Our focus is critical. This is what made all the difference in Mary's life. Her razor-sharp focus on God was a key component in her ability to remain content despite intense suffering. This is seen clearly in the Magnificat (Luke 1:46–55). Write down phrases from this passage that reveal the qualities of God that Mary dwelled on.

3. Mary's focus on God's goodness and greatness filled her heart with gratitude, which is the best antidote to discontent. A heart full of gratitude leaves no room for doubt, dissatisfaction, and unhappiness. In addition to her focus on God, Mary focused on who God had created her to be. She never lost sight of her God-given worth. Reread the Magnificat, noting all the things Mary said that refer to her own dignity.

4. Is there an area in your life where you are struggling to remain content? Write it below.

   I really want . . .

If I could receive what I'm longing for, I'd feel more . . .

Circle any that apply:

Secure
Peaceful
Happy
Fulfilled
Self-confident
_____ (other)

5. Just like Mary, you have a choice between dwelling on your if-onlys and what-ifs and focusing on what God has already done for you, and what He is doing right now. You also have a choice in terms of how you determine your worth and identity. We will always be tempted to define ourselves by what we have, what we're accomplishing, or our reputations. Mary allowed herself to be defined by God, not by her circumstances.

   A. Following Mary's example, can you list qualities of God or examples of His faithfulness to you today?

   B. Following Mary's example, can you describe who you are in God's eyes? Can you describe your own God-given worth?

Quiet your heart and enjoy His presence. . . . He is good. He is faithful. He is for you.

We often don't realize how much our discontent is holding us back from being the women that God created us to be. It's as if we're in a holding pattern, waiting for certain circumstances of our lives to change so that we can really start living the life that God has for us. But this is never God's plan. He wants us to engage fully in the moment, trusting that whatever He is allowing, giving, or withholding is ultimately for our good. This is really hard to do. But our ability to follow Mary's example, saying,

"I want what you want. I'll take your 'plan A' instead of all my own ideas," really will be impacted by what we choose to focus on.

Take a few moments to turn your answers to question 5 into a prayer. Praise is a key that unlocks the door to gratitude and joy!

Day Four
HIDING

Eve hid from God because of guilt. She knew she had sinned, and the shame drew her to turn away from God instead of running to Him to hide in His mercy. Because Mary was sinless, she never needed to hide out of guilt or shame. But throughout her life, there were periods of time when hiding Mary was very much a part of God's plan.

Read Matthew 2:13–18.

1. When God hid Mary and the Holy Family in Egypt, what was He protecting them from?

2. We read of many events around the birth of Jesus, but then the story goes quiet. We get a quick glimpse of Him at age twelve, and when Jesus comes on the scene next, He is in His thirties. During the time between those events, the Holy Family experienced years of a hidden life. What was taking place during that time? See Luke 2:41–52 and CCC 531 and 534.

3. Sometimes God hides His children to protect us. Other times it's because there is work He is doing that is best done in secret. Sometimes the hardest seasons of life are ones when we feel hidden. The world is passing us by, while God is working quietly within us. Seasons of inner growth always carry with them difficulties. We

often respond to them by asking God to take away what is hard. So why does He so often *not* remove the difficulty, instead giving us the strength to persevere? He sees the treasure at the end of the trail. Read Hebrews 10:35–36 and record any insights regarding endurance through times of hidden inner growth.

"Therefore do not throw away your confidence, which has a great reward. For you have need of endurance, so that you may do the will of God and receive what is promised" (Hebrews 10:35–36).

This verse was originally written in Greek. The word translated as "endurance" or "perseverance" is *hupomone* (hoop-om-on-ay). It means "a remaining behind, a patient enduring." When we persevere, we can feel as if the world is passing us by.

Other people are doing far more interesting things, while we slug it out, doing something that is difficult. Remaining behind, staying hidden, is hard. Perhaps you have decided to give up a career outside the home in order to raise your children. Perhaps you are parenting a child with special needs, and other kids are progressing at a rate beyond that of your child. Your sacrifice is hidden; you are remaining behind.

Perhaps you are dealing with an illness that keeps you from doing many things that feel exciting and meaningful. Your life is hidden; you are remaining behind.

Perhaps there is something you are longing for, and although you go through the motions of life, you feel as if you are not where you should be. As you wait to see if God will answer you as you desire, you feel you are remaining behind.

Perseverance means remaining behind, and it also means patiently enduring. So we don't give up, and we don't complain. We don't hide and remain behind resentfully. We do it *purposefully*. We do it while looking forward. Persevering always has in view a desirable end, a worthy goal, a divine reward.

4. In what area of life are you being asked to persevere? Do you believe that what you are doing is God's will for you?

If what you are doing is God's will for you, then God is calling you to persevere. He is asking you not to give up. For example, if you are being asked to persevere during a difficult time of mothering, then know it is God's will for you. That is living out your vocation with obedience. Are you being called to persevere as you care for your aging parents? That is God's will for you. You are living out the command to honor your father and mother.

Hebrews 10:36 reminds us that if we persevere in doing God's will, He promises something in the end: an eternal reward. He sees all that we do, and it is affecting our eternity. This life is not all that there is. We live as if our earthly life is everything, when it is so short in comparison to all the time we will spend in heaven.

Quiet your heart and enjoy His presence. . . . Amazing things happen as you hide yourself in Him.

God promises us an eternal reward when we persevere, when we stick with the ordinary duties of our lives when we'd rather be doing something different and more exciting. But God is so compassionate that He doesn't make us wait until heaven to be rewarded for our perseverance. There are fruits that we can see along the way. What is happening inside us as we do the hidden work of persevering?

"Perseverance must finish its work so that you may be mature and complete, not lacking anything" (James 1:4).

We need to always remember that God is much more concerned with the substance of our soul than with our comfort level. When we quietly persevere, we are maturing spiritually. We are growing up in ways that will serve us well in life. This is hidden progress. It doesn't earn us worldly accolades, but it's deeply satisfying when it occurs.

Author Gary Thomas shares the following thoughts on perseverance. Read them here and ask the Lord to give you His perspective on the purpose of your "bundle of difficulties."

There's only one way to develop perseverance: We have to surrender to God as we feel pushed past the human breaking point. We have to reach the threshold of exhaustion, and then get pushed even further. One trial can help us deal with fear. Two trials can lead to wisdom. But perseverance? That takes a bundle of difficulties. . . . If God gives us situations we already have the strength to handle, we won't have to grow in order to deal with them.[92]

Day Five
THE CONSEQUENCES

1. Compare the consequences of Eve's disobedience and Mary's obedience. See CCC 494.

2. In what sense is our own adoption as daughters of God a consequence of Mary's obedience to God? See CCC 488 and Galatians 4:4–5.

3. What personal consequence did Mary experience because of her obedience to God's plan? See Luke 2:34–35 and John 19:25.

4. A beautiful consequence of Mary's obedience is seen at the foot of the cross. When Jesus was dying, every word He spoke caused Him excruciating pain. Yet "when Jesus saw his mother and the disciple there whom he loved, he said to his mother, 'Woman, behold, your son. Then He said to the disciple, 'Behold, your mother.' And from that hour the disciple took her into his home" (John 19:26–

---

[92] Gary Thomas, *Sacred Parenting: How Raising Children Shapes Our Souls* (Grand Rapids, MI: Zondervan, 2004), 145.

27). According to CCC 968, how did that offering of His mother affect us personally?

Quiet your heart and enjoy His presence. . . . He loves you lavishly, holding nothing back—not even His mother.

Mothers are fixers. When they see their children tied up in difficulty, their first instinct is to jump in and help sort things out. Our Blessed Mother is no different. If something in your life is tied up in knots, then pray the following prayer to your heavenly Mother, Mary.

Mary,

Full of the presence of God during your life, you accepted with great humility the holy will of the Father and the legacy of your son Our Lord Jesus Christ.

Evil never dared to entangle you with its confusion. Since then you have interceded for all of our difficulties. With all simplicity and patience you have given us an example of how to untangle the knots in our complicated lives. By being our mother forever, you arrange and make clear the path that unites us to Our Lord. Holy Mary, Mother of God and ours, with your maternal heart untie the knots that upset our lives. We ask you to receive in your hands [a person or your prayer request] and deliver us from the chains and confusion that have us restrained. Blessed Virgin Mary, through your grace, your intercession, and by your example, deliver us from evil and untie the knots that keep us from uniting with God, so that once free of every confusion and error, we may find Him in all things, have Him in our hearts, and serve Him always in our brothers and sisters. Mother of good counsel, pray for us. Amen.

Conclusion

For it was while Eve was yet a virgin that the ensnaring word had crept into her ear which was to build the edifice of death. Into a virgin's soul, in like manner, must be introduced that Word of God which was to raise the fabric of life; so that what had been reduced to ruin by this sex might by the selfsame sex be recovered to salvation. As Eve believed the serpent, so

Mary believed the angel. The delinquency which the one occasioned by believing, the other effaced by believing.[93] *—Tertullian*

Belief precedes action. Before we do something, we believe something. This was true for Eve and for Mary, and it's true for women today. Whom we listen to, the books we read, the music we hear, and the movies we watch all influence us more than we realize. What we feed on will ultimately shape our opinions, beliefs, and actions.

"Believing is an act of the intellect assenting to the divine truth by command of the will moved by God through grace" (CCC 155). This means that when we expose ourselves to divine truth, when we soak up God's perspective on things, we are strengthening our intellect. When God's truth is up in our heads, it strengthens our will to make the right choice because we want to.

Mary was careful about what she allowed her mind to dwell on. She pondered things, "reflecting on them in her heart" (Luke 2:19). Instead of just taking life as it came and reacting to circumstances in whatever way her emotions led her, she took the time to reflect on the big picture, on God's plan, on His faithfulness and goodness. The time she spent quietly pondering shaped her beliefs. With her beliefs rooted firmly in God's trustworthiness, faithfulness, and goodness, she was able to face enormous challenges with grace.

As our study comes to an end, you have a choice. What will you fill your mind with in the upcoming weeks? What is the next book you'll pick up? How will you spend your leisure time? Mary challenges us to make it count. Soak up truth. Keep reading your Bible.

In the words of Pope Benedict XVI, "I would like to suggest that you keep the Holy Bible within reach. . . . By so doing moments of relaxation can become in addition to a cultural enrichment also an enrichment of the spirit, fostering the knowledge of God and dialogue with him, prayer."[94]

Does this guarantee that we'll never make the wrong choice? No, but it increases the odds that we'll make the right ones. And for the times when we mess up, it's good to be reminded that "the favors of the LORD are not exhausted, his mercies are not spent. They are renewed each morning, so great is his faithfulness" (Lamentations 3:22–23).

---

[93] Tertullian, *On the Flesh of Christ*, ed., trans. Canon Ernest Evans (London, England: SPCK, 1956).

[94] Pope Benedict XVI, "General Audience," The Holy See, August 3, 2011, http://w2.vatican.va/content/benedict-xvi/en/audiences/2011/documents/hf_ben-xvi_aud_20110803.html

Mary reminds us of new beginnings. Fresh starts. Renewed hope. All because of the one who promises, "Behold, I make all things new!" (Revelation 21:5)

"I have been crucified with Christ; it is no longer I who live, but Christ who lives in me: and the life I now live in the flesh I live by faith in the Son of God, who loved me and gave himself for me" (Galatians 2:20).

My Resolution

In what specific way will I apply what I learned in this lesson?

Examples:

1. In order to remember my God-given dignity, I'll meditate daily on Ephesians 1:3–5.

2. To strengthen myself against temptation, I'll receive the sacrament of reconciliation this week.

   "Sacraments are like hoses. They are the channels of the living water of God's grace. Our faith is like opening the faucet. We can open it a lot, a little, or not at all."[95] —Peter Kreeft

3. I'll daily ask for Mary's intercession as I seek to persevere through my difficult circumstances.

My Resolution:

---

[95] Peter Kreeft, *Jesus Shock* (Singer Island, FL: Beacon Publishing, 2008), 117.

Catechism Clips

CCC 155 In faith, the human intellect and will cooperate with divine grace: "Believing is an act of the intellect assenting to the divine truth by command of the will moved by God through grace."

CCC 488 "God sent forth his Son," but to prepare a body for him, he wanted the free co-operation of a creature. For this, from all eternity God chose for the mother of his Son a daughter of Israel, a young Jewish woman of Nazareth in Galilee, "a virgin betrothed to a man whose name was Joseph, of the house of David; and the virgin's name was Mary."

The Father of mercies willed that the Incarnation should be preceded by assent on the part of the predestined mother, so that just as a woman had a share in the coming of death, so also should a woman contribute to the coming of life.

CCC 492 The "splendor of an entirely unique holiness" by which Mary is "enriched from the first instant of her conception" comes wholly from Christ: she is "redeemed, in a more exalted fashion, by reason of the merits of her Son." The Father blessed Mary more than any other created person "in Christ with every spiritual blessing in the heavenly places" and chose her "in Christ before the foundation of the world, to be holy and blameless before him in love."

CCC 494 At the announcement that she would give birth to "the Son of the Most High" without knowing man, by the power of the Holy Spirit, Mary responded with the obedience of faith, certain that "with God nothing will be impossible": "Behold, I am the handmaid of the Lord; let it be [done] to me according to your word." Thus, giving her consent to God's word, Mary becomes the mother of Jesus. Espousing the divine will for salvation wholeheartedly, without a single sin to restrain her, she gave herself entirely to the person and to the work of her Son; she did so in order to serve the mystery of redemption with him and dependent on him, by God's grace:

As St. Irenaeus says, "Being obedient she became the cause of salvation for herself and for the whole human race." Hence not a few of the early Fathers gladly assert . . . : "The knot of Eve's disobedience was untied by Mary's obedience: what the virgin Eve bound through her disbelief, Mary loosened by her faith." Comparing her with Eve, they call Mary "the Mother of the living" and frequently claim: "Death through Eve, life through Mary."

CCC 531 During the greater part of his life Jesus shared the condition of the vast majority of human beings: a daily life spent without evident greatness, a life of manual labor. His religious life was that of a Jew obedient to the law of God, a life in the community. From this whole period it is revealed to us that Jesus was "obedient" to his parents and that he "increased in wisdom and in stature, and in favor with God and man."

CCC 534 The *finding of Jesus in the temple* is the only event that breaks the silence of the Gospels about the hidden years of Jesus. Here Jesus lets us catch a glimpse of the mystery of his total consecration to a mission that flows from his divine sonship: "Did you not know that I must be about my Father's work?" Mary and Joseph did not understand these words, but they accepted them in faith. Mary "kept all these things in her heart" during the years Jesus remained hidden in the silence of an ordinary life.

CCC 968 Her role in relation to the Church and to all humanity goes still further. "In a wholly singular way she cooperated by her obedience, faith, hope, and burning charity in the Savior's work of restoring supernatural life to souls. For this reason she is a mother to us in the order of grace."

CCC 1997 Grace is a *participation in the life of God*. It introduces us into the intimacy of Trinitarian life: by Baptism the Christian participates in the grace of Christ, the Head of his Body. As an "adopted son" he can henceforth call God "Father," in union with the only Son. He receives the life of the Spirit who breathes charity into him and who forms the Church.

CCC 2003 Grace is first and foremost the gift of the Spirit who justifies and sanctifies us. But grace also includes the gifts that the Spirit grants us to associate us with his work, to enable us to collaborate in the salvation of others and in the growth of the Body of Christ, the Church. There are *sacramental graces*, gifts proper to the different sacraments. There are furthermore *special graces*, also called *charisms* after the Greek term used by St. Paul and meaning "favor," "gratuitous gift," "benefit." Whatever their character—sometimes it is extraordinary, such as the gift of miracles or of tongues—charisms are oriented toward sanctifying grace and are intended for the common good of the Church. They are at the service of charity which builds up the Church.

Verse Study

See Appendix 3 for instructions on how to complete a verse study.

Galatians 2:20

1. Verse:

2. Paraphrase:

3. Questions:

4. Cross-references:

5. Personal Application:

Lesson 22: Connect Coffee Talk

MARY – UNTYING THE KNOT

Accompanying DVD can be viewed at:
www.walkingwithpurpose.com/courses/videos
Select: *Discovering Our Dignity* – Talk 06 – Mary: Untying the Knot

The freedom Christ offers:

Galatians 5:1

John 10:10

But is this what we're experiencing?

1. What Stole Our Freedom?

It started with Eve. She was free to be all that any woman could ever wish. But what did she choose to become? She chose to put her will above God's. And when Eve made her choice, she ushered in what stole our freedom: _____.

What was the consequence? _____.

What do we call the ray of hope God gave to Eve in Genesis 3:15? The _____.

"At the very moment of the fall, the promise also begins."[96] —Pope Benedict

2. Freedom Found in Obedience

"The knot of Eve's disobedience was untied by Mary's obedience: what the virgin Eve bound through her disbelief, Mary loosened by her faith" (CCC 494).

> "Full of grace" therefore means, once again, that Mary is a wholly open human being, one who has opened herself entirely, one who has placed herself in God's hands boldly, limitlessly, and without fear for her own fate. It means that she lives wholly by and in relation to God. She is a listener and a prayer, whose mind and soul are alive to the manifold ways in which the living God quietly calls to her. She is one who prays and stretches forth wholly to meet God; she is therefore a lover, who has the breadth and magnanimity of true love, but who has also its unerring powers of discernment and its readiness to suffer.[97] —Pope Benedict

> In the final analysis it becomes clear that the sort of person the prisoner became was the result of an inner decision, and not the result of camp influences alone. Fundamentally, therefore, any man can, even under such circumstances, decide what shall become of him—mentally and spiritually. He may retain his human dignity even in a concentration camp. Dostoevski said once, "There is only one thing that I dread: not to be worthy of my sufferings." These words frequently came to my mind after I became acquainted with those martyrs whose behavior in camp, whose suffering and death, bore witness to the fact that the last inner freedom cannot be lost. It can be said that they were worthy of their sufferings; the way they bore their suffering was a genuine inner achievement. It is this spiritual freedom—which cannot be taken away—that makes life meaningful and purposeful.[98] —Viktor Frankl

God is in the business of turning what was meant to _____ you into _____ (Deuteronomy 23:5, RSV).

---

[96] Hans Urs von Balthasar and Joseph Cardinal Ratzinger, *Mary: The Church at the Source* (San Francisco: Ignatius Press, 2005), 51.
[97] Ibid., 68.
[98] Viktor Frankl, *Man's Search for Meaning* (New York: Washington Square Books, 1984), 86–9.

Questions for Discussion

1. Do you feel knotted up inside? Can you identify what is causing those knots? Do you have physical symptoms that accompany the feeling of unsettledness?

2. Can you identify any lies that are holding you back from freedom in Christ?

3. In what specific way is God asking you to walk in obedience today?

Appendices

Appendix 1
SAINT THÉRÈSE OF LISIEUX

Patron Saint of Walking with Purpose

Saint Thérèse of Lisieux was gifted with the ability to take the riches of our Catholic faith and explain them in a way that a child could imitate. The wisdom she gleaned from Scripture ignited a love in her heart for her Lord that was personal and transforming. The simplicity of the faith that she laid out in her writings is so completely Catholic that Pope Pius XII said, "She rediscovered the Gospel itself, the very heart of the Gospel."

Walking with Purpose is intended to be a means by which women can honestly share their spiritual struggles and embark on a journey that is refreshing to the soul. It was never intended to facilitate the deepest of intellectual study of Scripture. Instead, the focus has been to help women know Christ: to know His heart, to know His tenderness, to know His mercy, and to know His love. Our logo is a little flower, and that has meaning. When a woman begins to open her heart to God, it's like the opening of a little flower. It can easily be bruised or crushed, and it must be treated with the greatest of care. Our desire is to speak to women's hearts no matter where they are in life, baggage and all, and gently introduce truths that can change their lives.

Saint Thérèse of Lisieux, the little flower, called her doctrine "the little way of spiritual childhood," and it is based on complete and unshakable confidence in God's love for us. She was not introducing new truths. She spent countless hours reading Scripture and she shared what she found, emphasizing the importance of truths that had already been divinely revealed. We can learn so much from her:

> The good God would not inspire unattainable desires; I can, then, in spite of my littleness, aspire to sanctity. For me to become greater is impossible; I must put up with myself just as I am with all my imperfections. But I wish to find the way to go to Heaven by a very straight, short, completely new little way. We are in a century of inventions: now one does not even have to take the trouble to climb the steps of a stairway; in the homes of the rich, an elevator replaces them nicely. I, too, would like to find an elevator to lift me up to Jesus, for I

am too little to climb the rough stairway of perfection. So I have looked in the books of the saints for a sign of the elevator I long for, and I have read these words proceeding from the mouth of eternal Wisdom: "He that is a little one, let him turn to me" (Proverbs 9:16). So I came, knowing that I had found what I was seeking, and wanting to know, O my God, what You would do with the little one who would answer Your call, and this is what I found:

"As one whom the mother caresses, so will I comfort you. You shall be carried at the breasts and upon the knees they shall caress you" (Isaiah 66:12–13). Never have more tender words come to make my soul rejoice. The elevator which must raise me to the heavens is Your arms, O Jesus! For that I do not need to grow; on the contrary, I must necessarily remain small, become smaller and smaller. O my God, You have surpassed what I expected, and I want to sing Your mercies. (Saint Thérèse of the Infant Jesus, *Histoire d'une Ame: Manuscrits Autobiographiques* [Paris: Éditions du Seuil, 1998], 244.)

Appendix 2
SCRIPTURE MEMORY

"The tempter approached and said to him, 'If you are the Son of God, command that these stones become loaves of bread.' He said in reply, 'It is written: One does not live by bread alone, but by every word that comes forth from the mouth of God" (Matthew 4:3–4).

Jesus was able to respond to Satan's temptations because He knew God's truth. When He was under fire, He didn't have time to go find wisdom for the moment. It had to be in His head already. He had memorized Scripture, and found those words to be His most effective weapon in warding off temptation.

Do you ever feel tempted to just give in? To take the easy way when you know the hard way is right? Does discouragement ever nip at your heels and take you to a place of darkness? If you memorize Scripture, the Holy Spirit will be able to bring God's truth to your mind just when you need to fight back.

Ephesians 6:17 describes Scripture as an offensive weapon ("the sword of the Spirit"). How does this work? When negative thoughts and lies run through our minds, we can take a Bible verse and use it as a weapon to kick out the lie and embrace the truth. Verses that speak of God's unconditional love and forgiveness and our new identity in Christ are especially powerful for this kind of battle. When we feel defeated and like we'll never change, when we falsely assume that God must be ready to give up on us, the Holy Spirit can remind us of 2 Corinthians 5:17: "If anyone is in Christ, [she] is a new creation. The old has gone. The new has come!"

That's not the only way memorized Scripture helps us. The Holy Spirit can bring one of the truths of the Bible to our mind just before we might make a wrong choice. It's like a little whisper reminding us of what we know is true, but there's power in it, because we know they are God's words. For example, in the midst of a conversation in which we aren't listening well, the Holy Spirit can bring to mind Proverbs 18:2: "Fools take no delight in understanding, but only in displaying what they think." This enables us to make a course correction immediately instead of looking back later with regret. As it says in Psalm 119:11, "I have hidden your word in my heart *that I might not sin against you.*" (emphasis added)

You may think of memorizing Scripture as an activity for the über-religious, not for the average Christian. A blogger at She Reads Truth (shereadstruth.com) described it this way: "Recalling Scripture isn't for the overachievers; it's for the homesick." It's for those of us who know that earth isn't our home—heaven is. It's for those of us who don't want to be tossed all over the place by our emotions and instead long to be grounded in truth.

But how do we do it? Kids memorize things so easily, but our brains are full of so many other bits of information that we wonder if we're capable of doing it. Never fear. There are easy techniques that can help us to store away God's words in our minds and hearts. Pick a few that work for you. YOU CAN DO IT!

Discovering Our Dignity **Memory Verses:**

"Trust in the Lord with all your heart, on your own intelligence do not rely; in all your ways be mindful of him, and he will make straight your paths" (Proverbs 3:5–6).

"There is no fear in love, but perfect love drives out fear" (1 John 4:18).

1. Learning Through Repetition

Every time you sit down to do the first eleven lessons, begin by reading one of the memory verses for *Discovering Our Dignity*. Then begin the remaining eleven lessons by reading the other memory verse. The more you read it, the sooner it will be lodged in your memory. Be sure to read the reference as well. Don't skip that part—it comes in handy when you want to know where to find the verse in the Bible.

2. Learning Visually

Write the memory verse lightly *in pencil* on a piece of paper. Read the entire verse, including the reference. Chose one word and erase it well. Reread the entire verse, including the reference. Choose another word, and erase it well. Reread the entire verse, including the reference. Repeat this process until the whole verse has been erased and you are reciting it from memory.

3. Learning Electronically

Go to our website under Courses and save the *Discovering Our Dignity* Memory Verse Image to your phone's lock screen. Practice the verse every time you grab your phone.

4. Learning by Writing It Down

Grab a piece of paper and write your verse down twenty times.

5. Learning by Seeing It Everywhere

Display the gorgeous WWP memory verse cards somewhere in your house. Recite the verse each time you pass by it. But don't stop there. Write your verse down on index cards and leave it in places you often linger: the bathroom mirror, the car dashboard, the coffee pot, whatever works for you.

6. Learning Together

If you are doing this Walking with Purpose™ study in a small group, hold each other accountable and recite the Memory Verse together at the start and end of each lesson. If you are doing this study on your own, consider asking someone to hold you accountable by listening to you say your verse from memory each week.

Trust in the Lord with all your heart on your own intelligence do not rely; in all your ways be mindfull of Him & He will make straight your paths

>> PROVERBS 3:5-6 <<

Appendix 3
HOW TO DO A VERSE STUDY

A verse study is an exciting Bible study tool that can help to bring the Scriptures to life! By reading, reflecting on, and committing a verse to memory, we open ourselves to the Holy Spirit, who reveals very personal applications of our Lord's words and actions to our daily lives.

Learning to do a verse study is not difficult, but it can be demanding. In this Walking with Purpose™ study, a Bible verse has been selected to reinforce a theme of each lesson. To do the verse study, read the verse and then follow these simple instructions. You'll be on your way to a deeper and more personal understanding of Scripture.

- **Read the verse and the paragraph before and after the verse.**

- **Write out the selected verse.**

- **Paraphrase.**
  Write the verse using your own words. What does the verse say?

- **Ask questions.**
  Write down any questions you have about the verse. What does it say that you don't understand?

- **Use cross-references.**
  Look up other Bible verses that help to shed light on what the selected verse means. A study Bible will often list cross-references in the margin or in the study notes. Another excellent resource is Biblehub.com. This website allows you to enter a specific Bible verse and it will provide many cross-references and additional insights into the passage of Scripture you selected. Record any insights you gain from the additional verses you are able to find.

- **Make a personal application.**
  What does the verse say to you personally? Is there a promise to make? A warning to heed? An example to follow? Ask God to help you find something from the verse that you can apply to your life.

The recommended Bible translations for use in Walking with Purpose™ studies are: The New American Bible, which is the translation used in the United States for the readings at Mass; The Revised Standard Version, Catholic Edition; and The Jerusalem Bible.

A SAMPLE VERSE STUDY

1. **Verse:**
   John 15:5: "I am the vine, you are the branches. Those who abide in me and I in them bear much fruit, because apart from me you can do nothing."

2. **Paraphrase:**
   Jesus is the vine, I am the branch. If I abide in Him, then I'll be fruitful, but if I try to do everything on my own, I'll fail at what matters most. I need Him.

3. **Questions:**
   What does it mean to abide? How does Jesus abide in me? What kind of fruit is Jesus talking about?

4. **Cross-references:**
   John 6:56: "He that eats my flesh, and drinks my blood, abides in me, and I in him." This verse brings to mind the Eucharist, and the importance of receiving Christ in the Eucharist as often as possible. This is a very important way to abide in Jesus.

   John 15:7: "If you abide in me, and my words abide in you, ask for whatever you wish, and it will be done for you." How can Jesus' words abide in me if I never read them? I need to read the Bible if I want to abide in Christ.

   John 15:16: "It was not you who chose me, but I who chose you and appointed you to go and bear fruit that will remain, so that whatever you ask the Father in my name he may give you." Not all fruit remains. Some is good only temporarily—on earth. I want my fruit to remain in eternity—to count in the long run.

   Galatians 5:22–23: "The fruit of the Spirit is love, joy, peace, patience, kindness, generosity, faithfulness, gentleness, self-control." These are some of the fruits that will be seen if I abide in Christ.

5. **Personal Application:**

I will study my calendar this week, making note of where I spend my time. Is most of my time spent on things that will last for eternity (fruit that remains)? I'll reassess my priorities in light of what I find.

Appendix 4
WHO I AM IN CHRIST

Do you wonder who you are? Do you struggle to define your worth by the right things? Read the following verses and rest in the truth that you are God's beloved daughter. You are worthy. You are accepted. You are loved.

I Am God's Beloved Daughter and That Is Enough

"In love, [God] destined us for adoption to himself through Jesus Christ" (Ephesians 1:4–5).
I am not an orphan. I am God's beloved daughter.

"The one begotten by God he protects, and the evil one cannot touch him" (1 John 5:18b).
I am God's daughter. He protects me. The evil one cannot touch me.

"For in [Jesus] dwells the whole fullness of the deity bodily, and you share in this fullness in him, who is the head of every principality and power" (Colossians 2:9–10).
I am complete in Christ.

I Am a New Creation

"So whoever is in Christ is a new creation: the old things have passed away; behold, new things have come" (2 Corinthians 5:17).
I am a new creature in Christ.

"No longer I, but Christ lives in me; insofar as I now live in the flesh, I live by faith in the Son of God who has loved me and given himself up for me" (Galatians 2:20).
Christ lives in me.

"Put on the new self, which is being renewed, for knowledge, in the image of its creator" (Colossians 3:10).
I am done with my old life. My new self is being made in the image of my Creator.

I Am Forgiven

"In him we have redemption by his blood, the forgiveness of transgressions, in accord with the riches of his grace that he lavished upon us" (Ephesians 1:7–8).
I am forgiven of all my sins.

"He himself bore our sins in his body upon the cross, so that, free from sin, we might live for righteousness. By his wounds you have been healed" (1 Peter 2:24).
I am healed by Christ's wounds.

"If we acknowledge our sins, he is faithful and just and will forgive our sins and cleanse us from every wrongdoing" (1 John 1:9).
When I confess my sins, God forgives me. Every time.

I Am Free and Fully Alive

"But God, who is rich in mercy, because of the great love he had for us, even when we were dead in our transgressions, brought us to life with Christ (by grace you have been saved)" (Ephesians 2:4–5).
I am alive with Christ, saved by grace.

"For the law of the spirit of life in Christ Jesus has freed you from the law of sin and death" (Romans 8:2).
I am free from the law of sin and death.

I Am Strong and Courageous

"In justice shall you be established, far from oppression, you shall not fear, from destruction, it cannot come near" (Isaiah 54:14).
I am free from oppression, and fear will not master me.

"The one who is in you is greater than the one who is in the world" (1 John 4:4).
The One in me is greater than the evil one.

"For God did not give us a spirit of cowardice but rather of power and love and self-control" (2 Timothy 1:7).
God has not given me a spirit of fear, but one of power, love, and a sound mind.

"In all circumstances, hold faith as a shield, to quench all the flaming arrows of the evil one" (Ephesians 6:16).
I can quench all the fiery darts of the evil one with my shield of faith.

"I can do all things through Christ who strengthens me" (Philippians 4:13).
I can do all things through Christ.

"In all these things we conquer overwhelmingly through him who loved us" (Romans 8:37).
I am more than a conqueror through Him who loves me.

"They conquered him by the blood of the Lamb and by the word of their testimony; love for life did not deter them from death" (Revelation 12:11).
I am an overcomer by the blood of the Lamb and the word of my testimony.

I Am Filled with God's Peace

"We have the mind of Christ" (1 Corinthians 2:16).
"Have among yourselves the same attitude that is also yours in Christ Jesus" (Philippians 2:5).
I have the mind of Christ.

"Then the peace of God that surpasses all understanding will guard your hearts and minds in Christ Jesus" (Philippians 4:7).
I have the peace of God that surpasses all understanding.

Appendix 5
CONVERSION OF HEART

The Catholic faith is full of beautiful traditions, rituals, and sacraments. As powerful as they are, it is possible for them to become mere habits in our lives, instead of experiences that draw us close to the heart of Christ. In the words of John Paul II, they can become acts of "hollow ritualism." We might receive our first Communion and the sacraments of confession and confirmation, yet never experience the interior conversion that opens the heart to a personal relationship with God.

Pope Benedict XVI has explained that the "door of faith" is opened at one's baptism, but we are called to open it again, walk through it, and rediscover and renew our relationship with Christ and His Church.[99]

So how do we do this? How do we walk through that door of faith so we can begin to experience the abundant life that God has planned for us?

Getting Personal

The word *conversion* means "the act of turning." This means that conversion involves a turning away from one thing and a turning toward another. When you haven't experienced conversion of heart, you are turned *toward* your own desires. You are the one in charge, and you do what you feel is right and best at any given moment. You may choose to do things that are very good for other people, but the distinction is that *you are choosing*. You are deciding. You are the one in control.

Imagine driving a car. You are sitting in the driver's seat, and your hands are on the steering wheel. You've welcomed Jesus into the passenger's seat, and have listened to His comments. But whether or not you follow His directions is really up to you. You may follow them or you may not, depending on what seems right to you.

When you experience interior conversion, you decide to turn, to get out of the driver's seat, move into the passenger's seat, and invite God to be the driver. Instead of seeing Him as an advice giver or someone nice to have around for the holidays, you give Him control of every aspect of your life.

More than likely, you don't find this easy to do. This is because of the universal struggle with pride. We want to be the ones in charge. We don't like to be in desperate need. We like to be the captains of our ships, charting our own courses. As

---

[99] Pope Benedict XVI, *Apostolic Letter: Porta Fidei*, for the Indiction of the Year of Faith, October 11, 2011.

William Ernest Henley wrote, "I am the master of my fate: I am the captain of my soul."

Conversion of heart isn't possible without humility. The first step is to recognize your desperate need for a savior. Romans 6:23 states that the "wages of sin is death." When you hear this, you might be tempted to justify your behavior, or compare yourself with others. You might think to yourself, "I'm not a murderer. I'm not as bad as this or that person. If someone were to put my good deeds and bad deeds on a scale, my good ones would outweigh the bad. So surely I am good enough? Surely I don't deserve death!" When this is your line of thought, you are missing a very important truth: Just one sin is enough to separate you from a holy God. Just one sin is enough for you to deserve death. Even your best efforts to do good fall short of what God has required in order for you to spend eternity with Him. Isaiah 64:6 says, "All our righteous acts are like filthy rags." If you come to God thinking that you are going to be accepted by Him based on your "good conduct," He will point out that your righteousness is nothing compared to His infinite holiness.

Saint Thérèse of Lisieux understood this well, and wrote, "In the evening of my life I shall appear before You with empty hands, for I do not ask You to count my works. All our justices are stained in Your eyes. I want therefore to clothe myself in Your own justice and receive from Your love the eternal possession of Yourself."[100]

She recognized that her works, her best efforts, wouldn't be enough to earn salvation. Salvation cannot be earned. It's a free gift. Saint Thérèse accepted this gift, and said that if her justices or righteous deeds were stained, then she wanted to clothe herself in Christ's own justice. We see this described in 2 Corinthians 5:21: "God made him who had no sin to be sin for us, so that in him we might become the righteousness of God."

How did God make Him who had no sin to be sin for you? This was foretold by the prophet Isaiah: "But he was pierced for our transgressions, he was crushed for our iniquities; the punishment that brought us peace was upon him, and by his wounds we are healed" (Isaiah 53:5).

Jesus accomplished this on the cross. Every sin committed, past, present, and future, was placed on Him. Now *all the merits of Jesus can be yours*. He wants to fill your empty hands with His own virtues.

But first, you need to recognize, just as Saint Thérèse did, that you are little. You are weak. You fail. You need forgiveness. You need a savior.

---

[100] Saint Thérèse of Lisieux, "Act of Oblation to Merciful Love," June 9, 1895.

When you come before God in prayer and acknowledge these truths, He looks at your heart. He sees your desire to trust Him, to please Him, to obey Him. He says to you, "My precious child, you don't have to pay for your sins. My Son, Jesus, has already done that for you. He suffered, so that you wouldn't have to. I want to experience a relationship of intimacy with you. I forgive you.[101] Jesus came to set you free.[102] When you open your heart to me, you become a new creation![103] The old you has gone. The new you is here. If you will stay close to me, and journey by my side, you will begin to experience a transformation that brings joy and freedom.[104] I've been waiting to pour my gifts into your soul. Beloved daughter of mine, remain confident in me. I am your loving Father. Crawl into my lap. Trust me. Love me. I will take care of everything."

This is conversion of heart. This act of faith lifts the veil from your eyes and launches you into the richest and most satisfying life. You don't have to be sitting in church to do this. Don't let a minute pass before opening your heart to God and inviting Him to come dwell within you. Let Him sit in the driver's seat. Give Him the keys to your heart. Your life will never be the same again.

---

[101] "If we acknowledge our sins, he is faithful and just and will forgive our sins and cleanse us from every wrongdoing" (1 John 1:9).

[102] "So if the Son makes you free, you will be free indeed" (John 8:36).

[103] "So whoever is in Christ is a new creation: the old things have passed away; behold, new things have come" (2 Corinthians 5:18).

[104] "I will sprinkle clean water over you to make you clean; from all your impurities and from all your idols I will cleanse you. I will give you a new heart, and a new spirit I will put within you. I will remove the heart of stone from your flesh and give you a heart of flesh" (Ezekiel 36:25–26).

Answer Key

Lesson 2, Day One
1. Man was created in God's own image.
2. It means that we have dignity. We are "the summit of the Creator's work" (CCC 343). We are God's masterpiece! We have souls, and have been given the capacity to choose. We have the freedom to choose good or evil.
3. While this list is by no means exhaustive, the culture around us says dignity comes from accomplishment, possessions, appearance, and a great reputation.
4. The woman is described as a helper suitable for the man. Answers will vary.
5. It says that man and woman were created for one another. The woman is described as "flesh of his flesh," man's equal, his nearest in all things, and his helpmate. She represents God, from whom our help comes.

Lesson 2, Day Two
1. The serpent deceived Eve through his cunning. The Greek word for *cunning* is defined as "shrewdness, skill, or craftiness." This has been his method from the beginning of time, and he continues to employ it today. He is skillful and crafty, and makes a study of the people he wants to destroy. He knows where we are weakest, and that is where he strikes. The Greek word translated in this verse as *deceived* also means "to seduce." He dangles something that is appealing. He parades before our eyes and in our imaginations the beautiful side of what is tempting us. He hides from us the consequences.
2. When Eve said, "You must not touch it," she was putting words in God's mouth that He had not said. Eve was careless with God's words. This is significant because getting lazy with the truth made her more vulnerable to deception.
3. Eve allowed her desires to drive her decision making. She "saw that the tree was good for food," that it was "pleasing to the eye" and "desirable."
4. Answers will vary.

Lesson 2, Day Three
1. God was generous to them. He said they could *freely* eat from any tree in the garden, except one.
2. Satan helped Eve shift her focus from God's generosity and all that He had given, to the one thing that He had withheld.
3. **Discontentment:** A longing for something better than the present situation.
   Contentment: Happiness with one's situation in life.
4. **A.** He said she would become "like God, knowing good and evil" (Genesis 3:5, RSV).
   B. He had taught her that eating from the tree of the knowledge of good and bad was the wrong choice, and that she had freedom in other areas. He had taught her the difference between good and evil.
   C. He had already made her in His image, or in His likeness. She was already like God.

Lesson 2, Day Four
1. They hid from Him.
2. He hid because he was afraid. He was afraid because he knew that he had committed an offense against God. Adam knew he was wrong. He was afraid of the consequence of his disobedience.
3. We hide from God when we turn away from Him instead of confessing our sin and running to Him for mercy. We also hide behind performance. We present our works and acts of service, but what God really wants is for us to present our hearts—our real selves. We hide behind words such as *fine*, and we fake feeling good when our hearts are aching. We can hide behind a tough exterior (in appearance or attitude) that gives the impression that we don't care, when inside we are desperate.

4. **Psalm 17:8** We are the apples of God's eye, and are kept hidden in the shadow of His wings.
    Psalm 27: 5 When we are in trouble, God will hide us in His shelter.
    Psalm 32:7 God is a hiding place for us—a refuge. He rings us round with safety.
    Psalm 119:114 God is our refuge and hiding place.
    Colossians 3:3 Our lives are hidden in Christ. That is our place of safe refuge.

Lesson 2, Day Five

1. They both responded by blaming someone else. Adam blamed Eve and Eve blamed the serpent. A better response would have been to take responsibility for their actions and admit their faults.
2. God promised that the offspring of "the woman" would be struck on the heel by Satan, but would deal Satan a mortal blow. The offspring of "the woman" is Jesus Christ. While Satan would wound Him, and it would appear that Satan was victorious when Jesus died on the cross, Jesus would rise again and destroy Satan and his work.
3. Childbirth would be painful. In addition, the previous harmony that Adam and Eve had experienced in their relationship would be marred. According to CCC 400, "The union of man and woman becomes subject to tensions, their relations henceforth marked by lust and domination."
4. In the garden, before the fall, work had not been a burden (CCC 378). From now on, work would be characterized by frustration and challenges.
5. God clothed Adam and Eve with animal skins.
6. They were banished from the Garden of Eden and no longer could experience intimacy with God. They were separated from their heavenly Father. They would no longer live forever. "Death makes its entrance into human history" (CCC 400).
7. Answers will vary.

Lesson 3, Day One

1. **Genesis 11:27–29** Sarai was from Ur of the Chaldeans, in Mesopotamia. Many consider this to be the city-state of Ur, located on the Euphrates River. It was a thriving commercial center, devoted to its patron god, Nunna, the Sumerian moon god.
    Genesis 11:30 Sarai was barren.
    Genesis 12:11, 14 Sarai was beautiful.
    Genesis 20:12 Sarai was Abram's half sister. They had the same father, but different mothers.
2. She left city life for a nomadic life. She left delicious food choices and shopping opportunities for the desert. She left family and the religion that she had grown up with. She probably wanted to be sure that it was really God who was communicating with Abram. She would have wanted to know why such a radical move needed to take place. She might have wanted details about what this new home would be like, but Abram couldn't answer that question.
3. God promised to make Abram a great nation and to bless him. He promised to make Abram's name great so that he could be a blessing. He promised to bless those who blessed Abram and curse those who cursed him. He promised that all the communities of the earth would be blessed through Abram. Genesis 12:3, "All the communities of the earth shall find blessing in you," is a reference to Jesus, who would be a descendant of Abram's. The first promise of the Redeemer was whispered in Genesis 3:15. We hear it promised again here.
4. **A.** Abram worried that the Egyptians would see how beautiful Sarai was, and kill him so they could have her.
    B. Abram's solution was for Sarai to say that she was his sister, so he wouldn't be seen as a threat.

C. He was most concerned with his own safety, not Sarai's. He abdicated his responsibility and placed her in harm's way in order to protect himself. This likely made Sarai feel vulnerable because she probably realized that he valued his own safety over hers.

5. Answers will vary.

Lesson 3, Day Two

1. **A.** God had promised that Abram would have a very great reward, but the one thing he and Sarai most wanted was being denied—they were childless.

   B. God promised that Abram would have a son. In fact, He promised that Abram's descendants would be so great, they'd be as many as the stars in the sky.

2. Sarai had Abram sleep with her maid, Hagar, so that Hagar would conceive Abram's child.

3. Hagar was probably part of the gift given to Abram when Sarai was taken into Pharaoh's palace.

4. In both cases, instead of waiting for God's solution, they took matters into their own hands. Both solutions brought temporary relief, but trouble later.

5. Hagar felt superior to Sarai when she conceived, and looked with contempt on her. Sarai's hurt over this caused her to mistreat Hagar, and Hagar to run away.

6. Answers will vary.

Lesson 3, Day Three

1. She was a slave—a piece of property, owned by Abram and Sarai. She had no rights. She probably felt used and discarded. Her heart must have sunk when she heard Abram say, "Your maid is in your power. Do to her whatever you please." Before this, she might have thought she had some value based on the baby she carried. Abram's words made it clear that she didn't matter. They valued what she could give them, but they didn't value her.

2. As a slave, she had to obey. She was pregnant not because of her own choices, but because she was a useful means to an end for Abram and Sarai. Whether or not what had happened was culturally acceptable, Hagar was a woman with real feelings. Her feelings of being abused and misused were based on true mistreatment.

3. **A.** They never refer to Hagar by name. They call her "my maid," "your maid," "she," and "her."

   B. God calls us by name, and says, "You are mine."

4. Hagar called God "a God of seeing" (RSV) or "the God of vision" (NAB).

Lesson 3, Day Four

1. **A.** God promised that Abram would be the father of a host of nations.

   B. God promised that He would give Abram a son by Sarai.

   C. He prostrated himself, showing respect to God, but laughed to himself at the thought of Sarai having a baby. He then said to God, "Let but Ishmael live on by your favor!" In other words, "Can't the blessing come through Ishmael?"

2. **A.** Every male was to be circumcised.

   B. He responded immediately. On that same day, all the males in his household were circumcised.

   C. Deuteronomy 30:6 states, "The Lord, your God, will circumcise your hearts and the hearts of your descendants, that you may love the Lord, your God, with all your heart and all your soul, and so may live." This type of circumcision goes right to the heart of a person—to his or her desires, attitudes, and priorities. What God most desired, and desires still, is that our hearts be marked by love for and devotion to Him.

   D. Answers will vary.

3. Three men visited them, one of whom was Yahweh. The other two were later revealed to be messengers (Genesis 19:1).
4. He said, "Is anything too marvelous for the Lord to do?"
5. Answers will vary.

Lesson 3, Day Five
1. Sarah is remembered as a woman of faith. Hebrews 11:11 tells us that it was through faith that she received power to conceive, even when she was past the age, because she considered faithful Him who had promised.
2. **Lamentations 3:22–23** God's mercy and favor do not run out. They are renewed every morning. We can never exhaust God's resources. He is always able to give us what we need.
   2 Corinthians 12:9 God doesn't wait until we are strong and worthy before He helps us. His power is made perfect in our weakness. It's as if our weakness makes room for His strength.
   Ephesians 1:11 (NAB) He chose us. When He chose us, He destined us for something consistent with His purposes. He wants to intervene in our lives and to keep us moving toward that destiny. He has a purpose for each of us.
   Jeremiah 29:11 God has a plan for each of us, and it's not a plan for disaster and misery. It's a plan to give us futures full of hope.
3. Faith is the assurance of things hoped for and the conviction that we will see things happen, even when we can't see how. Faith is a theological virtue. The theological virtues "are infused by God into the souls of the faithful to make them capable of acting as his children and meriting eternal life" (CCC 1813). This means that faith is a gift from God. It is what allows us to believe in God and believe all that He has said and revealed to us (CCC 1814).
4. Without faith, it is impossible to please God. Without faith, it's all up to us, and that's not a very appealing thought. Life without faith is *self*-sufficiency, but what happens when we fail? What happens when we're not enough? Faith grows when we admit, "I can't do this on my own. I need a source outside of myself to get me through." That source is God. Faith means that even if things seem to be out of control, we can trust that God is managing all, down to the last detail. Faith means that there is purpose and meaning, even in suffering. Faith means that this life isn't all there is. Eternity awaits us, where there will be no more sadness, death, mourning, or tears. Life is not just what we see with our eyes; there is more, so much more.
5. "Faith is a gift of God, a supernatural virtue infused by him. 'Before this faith can be exercised, man must have the grace of God to move and assist him; he must have the interior helps of the Holy Spirit, who moves the heart and converts it to God, who opens the eyes of the mind and "makes it easy for all to accept and believe the truth."'"

Lesson 4, Day One
1. He did not want her to be a Canaanite. The Canaanites were pagans, and Abraham worried that a pagan wife might lead Isaac away from God. He also wanted Isaac's wife to be from Abraham's own family. Lastly, she needed to be willing to relocate to where Abraham and Isaac lived. She would need to give up closeness to her own family in order to embrace Isaac's.
2. Answers will vary.
3. These verses tell us that what God values isn't the outward appearance of beauty or evidence of wealth; it's inner beauty. This inner beauty is described as a gentle and quiet spirit—the opposite of an inner spirit that is anxious or worked up. Where does this gentleness come from? It comes from a quiet trust in God and His provision. This charm never fades.
4. Answers will vary.
5. Eliezer requested that when he asked a girl to give him a drink at the well, if she offered to water his camels, too, she'd be the one. She'd be the girl for Isaac.

6. When she saw a need, she took immediate action to fulfill it. She was hardworking and willing to go the extra mile. She was hospitable, offering her home to a stranger. She had a heart that was willing to serve and do more than what was expected.

Lesson 4, Day Two

1. She might have felt amazed that God had a plan for her life. As she heard the way in which she was an answer to a prayer, she probably felt special and singled out. She must have wondered what Isaac was like. She probably was excited to hear of Abraham's wealth.

2. **A.** He gave her gold and silver jewelry and articles of clothing. He also gave costly gifts to Rebekah's mother and to her brother.

   B. He describes the Church as betrothed to one husband, Christ.

   C. We, the Church, His bride, are to be clothed in righteous deeds.

   D. God has clothed us with a robe of salvation. Through our baptism, we are clothed in Christ. He gives us His very nature, placing it within our hearts, so that we can approach Him with dignity. He gives us the Holy Spirit, who dwells in us. He also pours spiritual fruits (love, joy, peace, patience, kindness, goodness, faithfulness, and self-control) into our hearts so that we have all that we need in order to make good choices and do righteous deeds.

3. Eliezer wanted to leave one day after he had arrived. Rebekah's family wanted her to stay with them for ten days. Rebekah agreed to leave immediately.

4. Answers will vary.

Lesson 4, Day Three

1. They blessed her by saying, "Our sister, be the mother of thousands of ten thousands; and may your descendants possess the gate of those who hate them!" (RSV)

2. No. Rebekah struggled with infertility.

3. God's thoughts and ways are not ours. They are higher than ours, and because of that, we often don't understand why He is doing what He's doing. His timing is also not always our timing.

4. **A.** Answers will vary.

   B. **Philippians 4:6–7** Instead of anxiously worrying, we are to take our needs to God in prayer. We should do this with a spirit of gratitude, thanking God for the things that we do have. God promises to fill us with a peace that is beyond human understanding if we will do this.

   Philippians 4:8 We are to dwell on the things that are good. Our minds should stay focused on our blessings.

   Philippians 4:11–13 As difficult as it may be, we are to be content regardless of our circumstances. It may seem impossible for us to accept our situation as it is, but God promises that we can do all things through Christ who strengthens us.

5. Answers will vary.

Lesson 4, Day Four

1. Each baby represented a nation. The two babies would be divided. One would be stronger than the other, and the older would serve the younger.

2. **Esau:** Firstborn, very hairy from birth, a hunter, preferred by Issac

   Jacob: Born grasping Esau's heel, quiet man, homebody, preferred by Rebekah

3. A parent might prefer one child to the other because that child is more compliant, has an easier personality, shares the parent's interests, excels and makes the parent proud, or is physically more appealing. Favoritism fuels rivalry within the family, and destroys unity. It breeds jealousy and comparison. It pits one child against the other and encourages them to compete with one another instead of building up and loving each other.

4. CCC 1803 describes a virtue as "an habitual and firm disposition to do the good," allowing a person not just to "perform good acts, but to give the best of himself." "The virtuous person . . . pursues the good and chooses it in concrete actions." If we want to be the best people we can be, then we need to actively pursue the good, choosing it concretely. It won't just happen when we feel like it. We must choose it exactly when we least feel like it in order to grow in virtue.

5. Esau didn't appreciate the significance of the birthright. Instead of appreciating what had long-term blessing and value, he wanted whatever would give him instant satisfaction. He gave up his inheritance for instant gratification. In Hebrews 12:16, Esau is described as an immoral and irreligious man who was foolish enough to sell his birthright for a single meal.

6. We're tempted to compromise our lifestyles so that we don't stand out like sore thumbs. We want to blend in and be accepted by people. We're tempted to adopt the values of the culture around us, pursuing beauty, power, position, wealth, and reputation. We're tempted to sleep instead of getting up to pray. We're tempted to make choices based on what feels good, instead of being willing to live lives of self-sacrifice.

Lesson 4, Day Five

1. **Psalm 33:9–11** God, who created the world simply by His Word, can bring the wisest of human counsels to nothing. He can and will foil our plans if they aren't consistent with His.
   Proverbs 3:5–6 We are told not to rely on our own understanding, and instead to trust that God has the big picture and remains in control. He can make any path straight, no matter how crooked it appears to our eyes.
   Proverbs 14:12 What seems so right to us can actually be a path that leads to death.

2. Answers will vary.

3. He cried. He hated Jacob because Jacob had received the blessing through deception. His anger was so intense that he planned to kill Jacob.

4. We're to get rid of these emotions, replacing them with kindness, tenderheartedness, and forgiveness.

5. She gave up unity in her family and the closeness of her favorite son. In order to protect Jacob, she had to send him away. In Genesis 27:44, Rebekah urged Jacob to remain with her brother, Laban, "for a little while, until your brother's fury turns away." Jacob remained with Laban for twenty years. During this time, she never saw him. This left her only with Esau and his wives, who made life unpleasant for her (Genesis 26:35). She also damaged her marriage. Although Scripture doesn't record it, her part in the deception of Isaac must have eroded his trust in her.

Lesson 6, Day One

1. They had to wait until all the shepherds were there in order to remove the stone. The stone must have been very heavy.

2. He first went over and removed the stone from the mouth of the well and watered his uncle's sheep. He then kissed Rachel and burst into tears.

3. Leah and Rachel were sisters. Leah was older. She is described as having "weak eyes," and Rachel is described as being well formed and beautiful. The Hebrew word translated *weak* in English means "tender, delicate, or soft."

4. It's hard to grow up in the shadow of a beautiful sister. Even if your parents don't compare the two of you, you tend to compare yourself. Leah might have worried that she'd never get married, or that Rachel would marry first, which would have been very shameful in her culture. How hard or easy it would have been probably had a lot to do with Rachel's temperament. Did she point out the good things in Leah, building her up? Or did she relish her position as the

beautiful sister? Scripture doesn't tell us, but the upcoming story indicates that their relationship wasn't characterized by sweetness and wanting the best for the other.

5. Answers will vary.
6. They seemed to him but a few days because of his love for her.

Lesson 6, Day Two

1. **A.** In the previous lesson, we studied the intricate deception Jacob staged in order to receive the blessing that blind Isaac wanted to bestow on his favorite son, Esau. Now Jacob was the victim of a shady deal. The deceiver was deceived. Jacob got a big taste of his own medicine.
   B. Answers will vary.
2. If there had ever been any question in her heart of whether or not Jacob loved her, it was certainly answered by his reaction. His words, "How could you do this to me?" must have cut like a knife in her heart.
3. **Reuben:** The Lord saw my misery; now my husband will love me.
   Simeon: The Lord heard that I was unloved, and therefore He has given me this one also.
   Levi: Now at last my husband will become attached to me, since I have borne him three sons.
   Judah: This time I will give grateful praise to the Lord.
4. Leah expected that by providing Jacob with sons, she would earn his love. Unfortunately, she was disappointed. When she gave birth to Reuben, she hoped that Jacob would love her. By the time she had Levi, she was simply hoping that he'd be attached to her. Not until she gave birth to Judah do we see her focus shift from Jacob to God. By the time Judah was born, Leah's perspective had shifted from what she lacked to what she had. God had been generous to her, and she was grateful.
5. It's incredibly difficult to live in a marriage that is not characterized by mutual love and respect. A Christian marriage is supposed to be a picture to the world of the love that Christ has for His bride, the Church. Sin has marred that picture, and too many homes are very poor reflections of God's love. Just as Leah's focus shifted from what she didn't have to what God had given her, a woman going through this same heartache today can choose what she focuses on.

Lesson 6, Day Three

1. She was frustrated, angry, and bitter toward Jacob. She was so depressed that she even thought of death (Genesis 30:1).
2. In essence, he said, "Don't look at me! I'm not the one who determines these things. Look to God."
3. First of all, the Catholic Church acknowledges that struggling with infertility is truly suffering (CCC 2374). That being said, CCC 2378 says, "A child is not something owed to one, but is a gift." It's so difficult to understand why God would give this gift to someone who doesn't value it while not giving it to a couple who want nothing more than to raise children in a way that brings honor to God. Couples who have been unable to have children are encouraged to unite themselves with the Lord's cross, and perhaps adopt abandoned children or perform demanding services for others (CCC 2379). The cross is described in this Catechism passage as "the source of all spiritual fecundity." We rarely seek out the cross, hoping instead that we can become holy through less painful means. But the fact remains, when we suffer, when we experience the cross in our personal lives, we are given a unique opportunity to grow in godliness. Painful experiences can purify our hearts, preparing us for heaven, if we receive them with the right spirit. How difficult this is to do. So few are willing to view their struggles in this way. But for those who are willing to be purified by the cross, great spiritual fruit awaits in this life and the next.
4. Answers will vary.

5. CCC 2380 says that it is an image of the sin of idolatry. Quoting author Dee Brestin, "Adultery is a powerful word picture for sin, for idolatry, because this language awakens us to the truth that sin is not breaking the rules but breaking God's heart. It is getting into bed with other lovers—and of course He withdraws."[105]
6. Rachel's heart changed. She went from being a bitter, envious woman, angry with Jacob for her lack of children, to being a woman of prayer. She had turned her focus to God, recognizing Him as the source of fertility.

Lesson 6, Day Four
1. He saw that Laban's sons were jealous of his success and that Laban didn't regard him as favorably as before. Most important, God said to him, "Return to the land of your fathers and to your kindred, and I will be with you."
2. We're told to rejoice with those who rejoice, and to mourn with those who mourn.
3. Jacob knew that these blessings came from God. He acknowledged that God had not permitted Laban to harm him, and that He had taken away Laban's cattle and given them to Jacob. This is evidence of growth in Jacob's spiritual life, because when he was in Canaan, he felt that the best way to get the blessing was to deceive his father and do whatever it took to gain what he desired. While working for Laban, Jacob came to the end of his resources, and had to trust God to deliver him from his deceitful father-in-law.
4. Rachel and Leah felt cheated by their father, and said Jacob should do whatever God had said to do.
5. Answers will vary.
6. No. Jacob could have obeyed God in a more honorable manner. There's a difference between just doing what God wants and doing it in a way that pleases Him. Our methods need to be in keeping with godly character.

Lesson 6, Day Five
1. God had spoken to Laban in a dream (Genesis 31:24), telling him not to speak "a word to Jacob, either good or bad."
2. Jacob said that anyone found with Laban's gods would not live.
3. A menstruating woman and anything she sat on were considered unclean. She was lucky, as this saved her life.
4. Both Jacob and Laban agreed that they wouldn't pass the heap of stones in order to harm the other. Jacob agreed that he wouldn't harm Laban's daughters, Leah and Rachel, or take any wives besides them. Jacob and Laban marked the covenant by setting up stone pillars, which served two purposes: to identify the boundary between Laban's land and Jacob's, and to be a reminder of the covenant agreement that had taken place there.
5. After wrestling with Jacob all night, God gave him a new name. The name Jacob means "heel grabber" or "he who supplants" (to take somebody's place or position by force or intrigue). His new name, Israel, means "the one who struggles and overcomes." This new name symbolized how Jacob had changed.
6. Answers will vary.

---

[105] Dee Brestin, "The Punishment for Adultery," Dee Brestin Ministries, May 29, 2011, http://www.deebrestin.com/2011/05/the-punishment-for-adultery/.

Lesson 7, Day One

1. Rahab had to make a split-second decision. The spies had only just arrived when the king told her to give them up.

2. Rahab's belief in the Israelite God caused her to make the decision. Her words in Joshua 2:9 reveal this: "I know that the Lord has given you the land, and that the fear of you has fallen upon us, and that all the inhabitants of the land melt away before you." She went on to say that she and her people had heard the stories of all their victories, and she gave God credit for them. Most important, she said, "the Lord your God is he who is God in heaven above and on earth beneath." There was a lot about God that Rahab *didn't* know, but she bet her life on what she *did* know.

3. Answers will vary.

4. **A. Philippians 4:6–7** Many things we decide aren't specifically discussed in Scripture. This is where prayer comes in. God promises to give us peace that surpasses all understanding, even in the midst of uncertainty, if we present our requests to Him and trust Him to work His will in our lives.

   James 1:5 If we ask God for wisdom and guidance, He will faithfully give it.

   B. "Worldly wisdom" can encourage us to make decisions based on selfish ambition and jealousy. As followers of Christ, we are to make decisions that bring peace, that come from pure motives, and that are full of mercy.

   C. Throughout our lives, we'll make choices that will affect us for eternity. Some decisions might win us temporary gain but would mean eternal loss. Let's keep our eyes on how short our earthly life is and how long eternity lasts—and live that way! We often base a decision on what we feel like doing or what other people think of us. How much better it is if we can lift our perspective from the immediate benefits and costs of our decision to see what it all will look like in eternity.

Lesson 7, Day Two

1. The presence of God dwelled in a cloud above the wings of the cherubim. This was where He met with His people. But this was no casual meeting. Once a year on the Day of Atonement, the high priest entered the Most Holy Place, where the Ark of the Covenant was kept. He entered with the sole purpose of asking God's mercy for the Israelite people. He brought a blood sacrifice, which he sprinkled on the mercy seat. When Joshua told the Israelites to follow the ark, he was careful to stipulate that they were to leave a space between themselves and it. They were not to come near it. According to Numbers 4:4–6, when the Israelites moved camp, the priests were to take down the veil or curtain that separated the Holy Place from the Most Holy Place, and cover the ark with it. On top of that, they were to place a covering of goatskin, and over that a cloth of all blue.

2. **A.** Joshua told the people to sanctify themselves. The Hebrew word for *sanctify* is *qadash*, which means "to be set apart, kept holy, consecrated, or dedicated." The English definition of *sanctify* is "to make something holy, to free somebody from sin."

   B. We can receive the sacrament of reconciliation. If the Israelites were required to prepare before being near the presence of God above the Ark of the Covenant, surely we'll want to prepare before we receive God within our hearts. The Eucharist sanctifies us (or makes us holy) by strengthening us and wiping away venial sins. Christ revives our love for Him and gives us the strength to break disordered attachments to people and things and instead attach ourselves to Him. In receiving the Eucharist, we are receiving a gift of love through the presence of the Holy Spirit. This preserves us from future mortal sins, because the more united we are to Christ in love, the less we will be drawn to pull away from Him through sin.

3. God wanted to exalt Joshua in the eyes of the Israelites, so they would know that He was with Joshua as He'd been with Moses. He also wanted them to know that the living God was among them, and that He would *without fail* drive out their enemies before them.

4. It symbolized that God was going before them. God was the true leader of their army. The Israelites knew that conquering the Promised Land was a bigger task than they were able to achieve. God would need to go before them. The victory would be due to Him, not their own strength.

5. **A.** They had to get into the water. They had to step out in faith first.
   B. Answers will vary.

Lesson 7, Day Three

1. **A.** He asked each of them to take one stone from the midst of the Jordan, from the place where the priests' feet had stood, and to lay them down in the place where they were staying that night.
   B. It was to be a sign among the Israelites, and when their children asked in the future, "What do these stones mean to you?" they were to tell them that the waters of the Jordan were cut off before the Ark of the Covenant. The stones were to serve as a memorial.
   C. Joshua set up twelve stones in the midst of the Jordan, in the place where the feet of the priests had been.

2. He did this so all people of the earth might know that the hand of the Lord is mighty, so that they would fear the Lord forever.

3. We can recognize that all the good things we have done have their source in God. Our victories and accomplishments are due to the gifts from God that He's placed within us. We should always point to Him instead of to ourselves. We also want to live in a way that honors God. God dwells in us, and we want to act in a way that reflects His presence.

4. Answers will vary.
5. Answers will vary.

Lesson 7, Day Four

1. Circumcision had been the way that the Israelites were marked as God's people. Moses had circumcised the Israelites, but the young men of the new generation had not been circumcised. The use of "again" in verse 2 does not mean that a man was circumcised twice. It means that this was to be the second time in the Exodus that there was to be a large ceremony of circumcision.

2. If the Israelite men had been circumcised on the other side of the Jordan, it wouldn't have made much difference if they had taken some time to recover. But they were now on the side of the river near their enemies. They were vulnerable to attack.

3. The Israelites had no choice but to trust in God. This was an exercise of faith. The timing probably looked illogical to them, but they so wanted to be marked as God's followers and to do things His way that they were willing to trust Him for protection as they recovered. The people of Jericho placed their trust in their thick, tall walls. They also had a well within the walls, bringing them fresh water. They had just brought in the harvest, so food was plentiful. They were prepared for a long siege. Rahab knew these things, but also knew that God was greater than any man-made defense. She placed her trust in the Israelites' God.

4. Answers will vary.
5. **A.** Joshua showed respect by falling facedown in reverence, worshipping, and taking his shoes off. Moses had been told to take off his shoes in the presence of God before the burning bush.

B. We no longer take off our shoes to show respect, but we show respect with our bodies when we kneel and genuflect before the tabernacle. The way we speak of God shows our respect or our lack thereof. Preparing for Mass through reconciliation and pre-reading the Mass readings also shows respect. We refrain from eating one hour prior to receiving the Eucharist as a sign of respect, as well.

Lesson 7, Day Five

1. Her faith was being tested. Having to wait for action, day after day, must have been difficult. Fear must have continually nipped at her heart, whispering what-ifs. From the moment she hid the spies, she was in danger of being considered a traitor. She had invited her family to her house, so we can assume that they knew what she had done. She also might have worried that their confidence in God's rescue was waning, and that this might put her in further danger. It was probably an incredibly unsettling time.

2. As with all His miracles, God's purpose was to build trust and faith in the hearts of His people. He was showing them that He was on their side, but that His ways were different from theirs (Isaiah 55:8). In order for them to see God's miracles take place, total obedience was necessary.

3. The scarlet cord is the color of a lamb's blood, which was put over the doors of the Israelites' homes on the night of the first Passover. When the angel of death saw the lamb's blood, he passed by those houses and did not kill their firstborns (Exodus 12:1–13). With the Old Testament sacrifices, a lamb's blood brought the Israelites forgiveness (Leviticus 4:32–34, Hebrews 9:22). Most important, scarlet is the color of Christ's blood, which rescues us (Ephesians 1:7, Hebrews 9:22).

4. Rahab and her family were settled outside the Israelite camp. As Gentiles, they were ceremonially unclean. This was only a temporary situation, because Rahab eventually married Salmon (from the tribe of Judah), and made her home with the Israelites. At one time, all Gentiles were separated from God—alienated from His promises. According to Ephesians 2:13–14, "But now in Christ Jesus you who once were far off have been brought near in the blood of Christ. For he is our peace, who has made us both one, and has broken down the dividing wall of hostility."

5. Hebrews 11:31 draws attention to Rahab's faith, and James 2:25 lauds her for her works. Her faith was proven by her action, the rescue of the spies. Both were needed.

Lesson 8, Day One

1. As a result of their disobedience, God allowed the Israelites to be oppressed by the Canaanite king, Jabin. The general of his army was Sisera. Their military strength was undisputed because of their nine hundred chariots. The oppression was so terrible that people could no longer travel on the roads; it was completely unsafe. The Israelites had utterly lost their freedom.

2. The Israelites were commanded to drive out all the inhabitants of the land they were about to possess, specifically destroying their idols and pagan worship places. God did this in order to protect His people. According to Leviticus 18 and Deuteronomy 18:9–14, the Canaanites' religious practices were abominable. The people were taking part in incest, adultery, polygamy, bestiality, homosexuality, witchcraft, and child sacrifices to their god Molech. God knew that if His people were influenced by these practices, it would lead them down a destructive path.

3. They didn't obey. In some cases, they made the Canaanites work for them as forced laborers, but they didn't drive them out as God had commanded them.

4. Answers will vary.

Lesson 8, Day Two

1. Deborah was a prophetess judging Israel. Prophets had to be older than forty. A prophet spoke God's words to the people. A judge served as a military leader appointed by God to deliver His people from oppression. While few women are seen throughout the Old Testament in leadership positions such as this, it's interesting to note that of all the judges highlighted in the book of Judges, Deborah is painted in the best light.

2. All baptized Christians are given charisms. According to 1 Corinthians 12:7, "to each is given the manifestation of the Spirit for the common good." The grace of the gift of a charism is given to "the faithful of every rank" (CCC 951). These spiritual gifts aren't just reserved for the super holy or spiritual superheroes. No one is passed over. Everyone who has been baptized receives at least one of these gifts.

3. Charisms are given to directly or indirectly benefit the Church. They are to build her up, and should be used for the good of men and to meet the needs of the world. They are not to be used for one's own benefit. They should be outwardly, not inwardly, focused.

4. Romans 12:4–8: prophecy, pastoring, teaching, exhortation, giving, leadership, mercy; 1 Corinthians 12:4–11: wisdom, knowledge, healing, prophecy, discernment, speaking in and interpreting tongues; Ephesians 4:11–14: prophecy, evangelism, pastoring, teaching. Charisms not listed in these passages include administration, celibacy, encouragement, faith, help, hospitality, intercessory prayer, missions, and writing. This list is by no means exhaustive, but it is given to spark thought in terms of the many different gifts needed within the body of Christ. All are valuable and play an important role in the furthering of Christ's kingdom.

5. The one who prophesies is to use his or her words to build others up, offering encouragement and comfort. Deborah exercised her charism as it was intended to be used—for the benefit of others.

6. Answers will vary.

Lesson 8, Day Three

1. Deborah was sharing what the Lord, the God of Israel, had commanded. God's commands were specific, and required great courage. If Barak was going to head into battle as an underdog (which he was—even ten thousand men were no match for the nine hundred chariots), he needed to know he was following God's plan, not just Deborah's.

2. The chariots were surrounded by mud when unexpected torrents of water caused the Kishon River to flood. In those circumstances, chariots were no help at all.

3. **A.** Heber was not a Hebrew. He was related to Moses, but through Moses' Gentile wife. He was an ally of Jabin, the Canaanite king, which is surprising because of his connection to the Israelites through Moses. Many believe that it was Heber who informed Sisera of the Israelite army's whereabouts.

   B. If her husband was allied with the Canaanites, it's surprising that Jael would have gone against him, quietly sided with the Israelites, and killed Sisera.

4. Answers will vary.

   Job 42:2 God can do all things; none of His purposes can be hindered.

   Jeremiah 32:17 God created the world by His great might. Nothing is impossible for Him.

   John 14:13 Whatever we ask for in Christ's name, He will do. The key is recognizing what it means to "ask in Jesus' name." This means asking according to God's character and will. God won't give us what we want if what we're asking for is contrary to His nature. He won't give us things that He knows wouldn't be for our benefit.

Lesson 8, Day Four

1. They credited God with the victory. Immediately following their triumph, Deborah and Barak turned to God and praised Him. This reveals their humility. Humility isn't having a low opinion of yourself. It's seeing yourself as you actually are before God—seeing yourself as God sees you. They knew that their obedience was an aspect of the victory, but always kept in mind that without God and His intervention, they never would have won.

2. **Mark 1:35** Jesus got up early and went to a deserted place to pray. He knew that He needed to be strengthened by His Father and to check His mission before He stepped out and ministered. We can't lead effectively if we have run out of strength. The source of our strength is God, and to lead well, we need to make time for consistent prayer.

   Acts 20:24 It's incredibly important that we take the time to recognize our strengths (our spiritual gifts that God has given us) so that we can discover the ministry, or the calling, that God has created each one of us for. Every baptized Christian is given spiritual gifts (charisms), and every baptized Christian is given a calling—a purpose. To discover what it is, we must fully surrender and be available to God. We must ask Him, "What is my mission? What is the purpose You created me for?" When we discover it, we are to pursue it and stay focused, despite obstacles and discouragement.

   Matthew 25:14–30 God holds us accountable for what we have done with the talents entrusted to us. When we don't discover and develop the spiritual gifts God has given us, we are burying our talent. How do we develop and stretch our gifts to the best of our ability? We should read and study all we can about that gift. We should keep our passion hot by taking opportunities to immerse ourselves in that area. Instead of being threatened by or jealous of people who are better than we are in our area of giftedness, we should spend time with those who are more advanced so that we can learn from them.

   1 Peter 5:5 It's essential that we confess pride when we find it in our lives, and that we do our very best to root it out of our hearts. The best way to find out if the spirit of pride has entered your heart is to ask those closest to you. Ask your spouse, those you lead, your children, your spiritual director, or your friends. Pride is subtle, and our ability to deceive ourselves is great. Sometimes it takes someone else to shed light on this area of our lives.

Lesson 8, Day Five

1. **A.** Deborah described herself as a mother in Israel.
   B. As a spiritual mother, she faced her people's worship of new gods. The oppression and war they were experiencing was a direct result of this apostasy.

2. Deborah was concerned with freeing her people from oppression and leading them back to God. Sisera's mother was focused on the spoils she hoped Sisera would bring back from the battle. She anticipated receiving an ornate shawl or two for herself, and a damsel or two for each man. This inference of rape is especially upsetting, particularly because she seems callous to its horror.

3. Our battle, or struggle, is not with flesh and blood, but with spiritual entities, described as principalities, powers, world rulers of this present darkness, and evil spirits in the heavens. When we step out and try to make a difference, Satan will do all that he can to discourage us from continuing. All sorts of obstacles will crop up, tempting us to give up.

4. We are protected by the armor of God. That armor is His truth (which we are to study and soak up), righteousness (our sin weakens us in the battle), the Gospel, faith, and salvation. Our one offensive weapon mentioned here is the sword of the Spirit, the Word of God. If we don't know Scripture, this sword will be of little use to us.

5. **Lamentations 2:19** God calls us to fervently pray for our children.

John 15:16 We are promised that if our prayers are aligned with God's will, He will intervene on our behalf.

James 5:16 The changes we want to see in the world can't happen without God's intervention. Prayer invites the power of God into hopeless situations, and brings change. God is always faithful to do His part. Our part is to confess our sins and then ask Him to intervene in our lives.

Lesson 9, Day One

1. **A.** A famine.
   B. He warned them that if they didn't obey Him, they'd experience sickness. They'd also experience drought, which causes famine.
2. **Genesis 19:30–38** The Moab nation was born out of an incestuous relationship between Lot (Abraham's nephew) and his oldest daughter—not the best beginning.
   Deuteronomy 23:3–6 Moabites weren't allowed to worship at the tabernacle because they hadn't let the Israelites pass through their land during the exodus from Egypt.
   Judges 3:12–14 Because the Israelites disobeyed God, He allowed Moab to take over Israel. The Israelites were in servitude to the Moabites for eighteen years.
3. She experienced a famine, she had to leave her home and go to a country that she probably didn't like, she was widowed, she lost both her sons, and she was left with two foreign daughters-in-law and no grandchildren.
4. She might deal with financial issues and a lower standard of living, or experience changes in social relationships in which she'd always been part of a couple. She might feel less significant, that her dignity has been affected by her loss. If she has defined herself by her relationship to a man, she might question her value as a person. Loneliness might be a constant companion.
5. God does not define any woman by her circumstances, relationships, or accomplishments. He looks at each of His beloved daughters and sees the difference she can make in the world.

Lesson 9, Day Two

1. Her struggle is sacred ground. Trying to find words that adequately describe this particular ache is difficult. Many women feel that they are excluded from the "club of motherhood," and experience the constant pain of seeing the reminders of their loss with pregnant women and babies all around them. It can cause a woman to question God's goodness, wondering why He won't answer a prayer that is simply a request for the opportunity to love and give more.
2. Answers will vary.
3. Naomi referred to the Hebrew custom of levirate, in which a brother would marry his childless, widowed sister-in-law so she could have children and carry on her deceased husband's name. "If brothers dwell together, and one of them dies and has no son, the wife of the dead shall not be married outside the family to a stranger; her husband's brother shall go in to her, and take her as his wife, and perform the duty of a husband's brother to her. And the first son whom she bears shall succeed to the name of his brother who is dead, that his name may not be blotted out of Israel" (Deuteronomy 25:5–6). Naomi was pointing out that she didn't have any more sons, and even if down the road she would have more, it wouldn't make sense for Ruth and Orpah to wait until those boys grew up to marry them. She encouraged them to go back home, to find husbands and security in Moab.
4. It was most sensible for them to return to Moab. Life in Israel appeared to be an acceptance of perpetual widowhood. They had no means of supporting themselves, and this would be even more challenging in a foreign country. Because of the history between Moab and Israel, they would possibly be discriminated against as undesirable foreigners. While Orpah might appear to lack loyalty, she did the sensible, expected thing.

5. Her decision to stay with Naomi wasn't just about family loyalty. It was about God. She had chosen to walk away from the gods of Moab and turn wholeheartedly to the God of Israel. What did she see in Naomi and Elimelech's family that caused her to long for their God? What drew her to Him despite seeing the suffering of His children? The passage doesn't say, but something about God made Ruth willing to take an enormous risk and to set aside her own future happiness, believing that He was worth it.

Lesson 9, Day Three

1. To glean was to gather grain left behind by reapers in a field. The Israelites were commanded not to gather every last bit of grain possible, but to leave some at the edges so that the poor and foreigners could come and glean what was left. This "divine welfare plan" required the gleaner to work for what he or she received, and counted on the honesty and generosity of the landowner.

2. **A.** Ruth happened to glean in the field of Boaz, a relative of Elimelech's.

   B. According to the Catholic Catechism 321, "Divine providence consists of the dispositions by which God guides all his creatures with wisdom and love to their ultimate end." Put simply, it means God is in control of all things, and He has a plan. He is guiding all people and events toward that plan with wisdom and love.

   C. Answers will vary for the two personal questions. Romans 8:28 assures us that we are always under the providential care of God, and regardless of what life throws at us, He is in control and working all things for our benefit. But if we aren't pursuing *His* purposes, then it won't always feel like it's for our best. We need to want His will more than our own comfort. Pursuing God's purposes will mean that we long to be more like Christ, and we'll recognize opportunities to grow in that regard in each and every circumstance we find ourselves. When we meditate on Romans 8:28, we're also reminded to thank God for all the good things that He sends us. "Every perfect gift is from above, coming down from the Father of lights with whom there is no variation or shadow due to change" (James 1:17).

3. Boaz didn't ask who Ruth was; rather, he asked whose she was. In response, Ruth's name wasn't given; instead, she gave her place of origin and her family connection.

4. He had heard of her sacrificing and risk taking on behalf of Naomi, and felt that she deserved reward.

5. Just as Elimelech was a blood relative of Boaz, Christ is a blood relative of the human race through the Virgin Mary. The kinsman redeemer had to have the purchase price necessary to help his needy relative. There was a purchase price for our redemption, too. That price was the death of the sinless sacrifice. Because Christ was the sinless Son of God, He was able to redeem the fallen human race. The kinsman redeemer had to be willing to redeem his relative. Jesus willingly laid down His life to redeem us. No one forced Him. He did it out of love.

Lesson 9, Day Four

1. She listened to an older, wise woman's advice and followed it. She bathed and anointed herself and put on her best clothes. She took a risk. She asked boldly for the help that she needed.

2. **A.** She was motivated by love. Her love for Naomi was so deep that she was willing to sacrifice and suffer for her. She also was motivated to do these good things because of her love for the God of Israel.

   B. According to CCC 1972, "The New Law is called a law of love because it makes us act out of the love infused by the Holy Spirit, rather than from fear." This means that our motivation for the good things we do should be love for God, rather than fear of God. This motivation, and the grace to act, both come from the Holy Spirit. We aren't to do the things we do because it's a ritual; rather, we are to act spontaneously, all of our good deeds being means by which we can show love to our dearest friend, Christ.

C. We receive the strength of grace to act as we should "by means of faith and the sacraments."

D. Answers will vary.

3. Boaz was honored that she wanted him instead of a young man. He paid her a high compliment by saying that everyone knew that she was a woman of worth. He promised to see what he could do about her request the next day, but said that there was a relative more closely related than he was. He'd first have to make sure that this relative didn't want to marry Ruth.

4. Boaz's mother was Rahab, the Gentile rescued from Jericho.

Lesson 9, Day Five

1. At first, it seemed like a great offer to the kinsman. It was an opportunity to add to his own acreage. But then Boaz reminded him of a few details: He would be buying the property, tending it, fathering a child with Ruth, and then passing the property on to that child, who would bear not his name, but that of Ruth's first husband, Mahlon. This caused him to have second thoughts, and he declined.

2. Boaz married her, and she gave birth to a son. She was also able to experience the thrill of bringing Naomi a new lease on life, and deep, abiding joy.

3. Not only were Ruth and Boaz the great-grandparents of the renowned King David, they were part of the lineage of the Savior of Israel, Jesus Christ.

4. Answers will vary.

Lesson 11, Day One

1. He is described as wealthy, harsh, and ungenerous.

2. You can't serve God and money. When you serve money, making it your focus, your source of security, and your joy, it's going to impact your relationship with God. Without a relationship with God and the sweetness of the indwelling Holy Spirit, it is easy to fall into patterns of self-centeredness, stinginess, and harshness.

3. **A. Psalm 24:1** Everything we have belongs to God. We are stewards entrusted with these things, and we are to use them for God's glory, not our own.

    2 Corinthians 9:7 God expects us to respond to His generosity to us (He gave us His only Son, holding nothing back) by being generous with others. He's not just concerned with our outward actions. He wants our hearts to be cheerful as we give.

    Luke 12:16–21 The tendency to hoard wealth and to accumulate stuff is strong in our culture. The disease of discontentment feeds these desires. Some of us need to ask ourselves the hard question, "How much is enough?" Is your basement and are your closets full of stuff that you don't use anymore? Could you give it away and bless others?

    CCC 2536 It's an important reminder that even though we might delude ourselves into thinking that if we just had "a little bit more," we'd be happy, it will never be enough. When a desire wells up in our hearts for something that belongs to someone else, we need to banish it from our hearts, and replace the jealous thought with something positive.

    B. Answers will vary.

4. This passage gives hope that things can change, but it strongly advises us not to try to bring that change through our words. The key is not for us to fix things or teach our spouses. It's the impact our own transformed lives can have on loved ones as they see the changes up close.

Lesson 11, Day Two

1. They had protected Nabal's sheep and shepherds. This was a common practice in Old Testament time. Although these protectors didn't charge a fee, it was expected that when sheep-shearing time came, they would be given a "tip."
2. Approximately six hundred men were with David.
3. His first comment was, "Who is David?" He then went on to insinuate that David and his men were no better than runaway slaves. The idea that Nabal wouldn't have known who David was is preposterous, considering the news that had spread about David when he killed Goliath as a young boy and freed the Israelites from the Philistines.
4. **Proverbs 11:2** Pride gets in the way of wisdom. If we want to grow in wisdom, we'll need to grow in humility.

   Proverbs 12:18 Reckless words pierce like a sword, but wise words bring healing.

   Proverbs 13:10 A wise woman can take advice. She doesn't just surround herself with people who will tell her what she wants to hear. Her humility invites honest feedback and constructive criticism.

   Proverbs 29:11 A wise woman knows that it's all about timing. Letting her anger settle before discussing hot-button topics, waiting until the other person is in the right place to hear what she has to say, not getting into things when exhausted—all these things show wisdom. By contrast, a foolish woman blurts out whatever she's thinking, venting her anger without self-control.

Lesson 11, Day Three

1. He was going to kill every male, even the boys, in Nabal's family and among his servants. He was going to kill innocent people, who'd had nothing to do with Nabal's stubborn refusal to help David.
2. She was humble, and immediately bowed to David. With her description of Nabal, she showed that she was loyal but not blind. She disarmed David by arriving with gifts. Her words showed respect and admiration for David and his leadership.
3. No. All he had done was listen to her. He hadn't committed to anything.
4. Answers will vary.
5. **A.** While Nabal's refusal to tip David and his men was rude and ungenerous, it wouldn't qualify as evil. David was focused not on God's kingdom, rights, and concerns, but on his own; not on God having been offended, but on personal offense. Righteous anger responds in a godly way. It always remains under control. Responding with a decision to kill innocent people is not expressing anger in a godly way.

   B. Answers will vary.

Lesson 11, Day Four

1. Answers will vary.
2. After hearing the disaster that Abigail had prevented, his courage "dried up within him," and God struck him dead.
3. It is in God's heart to want His people to repent before we face Him for judgment after death. He longs for everyone to reach out for the mercy that Christ offers. So He waits. But not indefinitely. Death comes to us all, and with that, a face-to-face meeting with our Creator.
4. Answers will vary.
5. In order for us to be forgiven by God, we need to forgive the people who have hurt us. This is something that takes place in the "depths of the heart." It's not about feelings ("It is not in our power not to feel or to forget an offense"); it's a decision we make in the core of our being, in our will. This decision may or may not be accompanied by emotions that "feel" forgiving. The key to bringing the emotions in line is found at the end of this catechism passage: "The heart

that offers itself to the Holy Spirit turns injury into compassion and purifies the memory in transforming the hurt into intercession." It is as we pray for someone who has hurt us that the Holy Spirit begins this healing work with our emotions and memories.

Lesson 11, Day Five

1. She might have felt vulnerable and powerless. Women during this time had no rights and no protection. The property of Nabal would not have passed to her care or ownership, so she didn't have a lot of options. If she had sons who were young, then they wouldn't have been able to provide for her. Being given the protection and respect of a man like David likely rescued her from dependence on the goodwill of others that may or may not have been enough to keep her comfortable and safe.

2. She showed faith, because she was sure of what she was hoping for. She was taking God at His word. God had chosen David to be King of Israel, and even though circumstances in this moment made it seem like it would never happen, she believed God would do what He said.

3. Just as Abigail would have to endure trials with David as she waited to reign with him, we have to persevere through trials. We sometimes have to suffer with Christ, believing that one day we'll reign with Him in heaven. We are promised an amazing future if we have the virtue of faith and take God at His word, believing His promises.

4. She showed humility by bowing to the ground and saying, "Your handmaid would become a slave to wash the feet of my lord's servants."

5. Mary gave a similar answer that revealed her humility when she said, "I am the handmaid of the Lord. May it be done to me according to your word."

Lesson 12, Day One

1. **A.** According to 2 Samuel 11:1, at the time, all kings went to war, but David decided to stay home. He ignored his primary responsibility to Israel—to lead and protect his people. His priorities were out of order; he was putting his personal comfort above his duty to serve his people.

   B. Answers will vary.

2. First, David ignored his responsibility as the Commander of Israel and stayed home while everyone else went to war. Second, he focused on and mentally indulged his desires. When he saw Bathsheba, instead of turning away, he continued to stare at her and dwell on thoughts of her. He played with the temptation instead of running from it.

3. "No temptation has overtaken you that is not common to man." This reminds us that the temptations we encounter have been faced by people throughout the centuries. We are experiencing nothing new or more difficult. "God is faithful, and he will not let you be tempted beyond your strength." We may think we don't have the strength to resist, but God promises that He'll make sure that we are never tempted beyond our strength. "But with the temptation [He] will also provide the way of escape, that you may be able to endure it." He always provides a way out. But it's up to us to take it.

4. She was married to a man of principle. He was loyal both to his king and to his fellow soldiers. During this time in history, it was considered dishonorable for soldiers to take part in sexual activity during their military service. He was determined to do the right thing, no matter how tempting David's offer must have been. His integrity was in sharp contrast to David's compromise.

Lesson 12, Day Two

1. His heart had grown so hardened to the reality of his sin that he didn't even recognize himself in the story. He had probably thought that he had gotten away with his affair.

2. **A.** He said that the man deserved to die, and should make fourfold restitution for the lamb. David's words regarding a "fourfold restitution" proved prophetic. Four of his sons were to die: the baby (2 Samuel 12:18), Amnon (2 Samuel 13:28–29), Absalom (2 Samuel 18:15, 19:1), and Adonijah (1 Kings 2:24–25).

   B. God said that the sword would never depart from David's house, evil would come up out of his own house, his wives would be given to other men in public view, and the baby born to him and Bathsheba would die.

3. CCC 2538 says that envy was at the root of David's sin, and it can lead to the worst crimes. "Envy arms us against one another. . . . If everyone strives to unsettle the Body of Christ, where shall we end up? We are engaged in making Christ's Body a corpse. . . . We declare ourselves members of one and the same organism, yet we devour one another like beasts." Envy destroys marriages, sibling relationships, and friendships, and can lead nations to war against one another for the purpose of expanding territory. It is especially destructive within the body of Christ. Instead of people in ministry supporting one another and spurring each other on to love and good deeds (Hebrews 10:24), they often react with jealousy and envy when one ministry has more success than another. How this must grieve the heart of God.

4. He was listing things that David should be grateful for: being anointed King of Israel (a gift from God), deliverance from Saul (God's protection), a home and wives (God's provision), and more unmentioned blessings. He was making the point that in coveting one of the few things he didn't have, David had lost sight of all that he had been given. An antidote to envy is gratitude. When we are feeling more aware of what we don't have than what we do, that is a sure call to our hearts to take some time to reflect on all our blessings.

Lesson 12, Day Three

1. He fasted seven days, and pleaded with God to spare the life of his child.
2. **A.** David fasted, and we fast, as a way of expressing interior penance, or sorrow for our sins.
   B. Answers will vary.
3. **A.** He washed, dressed, anointed himself, and went to the house of the Lord to worship God.
   B. Answers will vary.
4. Her grief would have been complicated by regret and guilt. She probably longed for a "do-over" button, something that would allow her to make better choices. But that wasn't without its complications either, because wouldn't that be the same as wishing her beloved baby had never been born? Conceiving again would have brought comfort, but another child would never replace the one she had lost. The gift of Solomon might have softened her grief and brought joy into her life, but the loss of her first son with David would have left a hole in her heart forever.

Lesson 12, Day Four

1. Full of self-confidence and good looks, Adonijah boldly announced, "I shall be king!" Like his brother Absolom had earlier (2 Samuel 15:1, 6), Adonijah produced a display of power when he gave himself chariots, horses, and fifty men to run in front of him. He got the support of the high priest Abiathar, which gave him religious sanction. He won over Joab, the leader of the military. His royal brothers appeared to support him as well, as evidenced by their presence at the sacrifices near En-rogel. He felt confident enough to make enemies by not including Nathan the prophet; the other high priest, Zadok; the warriors (David's trusted and feared men); or Benaiah (who served as the head of David's bodyguard); and most notably, his brother, Solomon. The exclusion of Solomon implies that Adonijah knew the throne had been promised to his younger brother.
2. He did nothing, as seen by the verse, "Yet his father would never antagonize him by asking, 'Why are you doing this?'" (1 Kings 1:6)

3. If Adonijah were allowed to seize the throne, he would consider Bathsheba and Solomon criminals. They would be threats to the throne, and would be treated as such.

4. God came to Solomon in a dream and said, "Whatever you ask I shall give you." Solomon replied with humility, admitting that he didn't know at all how to act. He asked God for a listening heart to judge his people and to distinguish between good and evil. He asked for wisdom. This pleased God. Solomon asked for something unselfish, which revealed his true character. God granted his request. He gave Solomon a heart so wise and discerning that no one before or after was to match his wisdom. In addition, God gave him what he didn't ask for: riches and glory. He also promised that if Solomon would walk in His ways, He would give him a long life.

5. When children are small, saturate their hearts with Bible stories. In these years, they are like sponges. Never again will they be so open to learning about their faith! There are fabulous books, DVDs, and CDs on the market to help you teach spiritual truths in a way that is appealing to children. Talk about God as you go about your day. When you see something beautiful, pray with the children in your life, thanking God for His creation. When you have needs, small or large, bring them to God in prayer. The more you talk about God, the more natural it will become. Pray daily for and with the children in your life. It will not only draw you closer to God and closer to these children; it will draw down God's strength and power on your behalf.

Lesson 12, Day Five

1. He assumed she had influence and that it would be hard for King Solomon to refuse his mother.
2. **A.** Bathsheba entered and bowed in homage to the king.
   B. Instead of Bathsheba bowing to him, King Solomon stood up to meet her and paid her homage.
3. The position at a leader's right hand was the place of highest honor.
4. **2 Kings 24:12** When King Jehoiachin of Judah surrendered to the King of Babylon, he did so with his mother and his ministers, officers, and functionaries.
   Jeremiah 13:18, 20 The prophet Jeremiah had a prophecy for the king and the queen mother, saying that they would come down from their thrones, and that their splendid crowns would fall from their heads. When the question is asked, "Where is the flock entrusted to you, your splendid sheep?" it implies that the king and queen mother shepherded the people together.
5. Mary is our queen mother, and she serves as our advocate, interceding on our behalf. When the angel Gabriel appeared to Mary in Luke 1:31–33, she was told that she would have a son who would be given the throne of David, his father. "If an ancient Jew heard of a woman in the house of David giving birth to a new Davidic king, he would easily conclude that she was a queen mother. And that's exactly the vocation to which Mary is being called at the Annunciation."[106]

Lesson 13, Day One

1. Amnon; Ahinoam; Daniel; Absalom; Talmai, King, Geshur; Tamar
2. She was beautiful and a virgin.
3. **A.** Instead of keeping his eyes on one woman, David's eyes roamed. He found it hard to resist a beautiful woman. When he saw Bathsheba bathing, he looked, inquired about her, and then sent for her. Amnon saw Tamar, and instead of recognizing that his half sister could never be his wife, he became obsessed with her to the point of illness.

---

[106] Ibid., 91.

B. Answers will vary.

4. Answers will vary.

5. **Colossians 3:2** We need to continually remind ourselves that our time on earth is fleeting, but the decisions we make here will determine the quality of our eternity.

   1 John 4:4 When you feel like you can't resist temptation, that it is stronger than your resolve or inner strength, be reminded that the Holy Spirit dwells in you, and He is not only stronger than your temptation, He's stronger than Satan. Through His strength, you can resist.

   1 John 1:9 God always promises to forgive us. If we want to win the battle in our minds, we need to be as spiritually strong as we can possibly be. Unconfessed sin weakens us. It deadens our conscience and impedes the flow of grace in our lives.

   Philippians 4:8 We should compare our thoughts to this verse. We can choose to focus on what is true, honorable, just, pure, and lovely. We can focus on our blessings by making a list of them in order to draw our minds away from thoughts of what we don't have. Much that happens to us in life is out of our control, but not our thoughts. Where they roam and dwell is up to us.

Lesson 13, Day Two

1. **Proverbs 13:20** "He who walks with the wise grows wise, but a companion of fools suffers harm." Whether we like it or not, we are influenced by and grow to resemble our friends.

   Proverbs 27:17 One of the purposes of very close friends is to help us recognize blind spots, not to tell us what we want to hear.

   Proverbs 15:2 and 2 Timothy 2:16 "The tongue of the wise commends knowledge, but the mouth of the fool gushes folly" (Proverbs 15:2). We're encouraged in 2 Timothy to avoid profane, idle talk because it'll lead to more and more godlessness. What are our conversations like with our dearest friends? Do they consist solely of idle, superficial chitchat, or are we encouraging one another to grow into more holy women?

   Proverbs 22:24 "Do not make friends with a hot-tempered man, do not associate with one easily angered, or you may learn his ways and get yourself ensnared." Not everyone is going to be a good influence on us. A wise man can overlook an insult (Proverbs 12:16). If we know that a friend has a hot temper, consider this a red flag.

2. Answers will vary.

3. Sin can be like a snowball on a hill, gaining speed and destructive power the longer it goes unchecked. This is a reminder to us to stop temptation before it starts rolling down the hill—before momentum makes stopping much harder. The more we give in to temptation, the stronger and more destructive it will become.

Lesson 13, Day Three

1. Answers will vary.

2. He called her "this woman" and had his servant throw her out, bolting the door behind her. He did this in a public, shameful way, guaranteeing that people would know she was no longer a virgin, thereby ruining her chances of ever marrying. This would mean never having children. He treated her like a piece of trash.

3. Tamar was wearing a long robe, which was the attire of a virgin princess. When she was thrown out of Amnon's chambers, she tore her robe, symbolizing her grief and disgrace. Her robe had represented her dignity. Amnon had torn that away from her, and in doing so, had torn her heart irreparably. She put ashes on her head and wailed loudly, mourning all that she had lost.

4. **Amnon:** He not only raped Tamar; he blamed her for his own sin and ruined her reputation. He took no responsibility for his crime, and showed no regret or repentance.

Absalom: While Absalom clearly loved his sister and was furious that she had been treated this way, his response to her would have increased her pain. Being told to "keep still now" and "not take this so to heart" must have felt like additional knife wounds to an already bleeding heart. A far better response would have been, "I love you. I see you no differently now. I support you. I am here for you."

David: While David was furious, and that was certainly an appropriate emotion, *he did nothing*. He didn't want to "antagonize" Amnon; David "loved him because he was his firstborn." In addition, David knew that he was guilty of sexual sin as well. Perhaps he felt disqualified from holding his son to a high standard, because of his own sin. What tragic consequences resulted from his silence. We can make the same error in parenting when we feel like our past mistakes mean we can no longer stand for the truth. Tragedy results, and the ones who pay are our precious children.

5. She was devastated and remained in the house of her brother Absalom. Other translations refer to Tamar as a "desolate woman."

Lesson 13, Day Four

1. Two years had passed since the assault on Tamar.
2. **Tamar:** From what we see in Scripture, she never recovered, and carried her shame the rest of her life. She probably felt trapped with no future, possibly bitter, trying to find a new role, a "new normal."

   Amnon: He probably thought he had gotten away with his sin. He hadn't lost favor with his father; he still appeared to be in line to the throne. There was no consequence for his behavior. There was still no evidence of sorrow or repentance.

   Absalom: Absalom may have "said nothing, good or bad, to Amnon; but Absalom hated Amnon for having humiliated his sister Tamar" (verse 22). He may have been silent, but he was quietly plotting his revenge on her behalf.

   David: It appears that David remained aware of the possibility of fallout from Amnon's sin, seen in his hesitation and questioning why Absalom would have requested that Amnon come to his banquet.

3. **CCC 678** It may seem like evil is triumphing and that people are getting away with horrible things, but "Jesus announced the judgment of the Last Day in his preaching. Then will the conduct of each one and the secrets of the heart be brought to light. Then will the culpable unbelief that counted the offer of God's grace as nothing be condemned." One day, all will be made right. One day, God will judge, and the way we have loved the people God has placed in our path will be brought to light.

   CCC 1861 Although we can judge an act to be wrong and immoral, "we must entrust judgment of persons to the justice and mercy of God." Judgment and punishment must remain in the hands of God.

4. We are supposed to reflect God and forgive. We are to show mercy to others, even as God has shown mercy to us. It's impossible for us to do this in our own strength. It is done through the inner working of the Holy Spirit. "Only the Spirit by whom we live can make 'ours' the same mind that was in Christ Jesus."

Lesson 13, Day Five

1. He was told that all his sons had been killed by Absalom.
2. Jonadab told David that it was only Amnon who had died, and then pointed out that Absalom had been intent on this ever since Amnon humiliated Tamar. He relayed this fact as if he had nothing to do with it, when the rape was his suggestion in the first place. A further question

remains: How did he know this was Absalom's intent? Had he been Absalom's confidant? If so, he did little to protect his "friend" Amnon.

3. He fled to his maternal grandfather, the King of Geshur, and stayed for three years.
4. He initially intended to go out against Absalom, but his anger cooled as his grief lessened.
5. **A.** Absalom made a play for the throne, gathering men around him, conspiring to take his father's place.
   B. During the battle to win the throne, Absalom's beautiful, thick hair was caught in a tree, leaving him hanging, defenseless. Joab and his armor bearers found him there and killed him.

Lesson 15, Day One
1. **A.** She might have dealt with anxiety and feelings of insecurity. Perhaps she felt like she didn't know where she belonged. She no doubt felt alone.
   B. Answers will vary.
2. Perfect love drives out fear.
3. Because of God's love for us, we were destined to be adopted by Him.
4. I will not leave you an orphan. I will come to you.
5. We do not have a spirit of slavery, which leads to fear. We are adopted daughters. This truth should give us the confidence to call God Abba, which means "Daddy."

Lesson 15, Day Two
1. She was clearly "beautifully formed and lovely to behold" (Esther 2:7), but she also exemplified character. She showed discretion in not blurting out everything about herself (Esther 2:10). She was humble and teachable, listening to Mordecai's advice (Esther 2:10) and taking only the things that the royal eunuch Hegai suggested (Esther 2:15).
2. Answers will vary.
3. **Proverbs 31:25** Qualities of inner beauty: strength, dignity, trust in God, no fear of the future
   Proverbs 31:26 Qualities of inner beauty: wise words, kind instruction
   Proverbs 31:30 Qualities of inner beauty: fear of the Lord (which means respect for Him)
4. **A.** Answers will vary.
   B. Answers will vary.

Lesson 15, Day Three
1. Haman was the son of Hammedatha the Agagite.
2. Haman sought to destroy all the Jews—not just Mordecai. Answers will vary.
3. Haman not only portrayed the Jewish people as a bunch of lawbreakers, he also promised to deposit ten thousand silver talents in the royal treasury. It's likely he planned to use all he plundered from the Jews to make this substantial deposit.
4. No one was advising the king beyond Haman.
5. Answers will vary.

Lesson 15, Day Four
1. The decree said they were to destroy, kill, and annihilate all the Jews, young and old, including women and children, on one day, the thirteenth day of the twelfth month, Adar, and to seize their goods as spoils. After the decree was sent out, King Ahasuerus and Haman sat down to drink, but the city of Susa was thrown into confusion.
2. Mordecai tore his garments, put on sackcloth and ashes, and went throughout the city crying loudly and bitterly. In the provinces, the Jews went into deep mourning, fasted, wept, lamented, and put on sackcloth and ashes.

3. Esther asked all the Jews in Susa to fast and pray on her behalf. She and her maids fasted, too. Every pang of hunger would have reminded Esther to pray. Each prayer would have intensified her dependence on the Lord, which would have released His power into her heart.

4. Answers will vary.

5. **Romans 8:31–32** God promises to give us what we need. We may think we can't face certain circumstances, but He promises that if it's courage we lack, He will provide it.

   Romans 8:38–39 Even the worst thing we can imagine is not powerful enough to separate us from God's love.

   1 John 4:18 There is no fear in love. Perfect love casts out fear. We are perfectly loved by God, which means that His presence in our hearts can drive out the fear. Love is stronger than fear.

Lesson 15, Day Five

1. Esther knew that if she approached the king without being summoned, the punishment was death. The only way she would escape was if the king chose to extend the golden scepter to her, showing mercy. She was afraid to count on that, though, because the king hadn't summoned her for thirty days. She no doubt wondered if he had grown tired of her. After all, he got rid of Queen Vashti earlier.

2. He didn't want to place the honor of a mortal above that of God. He refused to bow down to anyone but God.

3. **A.** The king's heart is channeled water in the hand of the LORD; God directs it where He pleases.

   B. He is the strong and mighty one. Nothing is impossible with God. He is the Lord of the universe. Everything is subject to Him. He governs hearts and events.

4. Answers will vary.

5. The most common yet most hidden temptation in prayer is our lack of faith. What we need to grasp in the depths of our hearts is the truth that apart from God, we can do nothing.

Lesson 16, Day One

1. The conception of Jesus took place during the betrothal period, when Mary was betrothed to Joseph. A betrothal was the period of time before a couple lived together.

2. People might have expected Joseph to divorce her and publicly shame her. His response to Mary's pregnancy was unusual, and only explained by his belief that God had spoken to him through his dream. God brought Joseph's mind back to the Old Testament prophecy by Isaiah that a virgin would "be with child and bear a son, and they shall name him Emmanuel" (Matthew 1:23).

3. Mary's virginity shows that God initiated the Incarnation. In addition, it makes clear the fact that Jesus has only God as Father.

4. Because of Christ, we are offered a new relationship with God. We can become His children. We don't become His children through a sexual union; it isn't through "human choice or a man's decision." Becoming God's daughter is a pure gift from Him. "The acceptance of this life is virginal because it is entirely the Spirit's gift to man" (CCC 505).

5. Answers will vary.

Lesson 16, Day Two

1. The Ark of the Covenant contained a gold jar of manna, the staff of Aaron, which had sprouted, and the tablets of the covenant.

2. When Mary was pregnant, she contained Jesus: the bread of life, the great high priest, and the Word made flesh.

3. Jeremiah the prophet said that the place would be unknown until God gathered His people and showed His mercy, and the glory of the Lord and the cloud would appear.
4. The glory of the Lord and the cloud covered the Tabernacle, which contained the Ark of the Covenant (also called the Ark of the Testimony).
5. Just as the glory of the Lord and the cloud covered the Tabernacle (which contained the Ark of the Covenant), the Holy Spirit covered Mary, and the power of the Most High overshadowed her.

Lesson 16, Day Three
1. She bowed in homage to the king.
2. When Bathsheba became the queen mother, she went to King Solomon, her son, and the king stood to meet her and paid her homage. Then he sat down on his throne, and a throne was provided for Bathsheba, the queen mother. She sat at his right hand, the place of highest honor.
3. When Bathsheba, the *gebirah* to King Solomon, came to him with her request, he replied by saying, "Ask it, my mother, for I will not refuse you" (1 Kings 2:20).
4. His royal throne was to last forever.
5. Jesus was a direct descendant of King David. The one who was to sit on David's throne throughout eternity was Jesus Christ. This makes Mary, as His mother, the *gebirah*, the "great lady," the queen mother.

Lesson 16, Day Four
1. "Mary approaches her son to intercede for the people—just as Bathsheba spoke to Solomon on behalf of Adonijah. Mary counsels her son about the matter at hand; yet she counsels others to obey *Him* and not her. Jesus, then, speaks to His mother as her superior; yet He defers to her suggestion—just as one might expect a Davidic king to grant the wish of his queen mother."[107]
2. Mary is our mother, and she intercedes for us in heaven. We ask her to pray for us, calling her our advocate, benefactress, and mediatrix.
3. In 1 Corinthians 3:9, Saint Paul stated, "We are God's coworkers." Couldn't God do all the work alone? Does He need us? God has no needs; He is utterly self-sufficient and all-powerful. But He has chosen to include us in the execution of His omniscient plan. This is part of the process of raising us as mature daughters of God. Mary certainly shared in the work of redemption as she fed God's Son, cared for His needs, and taught Him what she knew. She labored alongside Christ all the way to the cross. In Colossians 1:24 we read, "Now I rejoice in my sufferings for your sake, and in my flesh I am filling up what is lacking in the afflictions of Christ on behalf of his body, which is the church." This is an interesting verse, on which the phrase "offer it up" is based. It means that we can offer our sufferings up to God, and He unites them with Christ's sufferings. When we do this, we are coworkers with Christ. As Mary accompanied her son to the cross, encouraging Him with her every look and word to persevere, she co-labored with Him. Was her suffering equal to His? Certainly not. We never refer to Mary as our savior. That is an honor certainly reserved for Christ alone. But nor do we downplay the significance of all that she gave and the difference she made in Christ's life.
4. Answers will vary.
5. The "hour" that Jesus was referring to was the hour of the cross. Jesus and Mary both knew that when He stepped out and performed such a noticeable miracle, His quiet years as a carpenter would be over. The time of His public ministry would begin. When He said, "Woman, how does

---

[107] Scott Hahn, *Hail, Holy Queen* (New York: Doubleday, 2001), 83.

your concern affect me?" it affected Him greatly. Her concern over the lack of wine, her prodding Jesus to step out at this time, set in motion His walk to Calvary.

Lesson 16, Day Five

1. This verse is called the protoevangelium, and it's the first mention of the gospel in Scripture. Satan would strike at Christ's and Mary's heels; there would be suffering, pain, and death for Jesus. But Mary's self-sacrificial yes and especially Jesus' self-sacrifice on the cross would deliver a mortal blow to Satan, a fatal head wound. Picture your strong heavenly Mother and Brother slamming their feet on the head of the serpent. Think of the courage and strength it required.

2. The three key individuals in this passage are the woman, the dragon, and the child. The woman represents Mary, the dragon represents Satan, and the child represents Christ.

3. Answers will vary.

4. Mary's offspring are those who keep God's commandments and bear witness to Jesus. This is a description of the Church. This is us. The dragon went off to wage war against the Church, which means he wars against us. And this causes our heavenly Mother to rise up to come to our aid.

5. Answers will vary.

Lesson 17, Day One

1. She was courageous. She exemplified genuine faith, evidenced by her trust in God's provision. She was selfless. She was worshipful, considering God worthy of earthly sacrifice.

2. Jesus sat close enough to observe rich people putting in large sums, and the poor widow putting in two small coins worth a few cents. He considered these actions worthy of a lesson for His disciples. Many words Jesus spoke never made it into our Bible, but these did. Far from considering our spending and giving to be unrelated to our spiritual lives, Jesus took time to teach about the beauty of sacrificial giving.

3. Answers will vary.

4. Answers will vary.

5. What "loving your neighbor as yourself" looks like will vary from person to person. Yet we all can identify basic needs we are sure to meet for ourselves and our children (clothing, shelter, food, water). These basic needs should be met in the life of every person God has created. Perhaps less luxury in our lives means basic needs could be met in the lives of the poor around us.

Lesson 17, Day Two

1. The widow gave all she had, her whole livelihood.

2. Answers will vary.

3. Jesus told us not to worry about our lives, what we'll eat, what we'll drink, our bodies, and what we'll wear. He pointed out that God takes care of the birds and flowers, which don't have souls. Think of how much more He will take care of His children! He promises to meet our material needs (*needs*, not wants) and asks us to focus on the things that have eternal value instead of worrying about food, drink, and clothes.

4. We get in trouble when we start to value the temporal more than the eternal. We take a step deeper down when we attribute our success to ourselves instead of recognizing that "all good giving and every perfect gift is from above, coming down from the Father of lights" (James 1:17). When we consider our source of security to be our possessions, our retirement funds, our investments, etc., we are on very shaky ground. It's hard to have faith in God and to see our need for Him when we have total faith in ourselves. "The Lord grieves over the rich, because they find their consolation in the abundance of goods" (CCC 2547).

5. We can pray instead of rushing into activities. We can forgo luxuries, trusting that God is wonderful enough to satisfy our cravings. We can put Him first with our time—making Mass the highest priority on a Sunday instead of sporting events, and taking advantage of the sacrament of confession frequently. We can make the reception of the sacraments as important as filling our car with gas, because we recognize that without God's grace, we can't accomplish anything of eternal value. We can step out and obey God in areas that seem risky, trusting that He will provide us with the strength and resources for whatever He asks of us. We can cultivate gratitude for God by thanking Him for the little gifts He gives us in everyday life.

Lesson 17, Day Three

1. Both had a desire to do the right thing, but the rich young ruler was too attached to his possessions and money to depend totally on God. The poor widow showed an amazing detachment from temporal comforts, trusting that if she honored God first with her money, He would take care of her. God, of course, never promised either the rich young ruler or the poor widow to meet every want. And therein lies the rub. We may trust God completely to satisfy our needs, but our wants scream out for satisfaction, and we often wonder if we could cope if at least some of them weren't given to us.

2. No. Giving away everything is not something that Jesus required of everyone. Joseph of Arimathea was a wealthy man and a disciple of Jesus.

3. God knows each of our hearts. He knows what we consider our source of security. He knows what we credit with our success and prosperity. He knows what is most important to us. Whatever that is, that is our god. If money is that important to us, God knows it's getting in the way of our relationship with Him. We need to strive to attach ourselves to Him, and to detach ourselves from any idols that we have purposely or inadvertently set up to replace Him.

4. Answers will vary.

Lesson 17, Day Four

1. Jesus makes the point that whatever we're trying so hard to acquire and keep here on earth will one day rot. We can't take any of it with us. But generosity, sacrifice, giving . . . those actions "pay it forward," allowing us to store up reward for eternity. And that's a far better investment.

2. Answers will vary.

3. Answers will vary.

4. Answers will vary.

5. All that we have comes from God. We simply give what was given to us by God in the first place. It isn't ours. We are stewards, and God has entrusted us with riches so that we can be a blessing to others, not so we can hoard it or find our security in our possessions.

Lesson 17, Day Five

1. Riches can lead to pride and elitism. They can keep us from relying on God. Wealth is uncertain—it can be gone in a moment—and the fear of losing it can be paralyzing and can keep us from experiencing inner peace.

2. Ecclesiastes 5:12 says that the abundance of the rich allows them no sleep. The more we have, the more we have to worry about. The acquisition, upkeep, and updating of possessions can cause loss of sleep and anxiety when we wrongly augment the worth of riches. Riches can rob us of peace and contentment when the fear of losing them or not increasing them fills our minds and hearts.

3. We are to rely on God and be humble, recognizing that all we have is from Him. We're to do good, to be rich in good works, to be generous, ready to share, and as a result, live the abundant life that we were created for. And it's OK to enjoy what God has given! He richly provides us

with all things for our enjoyment. Finding a balance between a pursuit of pleasure and a refusal to enjoy life is directly linked to our prayer life. Closeness to God gives us a sensitivity to the nudges of the Holy Spirit so we recognize the times He wants us to give generously and the times it's OK to do something special for ourselves.

4. The more we seek the things that matter to God, the more we'll experience true abundance and true life. "Seek first the kingdom of God and his righteousness, and all these things will be given you besides" (Matthew 6:33).
5. Answers will vary.

Lesson 19, Day One
1. She welcomed Jesus and was serving Him, both of which were right and good things to do. She spoke to Jesus honestly about her concerns instead of stuffing her emotions—that was also good.
2. Martha asked Jesus, "Lord, do you not care that Mary isn't helping me?" Jesus replied that Martha's anxiety and worry weren't appropriate for the circumstances and that Mary's choice to sit at His feet was the better one.
3. **Psalm 46:11, NAB** Be still and know I am God.
   1 Samuel 16:7 Man looks on the outward appearance, but God looks on the heart.
   Luke 12:33–34 God wants us to be generous and invest in heaven, not earthly riches that we can't take with us into eternity.
4. Answers will vary.

Lesson 19, Day Two
1. **A.** Answers will vary.
   B. Answers will vary.
2. God is my rock, my salvation, my fortress, my refuge. My hope comes from Him, not from peaceful, perfect circumstances. I can pour out my heart to Him.
3. According to 2 Thessalonians 3:16, we receive peace when the Lord of peace gives it to us. We are to cast our worries on the Lord, which requires humbling ourselves under His mighty hand.
4. Jesus says that we are to come to Him for rest. We are to take His yoke upon us and learn from Him. His yoke is easy and His burden is light.
5. Answers will vary.

Lesson 19, Day Three
1. In John 11:22, Martha said, "Even now, I know that whatever you ask of God, God will give you." In John 11:27, she said, "I have come to believe that you are the Messiah, the Son of God, the one who is coming into the world."
2. We have to listen. Listening to God's voice means that we "turn our ears" to His wisdom and "incline our hearts" toward understanding things from His perspective. We are to ask for this kind of wisdom, to seek it like silver or hidden treasure.
3. We have to act on what we hear.
4. Answers will vary.

Lesson 19, Day Four
1. Martha was concerned that if they removed the stone in front of the tomb, it would smell terrible because Lazarus had been dead four days. Jesus promised Martha that if she would believe, she would see the glory of God.
2. All it took was Him speaking the words, "Lazarus, come out!"
3. Lazarus was wrapped in burial clothes. Jesus told the people to untie him and let him go.

4. Answers will vary.

Lesson 19, Day Five

1. Martha was serving dinner.
2. Our motive should be to do everything for the glory of God.
3. Answers will vary.
4. **Honoring:** When we work, we showcase the many gifts God has placed within us. Example: A person with the gift of administration who works to organize her home or office is bringing glory to God as she uses those gifts.

   Redemptive: Being faithful to our daily work can be likened to carrying a cross. When a woman serves her family even when she is exhausted and doesn't feel appreciated, she is collaborating with Jesus in her selfless offering. When a woman does her job outside the home with integrity even though she could get away with cutting corners, she is collaborating with Jesus. She works with integrity because what matters most is what God sees and desires. These sacrifices are redemptive.

   Sanctifying: Faithful, hard work is a key way God makes us stronger and holy. Each choice to do what is right in regard to our work strengthens our will and causes us to grow in godliness. When it's hard to do this, we are most likely to depend on the Holy Spirit for help. He infuses His strength into our hearts and everything changes.
5. Answers will vary.

Lesson 20, Day One

1. Mary was sitting beside the Lord at His feet, listening to Him. Jesus said that only one thing was needed, and that Mary had chosen the better part.
2. **Exodus 14:14** The Lord fights for us. We only need to keep still.

   Isaiah 30:15 When we wait and sit calmly at the Lord's feet, He saves us. We receive strength in the quiet as we trust Him.

   2 Corinthians 3:18 When we gaze on the glory of the Lord, we are being transformed into His likeness. We are being made more like Him.
3. Answers will vary.
4. **Step 1:** Say, "Speak, Lord, your servant is listening."

   Step 2: Be attentive. Listen. Be silent. If there is something you must say, say it, but then be silent. Wait for God to teach you wisdom.
5. Answers will vary.

Lesson 20, Day Two

1. Mary was devastated. When she heard that Jesus was coming, all she could think was that it was too late. Her disappointment and grief immobilized her, keeping her from going out to greet Him. When Jesus called for her specifically, she came and threw herself at His feet. Gone was the attentive student, replaced by a messy, grief-stricken woman.
2. Jesus was deeply troubled, and wept with her.
3. Some saw this sharing of grief as something beautiful. Others said, "Couldn't this miracle worker have done something for him?" They were questioning both His ability to do something and His willingness to help.
4. Answers will vary.
5. Answers will vary.

Lesson 20, Day Three

1. The enemy of our soul—our opponent, the devil—prowls around like a roaring lion, looking for someone to devour.
2. Answers will vary.
3. **Psalm 32:3–5** "Because I kept silent, my bones wasted away; I groaned all day long. For day and night your hand was heavy upon me; my strength withered as in dry summer heat. Then I declared my sin to you; my guilt I did not hide. I said, 'I confess my transgression to the LORD,' and you took away the guilt of my sin."

   Proverbs 27:6 "Faithful are the wounds of a friend."

   Psalm 61:2–5, NAB "Hear my cry, O God, listen to my prayer! From the ends of the earth I call; my heart grows faint. Raise me up, set me on a rock, for you are my refuge, a tower of strength against the foe. Let me dwell in your tent forever, take refuge in the shelter of your wings."

   Psalm 139:23 "Probe me, God, know my heart; try me, know my thoughts."
4. Answers will vary.

Lesson 20, Day Four

1. **A.** The dinner party was given six days before Passover.
   B. Jesus was crucified during Passover.
   C. Yes. Jesus had actually told His disciples that He would be handed over and crucified on Passover.
2. It was a liter of costly perfumed oil made from genuine aromatic nard.
3. Judas felt it was an utter waste of money. He said the money could have been better spent on the poor, but John tells us that his motives weren't that pure. Judas was a thief in charge of the money bag; he stole from the contributions. Jesus told him to leave her alone. He commended her for her actions, saying that she had anticipated anointing his body for burial. He promised that everywhere the gospel would be proclaimed, what she had done would be told in memory of her.
4. Psalm 51:17 says, "The sacrifices of God are a broken spirit, a broken and contrite heart, O God, you will not despise."
5. Answers will vary.

Lesson 20, Day Five

1. God does not overlook our work anywhere, and that includes the little things we do to serve in our homes. He sees every act of love and remembers it.
2. Women have an inalienable dignity that comes to them directly from God, their Creator. "Man and woman are both with one and the same dignity 'in the image of God'" (CCC 369). God has given man and woman "an equal personal dignity" (CCC 2334).
3. He describes our mission as one of "greatness." This mission is critical if we want to see the world renewed and for believers to rediscover the true face of the Church.
4. Answers will vary.

Lesson 21, Day One

1. The angel Gabriel greeted Mary with the words "Hail, full of grace, the Lord is with you!"
2. According to CCC 492, "The 'splendor of an entirely unique holiness' by which Mary is 'enriched from the first instant of her conception' comes wholly from Christ: She is 'redeemed, in a more exalted fashion, by reason of the merits of her Son.'"
3. Romans 3:23 states, "All have sinned and fall short of the glory of God." Many argue against the teaching of Mary's immaculate conception by pointing to this verse. But does this verse state

that there are no exceptions? What about a baby? Or a child below the age of reason? What about Jesus? Exceptions to this verse exist. As a result, it is an ineffective argument against the dogma of the Immaculate Conception.

4. We are filled with grace at baptism, when we become God's beloved daughters. We receive the life of the Holy Spirit, who breathes love (charity) into us. We may feel like we can't love the way that Mary loved, but we're reminded here that the Holy Spirit breathes divine love into us. That's the love that we pass on to others. Yes, our fallen human nature lacks what is needed to love at all times. But God provides for us what we are lacking in ourselves. God continues to pour grace into our hearts through the sacraments. Additionally, we are filled with the grace of spiritual gifts, or charisms, that help us to live out our callings. "His divine power has given us everything we need for a godly life through our knowledge of him who called us by his own glory and goodness" (2 Peter 1:3).

5. We are blessed in Christ with every spiritual blessing. God chose us, before the foundation of the world. He chose us to be holy and blameless before Him. He destined us in love to be His daughters. He freely bestowed grace on us through Jesus.

Lesson 21, Day Two

1. Satan surely hoped that Mary would question what God's plan would cost her. He would have been thrilled if she had dwelled on all the reasons why this plan wasn't a good one. Was obeying God worth the loss of her reputation, the potential loss of her fiancé? Why would God allow the Messiah to start out life with a scandalous conception? Any or all of the questions could have gone through her mind, tempting Mary to doubt God's goodness and the wisdom of His plan.

2. Mary's heart's desire was to be available to God. Whatever His plan was, she wanted it. She held nothing back. Whatever it would cost, no matter what she would lose, she would trust. Her decision making was driven by trust, love, and a desire to see God's plan of redemption take place on earth

3. **A.** God wants us to use whatever gifts He has placed within us to serve others, being conduits of His grace to a world in desperate need of love and healing.

   B. According to 1 Corinthians 12:7, "to *each* [emphasis added] is given the manifestation of the Spirit." Every single follower of Christ has at least one spiritual gift. You may not know what that gift is. It may be lying dormant inside you. But it is there, and God wants you to discover it and use it for His purposes, at this time, in this generation.

4. Both Rahab and Bathsheba fell into sexual temptation and made the wrong choice. Rahab was a prostitute; Bathsheba had an affair that caused her husband to be killed. That's some serious baggage. Ruth was a Moabite, a pagan. She definitely lacked the good Israelite pedigree that everyone considered essential. Yet God never looked at these women as damaged goods. He took the broken pieces of their lives, put them all together again, and created something beautiful. God is not limited by our backgrounds, failures, and mistakes. If we will confess our sins and turn away from them and toward God, He can take our story and redeem it. God writes straight with crooked lines. But when we're tempted to define ourselves by our past, His plan is thwarted.

5. **Jeremiah 29:11** "For I know well the plans I have in mind for you—oracle of the LORD—plans for your welfare and not for woe, so as to give you a future of hope."

   Romans 8:37–39 "No, in all these things we conquer overwhelmingly through him who loved us. For I am convinced that neither death, nor life, nor angels, nor principalities, nor present things, nor future things, nor powers, nor height, nor depth, nor any other creature will be able to separate us from the love of God in Christ Jesus our Lord."

   Galatians 6:9 "Let us not grow tired of doing good, for in due time we shall reap our harvest, if we do not give up."

Lesson 21, Day Three

1. The timing of Mary's pregnancy (before her marriage) was replete with opportunities to say "if only" or "what if." She could have been very discontented with God allowing the census to be taken just when she needed to give birth. A long ride on a donkey is no one's desire when she is about to have a baby. She could have said "if only" there had been room in the inn so the birth could have been in a better place. Fleeing to Egypt so her baby wouldn't be killed wasn't pleasant either. Having to let Jesus go (surrendering her precious son to God's plan) could have utterly derailed her. Imagine all the what-ifs that accompanied releasing Jesus. Of course, He could have started His ministry whether or not His mother "released" Him, but we all know how hard it is for a mother to emotionally let go even if she has physically let go. Accompanying Jesus to the cross and watching His suffering and death is the worst thing we can imagine for a mother. She could have stood at the foot of the cross and cried out to God, "If only! If only you could have saved us all another way!" At each of these points, however, we never see Mary displaying discontent. She is, instead, an example of peace, trust, and surrender.

2. Mary always focused on the "greatness of the Lord" (v. 46), the great things the mighty one had done for her (v. 49), God's holiness and mercy (vv. 49–50), His unusual but perfect way of working out His plan (vv. 51–53), His provision for the lowly and hungry (vv. 52–53), and His utter faithfulness to His promises (vv. 54–55).

3. "He has looked upon his handmaid's lowliness; behold, from now on will all ages call me blessed. The Mighty One has done great things for me" (vv. 48–49). "He has thrown down rulers from their thrones but lifted up the lowly" (v. 52). Mary, the lowly handmaiden, was lifted by God to a throne as the queen mother.

4. Answers will vary.

5. **A.** Answers will vary.
   B. Answers will vary.

Lesson 21, Day Four

1. God was protecting them from the Massacre of the Innocents. King Herod had heard the prophecies of a new king being born in Bethlehem, and was threatened by the possibility of a usurper to his throne. He killed all baby boys in the vicinity of Bethlehem under the age of two to protect himself.

2. As Jesus grew from age twelve into adulthood, the Holy Family spent years hidden from view, sharing the kind of life experiences that most of us are familiar with. Nothing great to the outside observer—days filled with manual labor and ordinary experiences. In living those experiences, Jesus sanctified them, showing us that we can grow in holiness exactly where we are. "Mary 'kept all these things in her heart' during the years Jesus remained hidden in the silence of an ordinary life" (CCC 534).

3. When we remain confident that God is at work within us, we will later be rewarded. We need to persevere and endure, because when we continue to do God's will, even when it's hard, there's a reward for us

4. Answers will vary.

Lesson 21, Day Five

1. "Hence not a few of the early Fathers gladly assert . . . : 'The knot of Eve's disobedience was untied by Mary's obedience: what the virgin Eve bound through her disbelief, Mary loosened by her faith.' Comparing her with Eve, they call Mary 'the Mother of the living' and frequently claim: 'Death through Eve, life through Mary'" (CCC 494).

2. God wanted "the free co-operation of a creature" (CCC 488). Because of this, He didn't *demand* that Mary open her heart and womb to receive the Savior. She had a choice. When Mary said

yes, the way was made clear for the execution of God's plan of salvation, to send His Son "in the fullness of time" (Galatians 4:4). Jesus came to ransom us, so that we could be adopted as daughters of God.

3. One consequence Mary experienced because of her yes to God was deep personal suffering. Her yes led to Christ's yes. When Christ suffered on the cross, a sword pierced her heart. Mary, whose love wasn't defiled by self-interest or any sin, loved purely. Because of this, she felt the suffering of her son even more acutely.

4. With some of His final breaths, Jesus not only offered His mother to the disciple John. Throughout history, the Catholic Church has considered John to be symbolic of all of humanity. This is why she teaches that when Jesus offered Mary to John to be his mother, He also gave her to us. "She is a mother to us in the order of grace" (CCC 968).

Prayer Pages

Dear God,

Thank You for loving me unconditionally.
Help me to see myself through Your eyes.
Help me to remember that You started a good work
in me, and You promise to complete it.

Set me free from perfectionism, comparison, and fear.
May I get out from under others' expectations of me
and live for an audience of one.
Replace my worry with trust, my striving with rest,
the voice of condemnation with Your voice of
acceptance and blessing.

May I walk with dignity because the God of the Universe
has chosen to make His home in my heart.

Amen

Prayer Requests

Date:

Date:

Prayer Requests

Date:

Date:

Prayer Requests

Date:

Date:

Prayer Requests

Date:

Date:

Prayer Requests

Date:

Date:

Prayer Requests

Date:

Date:

Prayer Requests

Date:

Date:

Prayer Requests

Date:

Date:

Prayer Requests

Date:

Date:

Prayer Requests

Date:

Date:

Prayer Requests

Date:

Date:

Prayer Requests

Date:

Donation Information

Walking with Purpose expands when women in parishes respond to the inspiration of the Holy Spirit and step forward to serve their neighbors and friends through this ministry. As the ministry grows, so do the material needs of the Walking with Purpose™ organization. If you would like to contribute to Walking with Purpose, donations can be mailed to:

Walking with Purpose
PO Box 1552
Millersville, MD 21108

You can also donate online at www.walkingwithpurpose.com.
Walking with Purpose is a 501(c)(3) nonprofit organization.
Your gift is fully tax deductible.

*"See to it that no one misses
the grace of God"* Hebrews 12:15

It's time to stop talking about how there's nothing relevant out there for Catholic women.

IT'S TIME TO BE THE CHANGE WE WANT TO SEE.

You can bring **Walking with Purpose** to your parish!

IT'S EASY TO DO!

● **You've already got the skills needed!**
  - Personal commitment to Christ
  - Desire to share the love of Christ
  - Belief in the power of authentic, transparent community

● **We'll be there every step of the way, offering:**
  - Training
  - Mentoring
  - Course materials
  - Promotional materials

● **Do you think you have too many limitations to serve in this way?**
  Great! That's *exactly* where God wants us to start. If we will just offer Him *what we have*, He promises to do the rest. Few things stretch and grow our faith like stepping out and asking God to work through us. Say *YES*, and get ready to watch what He can do through imperfect women who depend on Him.

Learn more about bringing **Walking with Purpose** to your parish!

Email us at **infowwp@walkingwithpurpose.com** or
visit us at **WalkingwithPurpose.com/start**.

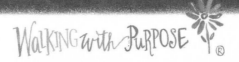

"For to the one who has, more will be given"
Matthew 13:12

THANK YOU

for sharing this journey with all of us at **Walking with Purpose.**
We'd love to stay connected!
We've got more encouragement and hope available for you!

FREE valuable resources:

- **Sign up for the Walking with Purpose Newsletter for a monthly reflection from Lisa Brenninkmeyer!**

- **Join our community on Facebook and Twitter for a daily boost!**

- **Subscribe to our blog for regular inspiration and participate in conversations by contributing your comments!**

The Walking with Purpose Bible study program is
just the beginning.

Go to **www.WalkingwithPurpose.com** to sign up
for the newsletter, subscribe to the blog, and find links
to the Facebook and Twitter communities.

OPENING YOUR HEART:
The Starting Point

Opening Your Heart: The Starting Point is our foundational 22-week course, designed for women who are new to Walking with Purpose as well as those with more experience in Bible study. Join us as we take a deeper dive into the core questions that we need to wrestle with if we want to experience all that God has for us.

Some of the questions we'll explore:

- How can I conquer my fears?

- What is the role of the Holy Spirit in my life?

- What does the Eucharist have to do with my friendship with Christ?

- What are the limits of Christ's forgiveness?

- Why and how should I pray?

- What is the role of suffering in my life?

- What challenges will I face in my efforts to follow Jesus more closely?

A DVD series on Priorities complements the course and is immensely practical and encouraging. *Opening Your Heart* is the perfect starting point as you seek to grow closer to God.

Find out more information about
Opening Your Heart: The Starting Point
at WalkingwithPurpose.com/open-your-heart-the-starting-point/

If you're interested in bringing Walking with Purpose
to your parish, contact us at
WalkingwithPurpose.com/start.

WALKING with PURPOSE

WALKING WITH PURPOSE COURSES

Opening Your Heart is our foundational course where we explore core questions that lead us to experience Christ personally within the context of the Catholic Church. (22 sessions)

Keeping in Balance focuses on creating balance within. (22 sessions)

Touching the Divine draws us into a deeper relationship with Jesus as we study the Gospel of John. (22 sessions)

Discovering Our Dignity gives us modern-day advice from women of the Bible. (22 sessions)

Living in the Father's Love reveals how deeply relevant the Gospels are to our relationships, both with God and with those we love. (6 sessions)

Beholding His Glory shows us how all Scripture points us to our Redeemer, Jesus Christ. (9 sessions)

For more information on all Walking with Purpose courses please visit us at
WalkingwithPurpose.com/courses.